Images from "Over There"

Personal Photography of America's Expeditionary Forces in WWI and Occupation

Stephen C. McGeorge, *Major US Army (Ret.)*

Other Schiffer Books on Related Subjects:

In a Strange Land: The American Occupation of Germany 1918–1923
by Alexander Barnes, ISBN: 978-0-7643-3761-1

Forgotten Soldiers of World War I: America's Immigrant Doughboys
by Alexander F. Barnes & Peter L. Belmonte, ISBN: 978-0-7643-5547-9

Uniforms, Equipment and Weapons of the American Expeditionary Forces in World War I by Brett Werner, ISBN: 978-0-7643-2431-4

Library of Congress Control Number: 2018937192

Designed by Jack Chappell
Cover design by Matt Goodman

Type set in P22 Cezanne/Lyon Text

ISBN: 978-0-7643-5635-3
Printed in China
Published by Schiffer Publishing, Ltd.
4880 Lower Valley Road
Atglen, PA 19310
Phone: (610) 593-1777; Fax: (610) 593-2002
E-mail: Info@schifferbooks.com
Web: www.schifferbooks.com

Contents

Introduction
4

Acknowledgments
5

Photography in the
Allied Expeditionary Force (AEF)
6

Conclusion
142

Bibliography
143

Introduction

This book has its genesis in a museum exhibit concept developed for the National Museum of the United States Army. I was asked by one of my colleagues who knew I collected Doughboy images if I would be willing to allow their use in an exhibit under development. I assented, and some months later the focus of the exhibit was refined. Simply put, the idea was to display a large number of photographs of soldiers as they appeared overseas either in France or in the post Armistice Army of Occupation in Germany. The overriding theme was to show what the personnel of the American Expeditionary Force (AEF) looked like while serving overseas, and specifically not as they appeared as newly uniformed recruits in the US, or in the common and often formal studio portrait taken just after their discharge from service. In selected cases where a photograph had significant biographical background on the subject, those might be reproduced in near life-size and placed in front of the "wall" of smaller, often anonymous, pictures of Doughboys. The exhibit could thus at once give the impression of a massive Army, yet one that upon closer examination was made up of individuals, each with their own personality and experience. These then would be examples of "personal" photography, the images of self, buddies, perhaps squad or section, kept by the individual soldier or perhaps sent to the folks back home. The subtext of many of the images is, "I'm alive, I made it. And here is the proof."

For the reasons above official Signal Corps photos were not selected, nor were the "formation" photographs, often taken in panoramic format. These, though interesting, are not nearly as personal as the individual and small group images. And frankly, the soldiers in such images had no say in composition or makeup of the participants. Again, the focus of the exhibit concept was to remain on the individual soldier.

Individual soldier photographs and in particular individual portraits were nothing new in 1918. From the practical inception of photographic processes in the 1850s, myriad soldiers had the "image taken" as keepsakes or to send to the folks at home. The important distinction between imagery of Civil War soldiers and the Doughboys of 1918 lies in photographic technology. "Johnny Reb" and "Billy Yank" had their pictures taken by bulky cameras, using wet plate processes, with the final images imprinted on glass, metal, or paper. Long exposure times dictated stiff poses and the bulk of equipment and materials needed generally required the sitter to have the image taken in a permanent or makeshift studio. The painted backdrop might depict the tented camp or some other martial site, but actual open air photography, at least for common portraits, is rarely seen.

Matthew Brady and his contemporaries developed travelling photographic laboratories and did accomplish a large body of outdoor photographic works taken in the field. In most of these works the subject is not the individual soldier, but more commonly documentary material. As is well-known, particularly in post battle images at Antietam and Gettysburg, the dead were sometimes physically rearranged to provide better composed photographic images of the horrors of war. The distinction seems to be this: in the nineteenth century photography was seen as a technical process to execute what formerly had been an entirely creative and artistic process; to whit drawing or painting a portrait or scene either from life or memory. By the early twentieth century, photography had graduated to a more purely documentary medium, capable of standing on its own merits and hence removed from artistic creative considerations.

To be sure, many images of the Doughboys retain the conventions of the earlier era. The painted backdrop, martial or pastoral, the carefully positioned chair, a stand or column bearing the props of flowers, books, or other knick-knacks all can be seen in Doughboy portraits executed in local photographer's studios. With far faster exposure time, poses however, are far more varied than one sees in Civil War photography. For example, I have yet to find a Doughboy image displaying the classic Napoleonic portrait pose of right hand stuffed into the coat front. More striking is the larger number of open air outdoor photographs. This is largely the result of changes in photographic technology, which made the process of taking the actual image far simpler, more portable, and less dependent on large apparatus and immediate development.

By the early twentieth century photography had graduated from reliance on solid negative plates to spooled film. This was a practical revolution in terms of camera portability and the speed of the process. Negative film was simply advanced and the next image taken. Once the spool was complete it was removed from the camera, developed, and the multiple images thereon printed. Exposure times were reduced, further allowing for less-stilted poses. These revolutions in technology provided the basis for popular, affordable amateur photography and the development of moving films. A very limited number of moving film images were taken of US Army activity during the Spanish-American War of 1898. Some twenty years later the Army Signal Corps produced some 900,000 feet of moving picture film of Army activity. Similarly with the advent of affordable box and vest pocket cameras every man could become his own photographer.

Acknowledgments

The debt of gratitude to those who have encouraged my study of military history is so long as to tax both my memory and the supply of ink on hand. First and foremost I must thank my wife, Barbara, who has long encouraged me to write more books than I read! In truth, she first saw the current work as a unique opportunity to embark on "my book." Likewise, my children MSgt. Herbert B. McGeorge, Megan, and Colin have never failed to encourage me.

Next must come the long list of colleagues, friends, and associates whom I deem "true believers," those who have long held to the certainty that World War I, and particularly the memory, deeds, and sacrifices of the men and women of the Allied Expeditionary Force (AEF) have always deserved more honor than they have yet been accorded. Among these are Maj. (Ret.) Peter G. Tuttle, Jim Hestick, Bill Munday, Col. (Ret.) Robert Dalessandro, Frederic Castier, Phil Richart, James Bond, Brett Werner, Mark Beveridge, Darrek Orwig, Doran Cart, Hayes Otoupalik, Rick Keller, Jim Hestick, Bill Hoffman, Tom Gudmestad, Brian Stewart, Jonathan Gawne, Alexander Barnes, and Thomas Fife. Of special note are those who have, as the Doughboys would have said, "Gone West," William L. Brown III, and Walter Keener—both were men who were truly gentlemen, scholars, and friends.

To Ken Smith-Christmas I owe special thanks; he first suggested using the Doughboy images in my collection for something greater than my personal amusement. Thanks, buddy!

My professional colleagues and coworkers also deserve my thanks for listening to my often-long-winded prattling on things Doughboy and AEF. Though they may not share in my fascination with World War I, they are, to a man, serious scholars and historians, and always ready with an encouraging word. Hearty thanks to Dr. J. Britt McCarley, Dr. Charles Cureton, Dr. Joseph Rainer, and Mr. Benjamin King.

In academia, Dr. Theodore Wilson, who saw me through my MA at University of Kansas in the 1990s, and has remained a mentor, friend, and sounding board ever since. Thanks also to my newest member of the true believers, Dr. Steven Trout at University of Southern Alabama. His interdisciplinary approach to the memory of the American experience of World War I is at once broad, meaningful, and fresh. On top of all that, he likes Doughboy photographs, too!

On the technical side, I owe a tremendous debt of gratitude to Martin Baldassari, photo researcher extraordinaire. He is at once a gifted technician, dogged researcher, and a fun guy to be around. His assistance in scanning and selecting images for this work, deciphering ninety-year-old captions and commentaries, and keen eye for detail was immensely helpful. Likewise, the editorial staff at Schiffer Books were a truly professional group who were a joy to work with.

Finally, I must thank the real subjects of this work—Doughboys. I am old enough to remember veterans of the AEF as other than a ghostly crowd of long-dead and nearly forgotten ancients or a mere dozen or so centenarians plus awaiting the final roll call. On my walks to kindergarten in Stamford, Connecticut, as a child, one of the crossing guards was missing the greater part of a hand. In retrospect, given his age at the time, he was clearly a veteran of World War I service.

Of the many AEF veterans I have been honored to know, two stand out. The first is Sergeant 1st Class Frederick B. Haines, Co. E, 1st Engineers (and for a short period, Acting Battalion Sergeant Major, 1st Battalion, 1st Engineers) 1st Division AEF. After years of cajoling at family gatherings, Uncle Fred finally opened up when I asked him where he was the night of November 2, 1917, when Cpl. Gresham, and privates Enright and Hay were killed by German trench raiders. He had not heard their names spoken in fifty years. That shock opened the door and he shared innumerable stories of his time in the 1st Division freely for years after. He and his barbed wiring detail were in "No Man's Land" that night, and had heard the Stroßtruppen pass through on their way into American lines.

The second is Cpl. Howard Verne Ramsey, 302nd Water Tank Train, 2nd Army AEF. I first met Howard when he was 103 years old, still living by himself and able to grant me a forty-five-minute video interview on his World War I experiences. His recollections of service in the AEF were as clear as if they had occurred yesterday, and the more poignant of them could still move him to tears. The comical ones could still provoke a hearty laugh. It was my honor to help convey his remains to their final resting place in a 1918 Liberty truck much like those he drove in France when he passed away a few weeks short of his 109th birthday.

Stephen C. McGeorge
Hampton, Virginia, November 2016

Photography in the Allied Expeditionary Force (AEF)

Within the first month after arrival in France in June 1918, General Headquarters (GHQ) AEF promulgated its initial guidance on control of responsibility for photographic work, and subsequent control of photographic images. GHQ AEF General Order (G.O.) No. 8, dated July, 5 1917, outlined the duties of the Headquarters AEF staff. The first mention of photography comes in description of the duties of the Intelligence Section, which assigns this staff section responsibility for censorship, including "Official photographs and moving pictures." In its description of Technical and Administrative Services, the Signal Corps Section is charged with "Photography of Military Operations."

Some five weeks after publishing the outline duties of GHQ AEF staff, GHQ AEF G.O. No. 22, dated August 18, 1917, delineated in detail policies covering "developing, censoring, storing, and distribution of still and motion pictures taken by the official photographers, US Army, and also by correspondents and authorized visitors in the Zone of the American Armies." In this General Order the Signal Corps was given control over photographic work by a variety of means. Among these were:

a. Establishment of the Signal Corps as the sole archival repository for photographic images.

b. Vesting the Signal Corps with the sole authority to develop films and plates at the Signal Corps plant.

c. Directing that all films and photographs be submitted to Press Officer, Intelligence Section, General Staff, for censorship before public release.

d. Firm prohibition of film development at any facility beside those described above, and retention of all rights to photographic materials, no matter the maker, to the Signal Corps.

In short, the regulatory guidance on photography in the AEF from the very outset of its existence, was designed to ensure that photography was effectively censored, and processing of photographic images carefully controlled.

By January 1918, further guidance on photography was required. GHQ AEF G.O. No. 15 dated January 24, 1918, revoked the previous general Order, G.O. No. 22. It specified that:

1. The Corps of Engineers is charged with technical photography related to construction, surveying and map reproduction.

2. The Air Service is charged with photography pertaining to map reconnaissance.

3. The Signal Corps is charged with general photography of military operations, and obtaining photographs to support a pictorial history of the present war.

The regulation further provided that: "Hereafter no photographs will be taken in the Zone of the American Army except by official photographers provided for in paragraphs 1, 2, and 3: by accredited or visiting correspondents, or members of photographic sections of allied armies duly authorized by these headquarters."

In seven more paragraphs the order directed that the Paris Signal Corps laboratory to be the sole facility to develop photographic images, that they would be censored by the Intelligence Section, General Staff GHQ AEF, and that for all practical purposes all photographic imagery was property of the United States. This G.O. certainly implies prohibition of personal photography by members of the AEF, although it is not explicitly addressed.

GHQ AEF General Order No. 146 dated September 1, 1918, was the most comprehensive guidance issued by GHQ AEF on censorship during the war. The order runs to nine pages and covers every aspect of censorship put in force in the AEF.

Section XII. PHOTOGRAPHIC CENSORSHIP opens with an unequivocal prohibition on personal photography:

(A) All members of the American Expeditionary Forces are forbidden to take photographs unless photography is part of their official duties. If cameras are in the possession of members of the American E.F. they may be kept (unloaded) in baggage (but are not to be used).

The general order continues with restatement of procedures for film developing, censorship and release of photographs nearly identical to earlier guidance. Paragraph (F) states, "Personal photographs may be sent if there is no suggestion of background that might connect any organization with any particular place."

Since all mail was censored any offending photographs would have been discovered. Very occasionally AEF photographs are found with a censors stamp applied directly to the image. Two examples I have seen are photographs of Lt. Quentin Roosevelt's gravesite, and 155 mm gun positions with guns emplaced, camouflaged and ready to fire.

GHQ AEF General Order No. 8 dated January 11, 1919, finally suspended ALL photographic censorship:

All members of the American Expeditionary Forces, including militarized civilians serving with the Army, and authorized civilians visiting the zone occupied by the American Army, are, during the period of the armistice, permitted to take photographs and moving pictures and to forward such photographs (negatives or prints) to the United States or other countries, except enemy countries, by the ordinary channels without restriction and without submitting them to censorship.

The implied, and later emphatic prohibition on personal photography in the AEF was not absolutely enforceable. Clearly some Officers and men in the AEF retained personal cameras despite orders and made images of their experiences. There really is no way to quantify how much personal photography was done during the war. Veterans organization magazines in post war era often contain advertisements for "photographic sets" for sale to those former Doughboys who didn't have a camera or followed the letter of General Order No. 146. Such stock photography sets are quite common.

GHQ AEF General Order No. 56 dated March 29, 1919, section II , 2. contained directions for the, "PURCHASE OF OFFICIAL PHOTOGRAPHS FOR PERSONAL OR PRIVATE USE" and reads as follows:

Photographs taken by the Signal Corps, American E.F. may be procured foe personal or private use at the price of fifteen cents per contact print by applying to the Photographic Section, Signal Corps, US Army, Washington, DC. In applying for these photographs the American E.F. file number, together with title or caption of the photograph should be furnished. These file numbers and tiles or captions may be obtained from the historical officer of each staff, section, division,, corps, and army in the American E.F. who has been issued an album and copies of all photographs pertaining to his respective organization or unit. In the event this information cannot be obtained from the historical officer, inquiries may be addressed to the Signal Corps Photographic Laboratory, Paris. Remittances should be made by money order, payable to Photographic Section, Signal Corps, US Army, Washington DC.

In May 1919, the War Department published the Catalogue of Official AEF. Photographs taken by the Signal Corps, USA (to be supplemented), War Department Document No. 903. This massive listing is the size of a good sized city telephone directory, and includes indexes by Military Unit, Persons, Places, Subjects, and includes the official caption of each photograph. It also includes detailed ordering instructions and prices ranging from fifteen cents for contact prints to one dollar for 20 x 24 inch enlargements. I am unaware of any printed supplement to the Catalogue ever being issued.

The issuance of such a catalog explains the relative commonality of official AEF photographs in the market today.

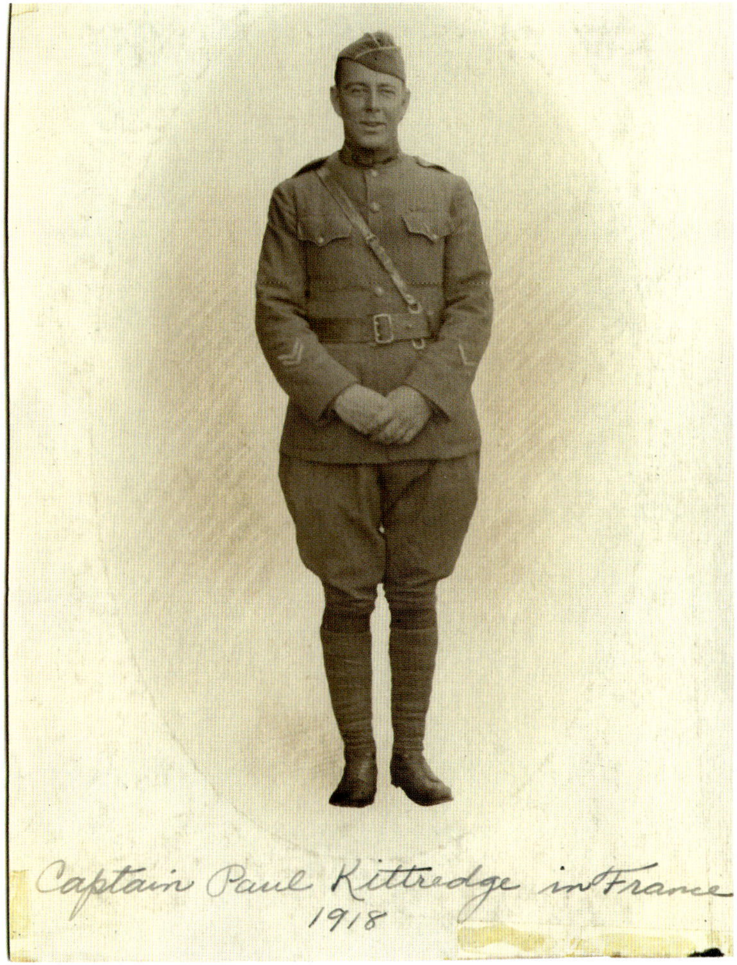

Capt. Paul Kittredge. Note two wound chevrons on his right sleeve. This is very likely Capt. Paul Edward Kittredge of Lowell, Massachusetts. Kittredge Park in Lowell was named in his honor. He was assigned to Company M, 101st Infantry, 26th Division, AEF. Kittredge was killed in action October 23, 1918. He was previously cited for bravery and devotion to duty for his actions at the St. Mihiel Salient, October 16, 1918. Kittredge is still "Over There," in the Meuse-Argonne American cemetery.

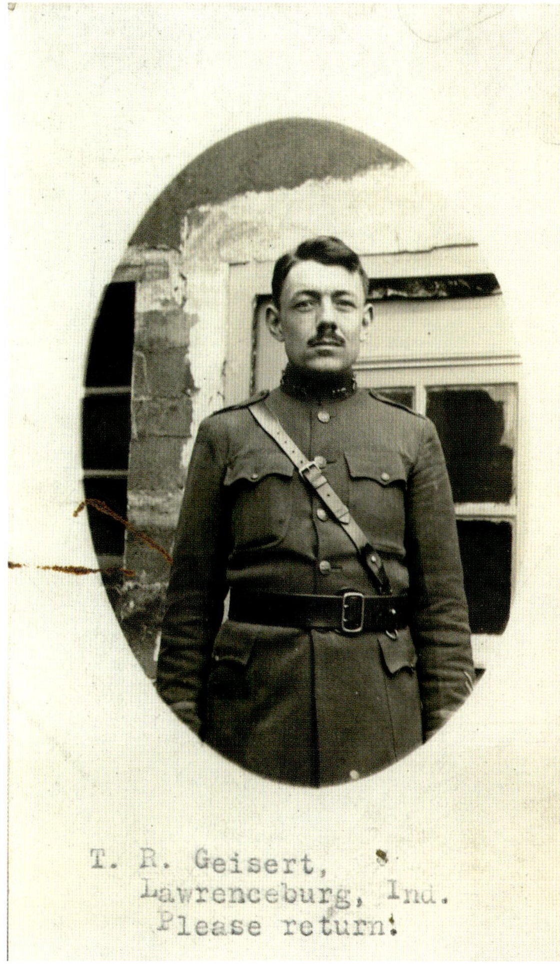

Lt. Thaddeus R. Geisert, Battery C, 305th Field Artillery, 77th Division, of 307 West High Street, Lawrenceburg, Indiana. He is wearing two war service chevrons, denoting one year of service in France, when the image was taken.

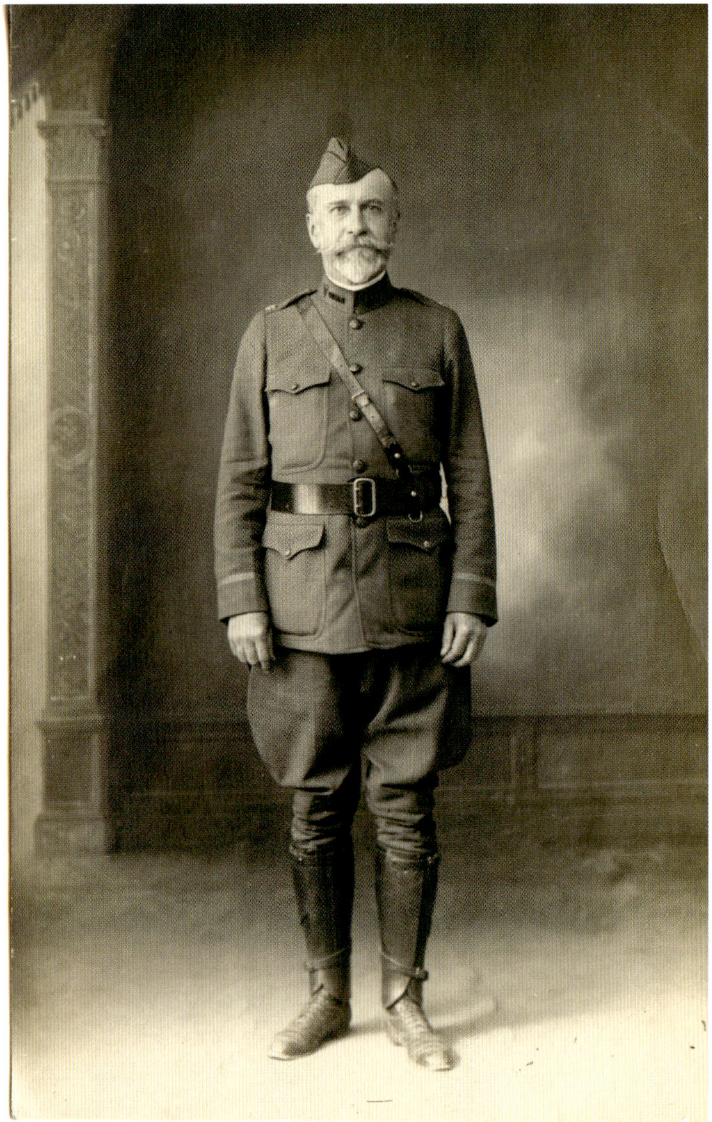

Maj. L. Vernon Briggs, Medical Corps, US Army image taken August 1918, in France. Lloyd Vernon Briggs was a 1899 graduate of the Medical College of Virginia, eventually specializing in psychiatry and criminal law. Practicing in Massachusetts, he was the father of what became known as "Briggs Law," that required mental examination of all persons indicted for felonies before trial. In military service he initially served at Ft. Devens, Massachusetts, and was responsible for neuro-psychiatric examination of new recruits. He was appointed Division Psychiatrist of the 76th Division National Army in January 1918. After the Armistice, he was assigned as Division Psychiatrist of 2nd Division, rising to the grade of lieutenant colonel. In a 1919 address to the American Medico-Psychological Association he commented at length on "war neurosis" cases he had observed, many of which would today be diagnosed as post traumatic stress disorder.

The Regulations for the Army of the United States 1913, Para. 286 stated, " The hair will be kept short and the beard neatly trimmed." The "beard neatly trimmed" part seems to have been interpreted (at least for enlisted men) as meaning clean shaven, with the possible exception of a moustache. Officers in the AEF and in the United States seem to have exercised much more latitude. While not common, senior officers are seen with fairly tame goatees and moustaches. For frontline soldiers the issue of facial hair carried with it the practical consideration that beards or even heavy stubble could prevent an adequate seal of the gas mask face piece.

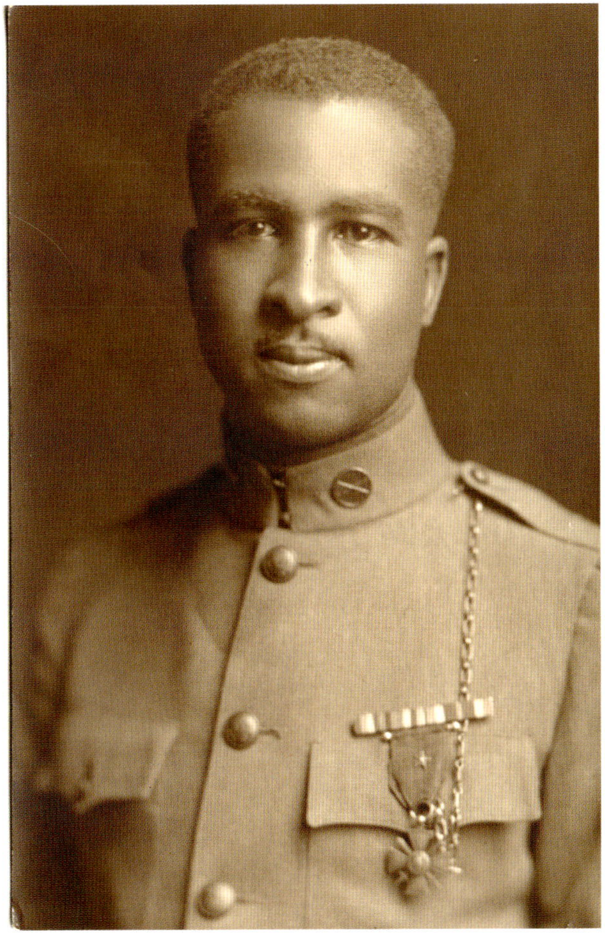

Cpl. Theodore C. Banks, Company L, 806th Pioneer Infantry. Cpl. Banks was one of two sons of Rev. Wilson P. Banks and his wife, Louisa. Rev. Banks was pastor of St. Johns Baptist Church, Salina, Kansas. The family resided at 334 North 5th Street, in Salina. Banks was twenty-two when inducted, and listed his occupation as cook. In this image he wears the Inter-Allied Victory ribbon, another unknown ribbon, and a Croix de Guerre with star. It was remarked in the period that only "handsome men" were allowed in the 806th Pioneer Infantry. Banks clearly met this standard. He served in France from September 1918, and was discharged in August 1919.

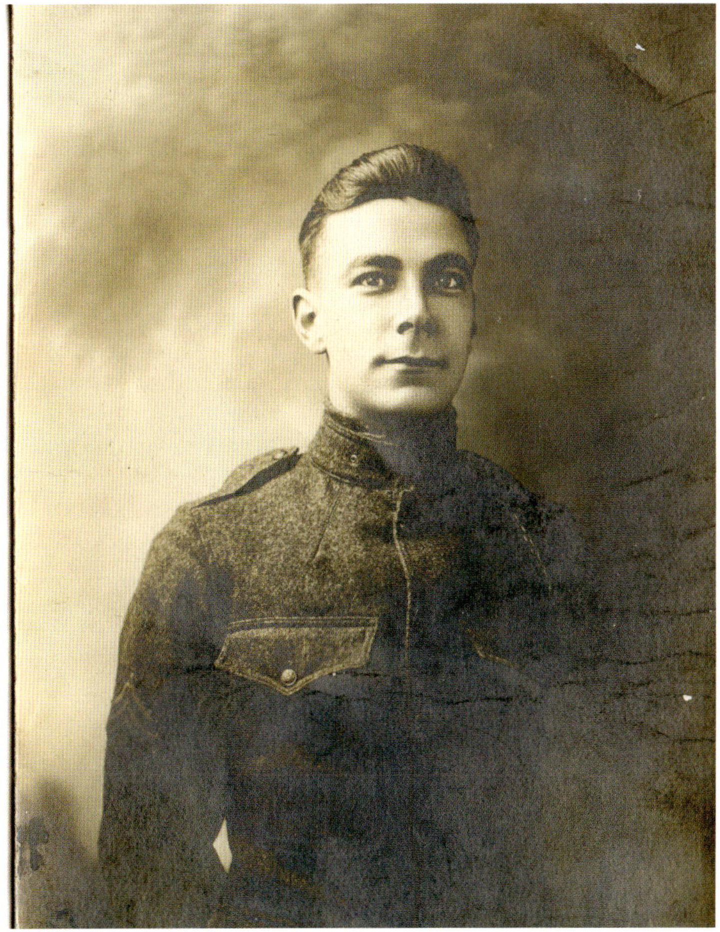

Sgt. Anthony M. Waldron, Company K, 132nd Infantry, 33rd Division, AEF; image taken November 10, 1918, one prior to the Armistice. It is interesting to note in the later part of fall 1918, and throughout the period of Occupation of Germany, how many Doughboys lack a complete set of collar and cap ornaments.

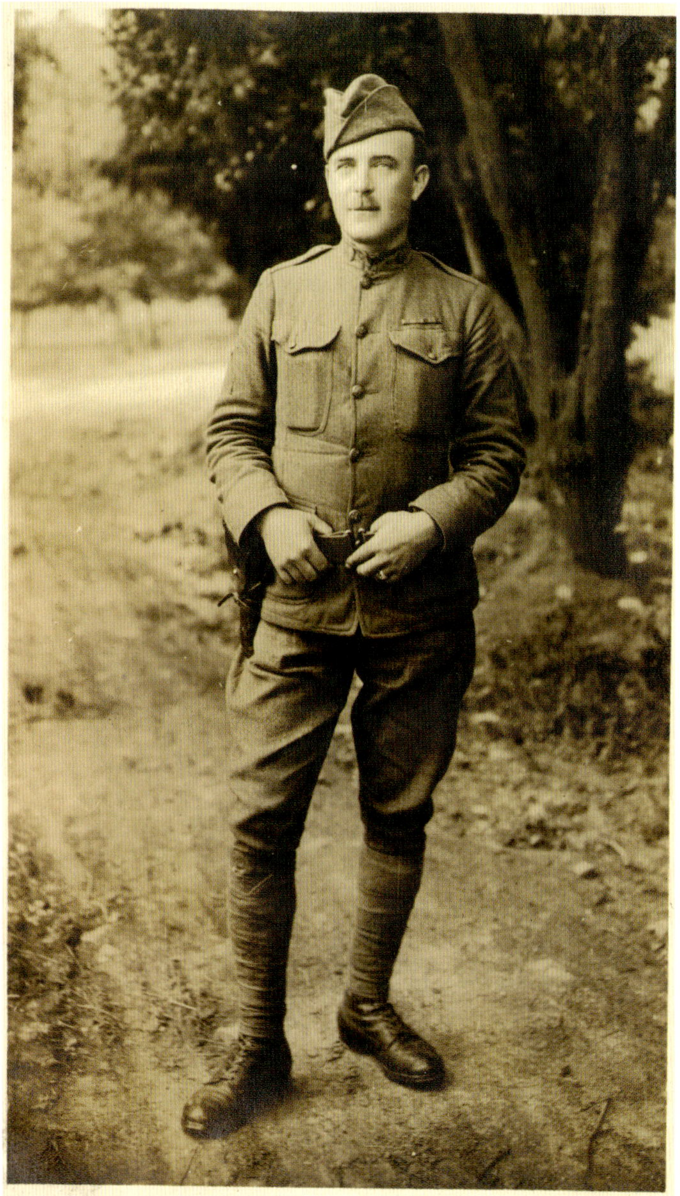

Sgt. William P. Finley, Battery F, 108th Field Artillery 28th Division AEF image, dated July 27, 1918. Finley was a pre-war National Guard member, and he is wearing the Mexican Border Service ribbon in this image, and one other unidentified ribbon as well. Finley listed his address at enlistment as 2220 Bonnafon Terrace, Philadelphia, Pennsylvania. The 108th Field Artillery was the 28th "Keystone" Division's heavy Artillery Regiment, armed with 155 mm Model 1916 Schneider howitzers. At the time this image was taken the 108th Field Artillery was nearing completion of their training on 155 mm howitzers at Camp de Meucon near Vannes, France. Less than a month after this image was taken the 108th would fire its first shot at the Huns on August 15, 1918, while serving in the Aisne-Marne region. Finley is wearing a newly issued overseas cap and appears to be wearing a pair of the pre-war smooth side out russet marching shoes.

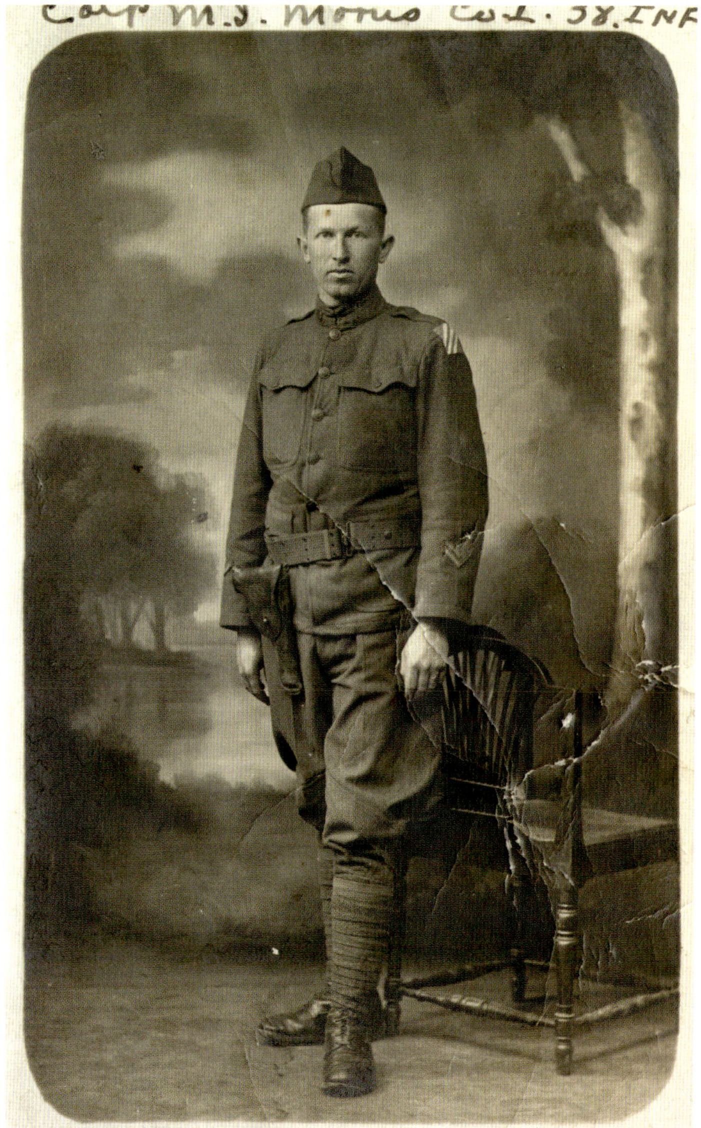

Cpl. M. J. Morris, Company I, 38th Infantry, 3rd Division AEF. Morris' inscription on the back states, "This is a picture I had taken just before I left I Co., 38th." Unfortunately, Morris did not provide a date, though the image was almost certainly taken in the Army of Occupation, since he is wearing the 3rd Division insignia. Also notable are his French style overseas cap, and one wound and two war service chevrons. While he is armed with a Model 1911 automatic pistol he isn't carrying any magazine pockets for it. It was the 38th Infantry Regiment, commanded by Col. Ulysses Grant McAlexander that was originally deemed the "Rock of the Marne" for their monumental efforts in stopping the German crossings of the Marne River near Mezy, in July 1918. It was only later that the sobriquet was expanded to apply to the 3rd Division as a whole.

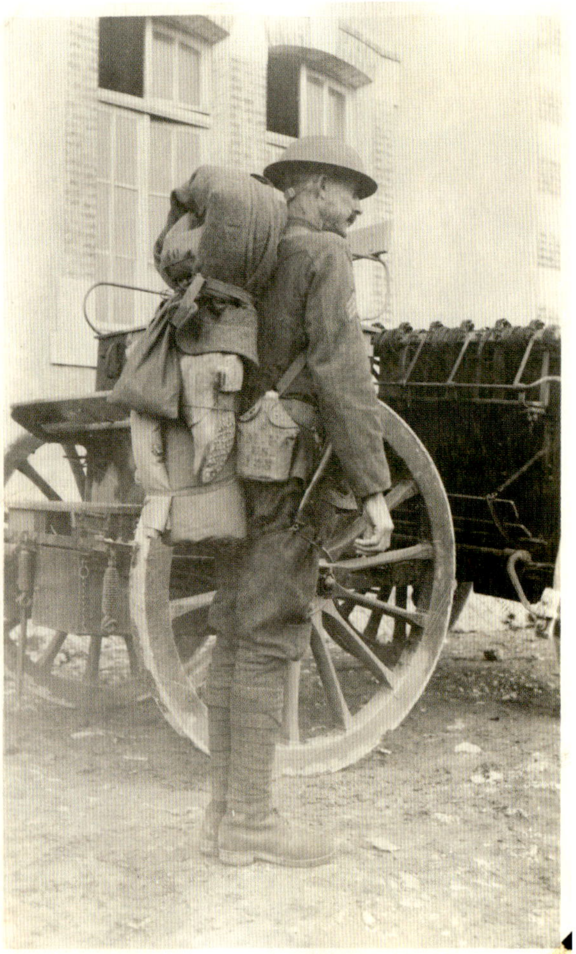

Identified as Sgt. Symonds, Battery C, 11th Field Artillery, 6th Division, AEF, this photo and its companion illustrate very well the shortcomings of the model 1910 Infantry equipment. The haversack/pack combination was incapable of conveniently accommodating any additional equipment it was not specifically designed to carry. Here we see the overcoat formed in a horseshoe roll tied over the top of the haversack, spare boots tied onto the body of the haversack, a slicker or raincoat rolled into a cylinder and secured under the pack straps, and for good measure a small ditty bag suspended by its strings just under the meat can pouch. The only thing Symonds seems not to be burdened with is an entrenching tool. The 11th Field Artillery was the sole element of the "Sight Seeing Sixth" Division to actually get into action in the war. Attached to the 58th Field Artillery Brigade, the 11th Field Artillery was armed with 155 mm Model 1916 Schneider howitzers and provided fire support to the 89th Division the last several weeks of the war. The 11th was described as the outfit that "Got to the Front God knows how; got ammunition God knows where; fired it at God knows what, and ended up on the banks of the Meuse, but God knows what measures it took to get there."

In the front view Sgt. Symonds' sidearm is clearly visible, a Model 1917 Revolver (either Colt or Smith and Wesson, it is impossible to tell), and the distinctive three-pocket pouch for carrying a total of eighteen .45-caliber rounds in their three-round, half-moon steel clips. He has the holster securely tied to his right thigh. On his lower left sleeve he wears a narrow brassard. This is most likely either the blue brassard for signal men or the red brassard for runners. His American small box respirator is slung on his left side and is prominently stenciled with his name. His name and service number are also hand-inked on the lower portion of the carry strap where it attaches to the bag proper. Barely visible is the cord used to loosely tie his helmet to his left epaulette. The cord looks to be either a canvas legging or breeches lace. This practice is rarely seen in the AEF, although there is an official Signal Corps image of an MP using the standard 1917 pistol lanyard in a similar manner. The mystery of why was resolved in a close reading of one of Leonard H. Nason's novels of the AEF—the idea of "dummy cording" the helmet to the body was to preclude losing one's helmet or having it touch contaminated ground in the process of rapidly donning the gas mask in a chemical attack!

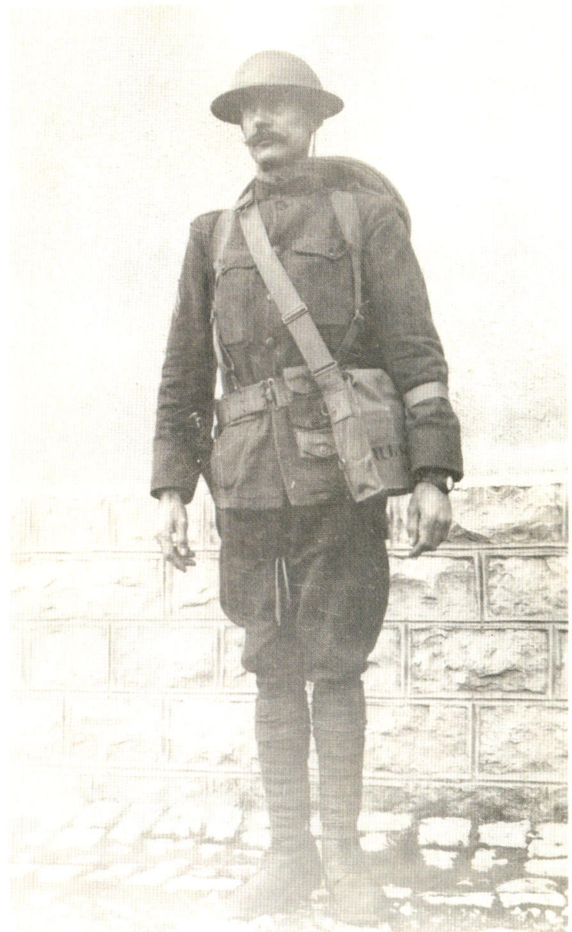

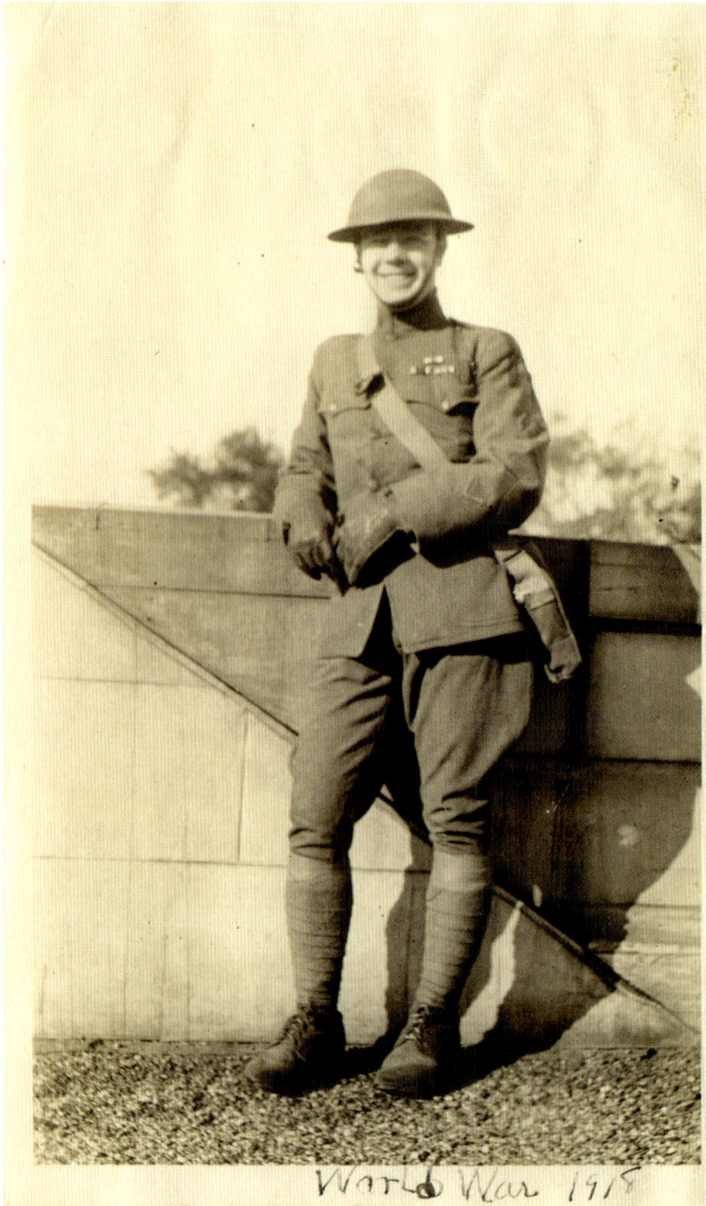

This smiling Doughboy is Sgt. Donald N. MacKubin of 723 Wister St., Germantown, Pennsylvania. MacKubin apparently served in a number of organizations before landing in the AEF. Before America's entry into the war he attended Cambridge University and was a member of the American Student Detachment there. Returning to the United States, he worked with the YMCA at both Camp Mills and Naval Base, Brooklyn, New York. Finally, in the US Army proper he served in Company K, 315th Infantry, 79th Division, AEF. He was cited for, "Gallantry in action and meritorious service," in the 79th Division G.O. No. 29, dated May 8, 1918. A graduate of Blair Academy, Blairstown, New Jersey, the school's memorial volume, Blair Academy in the Great War, claims he was also recommended for commission, based on gallantry in action. In this image he sports three ribbons, likely some of the many unofficial (and unauthorized) campaign and battle ribbons available after the Armistice. Also inexplicably, he appears to be wearing a 1st Army patch.

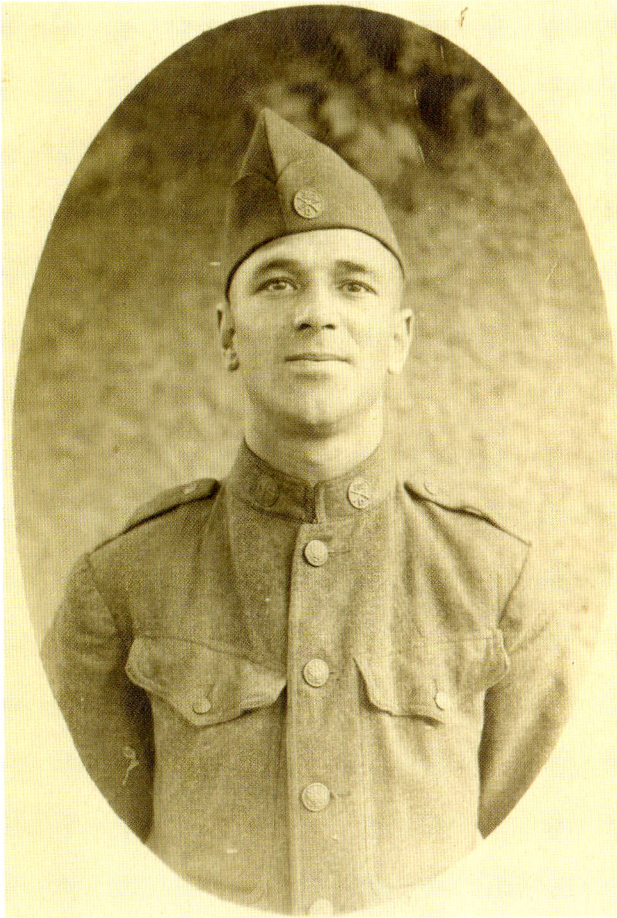

Cpl. Lewis Cross, Prisoner of War Escort (PWE) Company No. 227. While wearing collar ornaments for Company D, 302nd Infantry in this image, Cross was later assigned to PWE Company 227 working in Bretagne, France. He enclosed this image in a letter home to Miss Anna Howland, of Fall River, Massachusetts, in April 1919. In this letter he complains (as did many other Doughboys) of incessant rain in France. He also tells Miss Howland he has recently been informed of his mother's death in a letter from his brother. Hard news while serving overseas, even though Cross referred to her as invalid for years whose death he expected all the while in France.

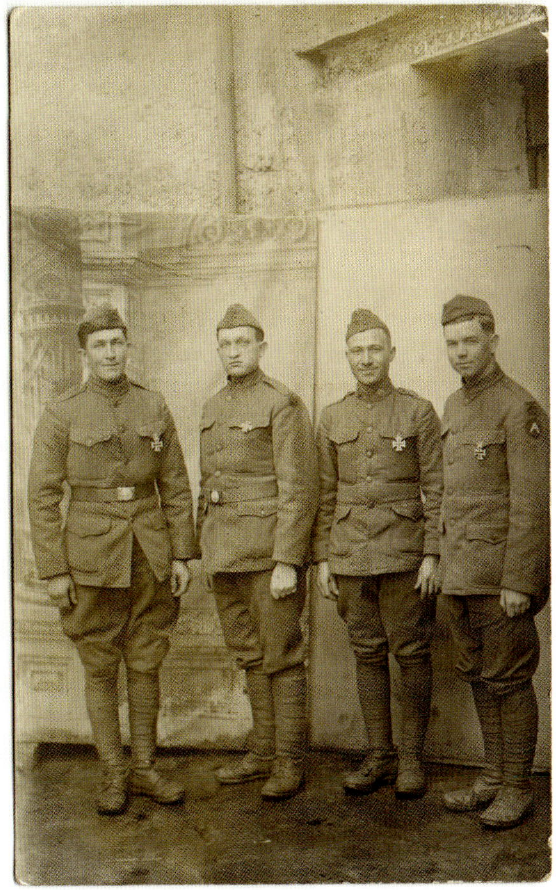

A handsome foursome of "Tough Hombres," Doughboys from Company G, 358th Infantry, 90th Division, AEF. From left to right they are: Pvt. Hover, Mechanic Gerler, and privates Klinger and Lombardo. All sport Iron Cross 2nd Class medals suspended from their pockets. In addition, Hover and Gerler proudly wear captured German belts. Pvt. Lombardo wears the double patch combination of 3rd Army and 90th Division. Three of the four are lacking any collar ornaments. None have ornaments for their overseas caps. Also interesting is the painted backdrop set up for the photo—against the exterior wall of a building!

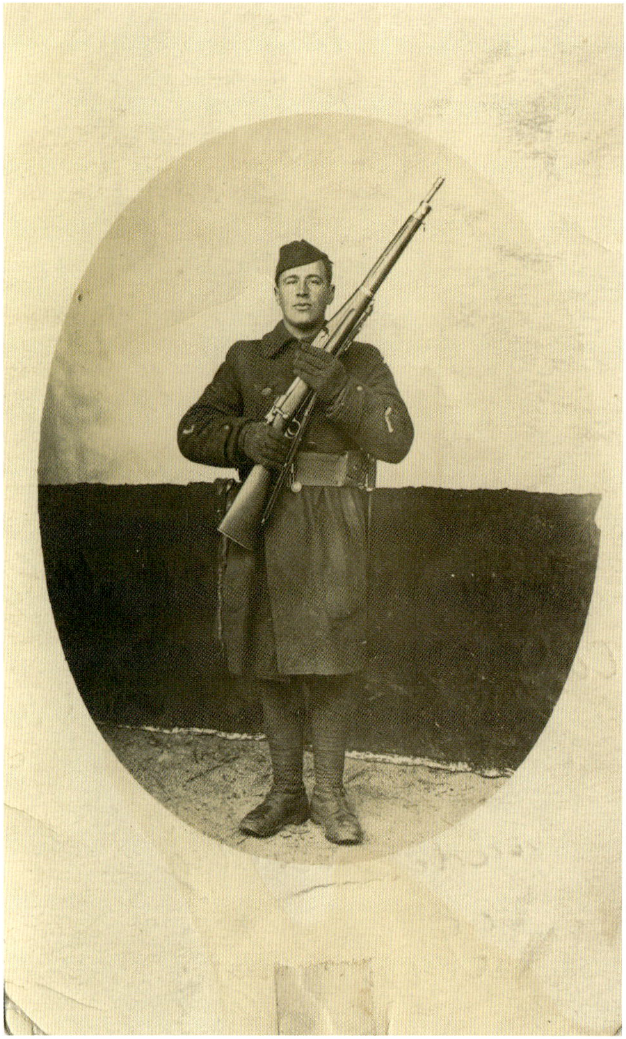

Sigurd G. Sandberg, of Company G, 38th Infantry, 3rd Division, AEF. Image taken at Neidermendig, Germany, during the occupation. Sandberg wears a single war service chevron and a wound chevron. It is quite possible he was one of the "Giants of the Marne" members of Company G, 38th Infantry who held the farthest forward positions near Mezy on the Marne, where the 38th Infantry repelled the best efforts of the German army to cross the river in mid-July 1918. Company G experienced tremendous losses in stopping repeated German assaults and engaged in fierce hand-to-hand combat with the Germans who made the crossing. Commanded by Capt. Jesse W. Wooldridge, Company G counted as trophies fifty-two machine guns carried by the Boche who crossed the Marne at Mezy, and advanced no further. Sandberg wears a 1917 pattern overcoat. He is armed with a Model 1903 Springfield rifle, apparently a rather early production gun as there are no visible stock reinforcing bolts. This indicates it is a pre-1910 production rifle. He also carries a Model 1911 pistol in the standard M1916 holster, with a very long coiled elk hide tie-down thong. He is wearing an early production cartridge belt, possibly the model 1912 cavalry experimental model with no visible snap for a magazine pocket for his pistol. His bayonet is worn on the belt and appears to be a model 1905 bayonet carried in a model 1917 scabbard. This substitution is occasionally seen in AEF images.

An interesting image and difficult to date. This Doughboy, having his canteen filled by a young (presumably) French girl, is wearing no war service chevrons, but he wears the marksman bar/badge over his left pocket. He also appears to be wearing both a rifle cartridge belt and a pistol belt. The pistol magazine pouch appears to be one of the earlier eagle snap variants. Most troubling is the complete absence of any gas mask. The narrow strap of the French M-2 mask bag is not evident, nor is the broader web strap of a small box respirator. His fixed bayonet is evidently a pre-1917 "bright blade" model 1905 version. Why a fixed bayonet, pistol, and rifle cartridge belt (clearly empty), and no gas mask?

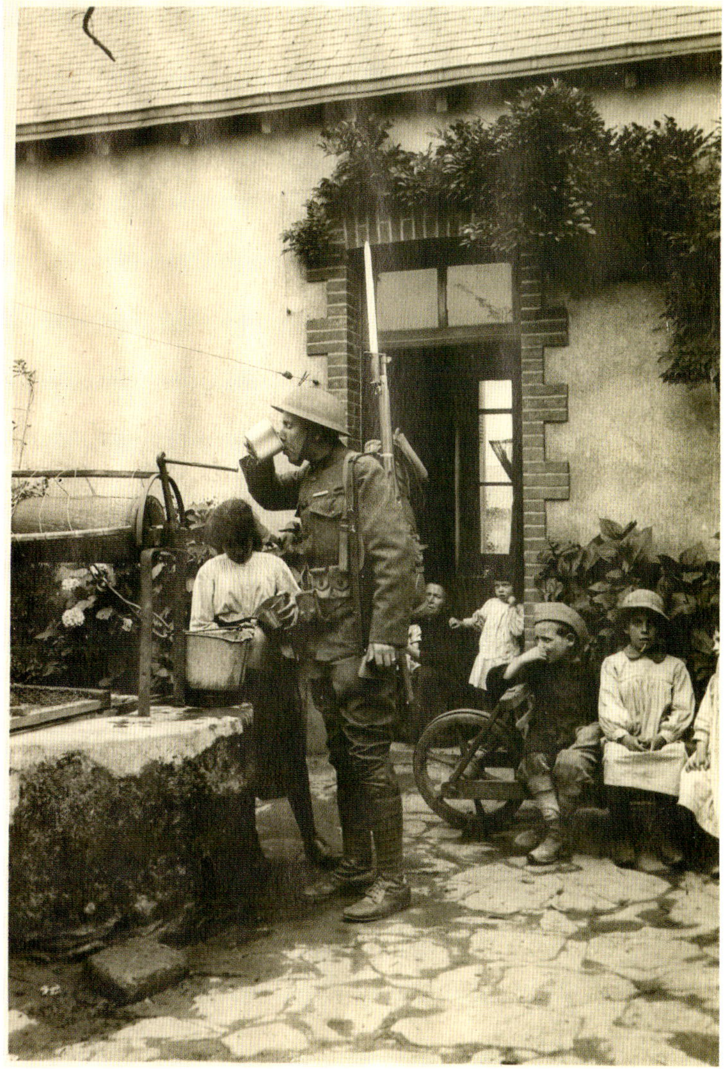

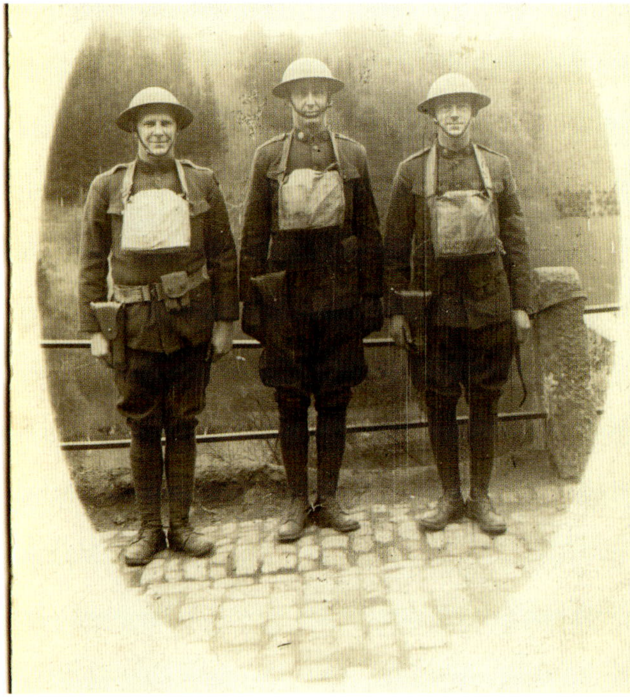

A trio of dapper 89th Division MPs. The 89th Division shoulder sleeve insignia is barely visible on the Doughboy on the left. All three are wearing the most common type of MP brassard observed in use in the AEF, red letters MP on a dark blue background. They also wear the scarlet cloth strips on the collar, distinctive insignia of members of the Military Police Corps. The scarlet stripes were prescribed for wear by GHQ AEF G.O. No. 152, dated September 10, 1918. Armed with Model 1911 pistols, all three are wearing only the pistol holster and magazine pocket on the pistol belt. Interestingly, they are wearing the small box respirator in the alert position despite the fact the image was taken after hostilities in the Army of Occupation. They are identified as Rastus Crull, John Cantwell, and Grove Hand.

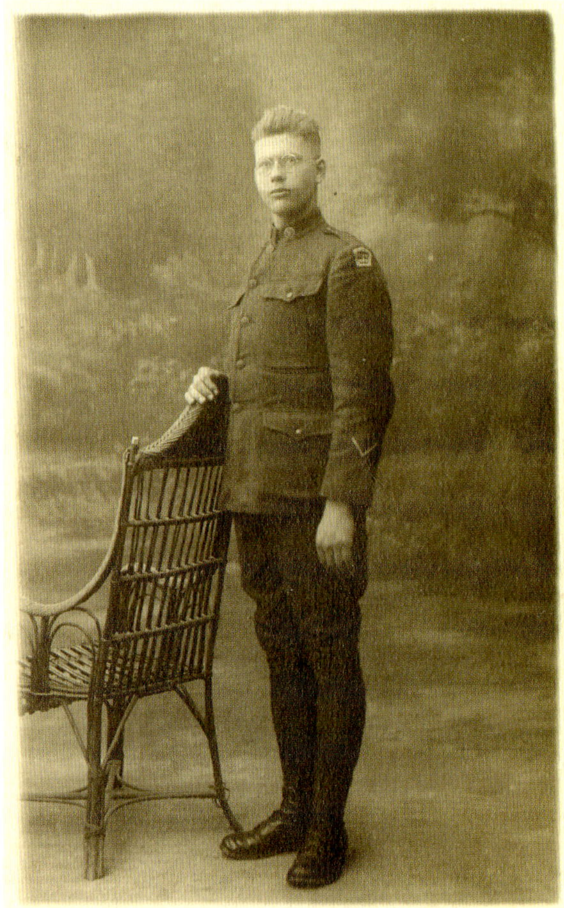

A member of the Services of Supply as evidenced by his shoulder sleeve insignia, this anonymous Doughboy wears a Medical Corps collar disk. He is wearing the standard issue American Optical Company. No. 5468, 40 mm standard spectacles. These were industry standard spectacles and were purchased for soldiers from larger optical supply houses on a regional basis while soldiers were undergoing initial training in the United States.

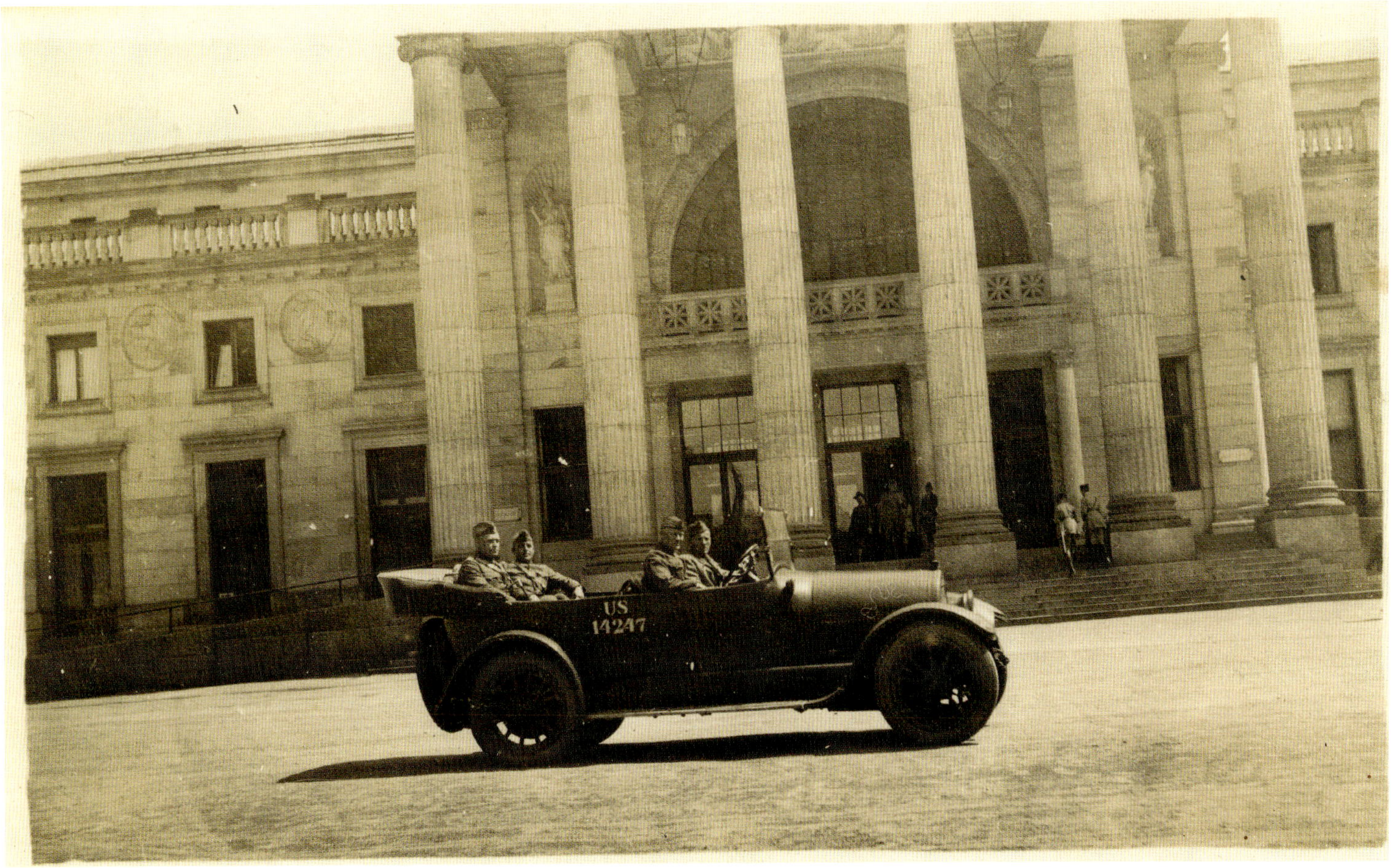

A typical AEF staff car. In this case the machine appears to be a Cadillac. The most common staff cars used in the AEF were the Ford Model T and the Dodge, both touring and closed models, in the light category, and the Cadillac being the most common car in the heavy category. The Cadillac is easily identifiable by the presence of the two cowling lights mounted on the hood just in front of the windshield stanchions. A total of 1,503 Cadillac cars were shipped overseas of both the "limousine" and "open" body styles. This vehicle is the open or touring style body. As evidenced by their Sam Browne belts the two occupants in the rear of the vehicle are officers, one of whom is holding a riding crop. In front appear to be an enlisted driver and assistant. The "1" prefix to the US registration number, 14247 on the hood further identifies the vehicle as a passenger car, and the remaining digits were supposed to reflect the consecutive number of arrival of the car in France. This vehicle numbering system was prescribed in GHQ, AEF Bulletin No. 90, dated November 11, 1918. This bulletin revoked earlier guidance issued by Chief Quartermaster, AEF, in September, 1917, but from photographic evidence appears that the basic vehicle numbering system must have been similar, if not identical.

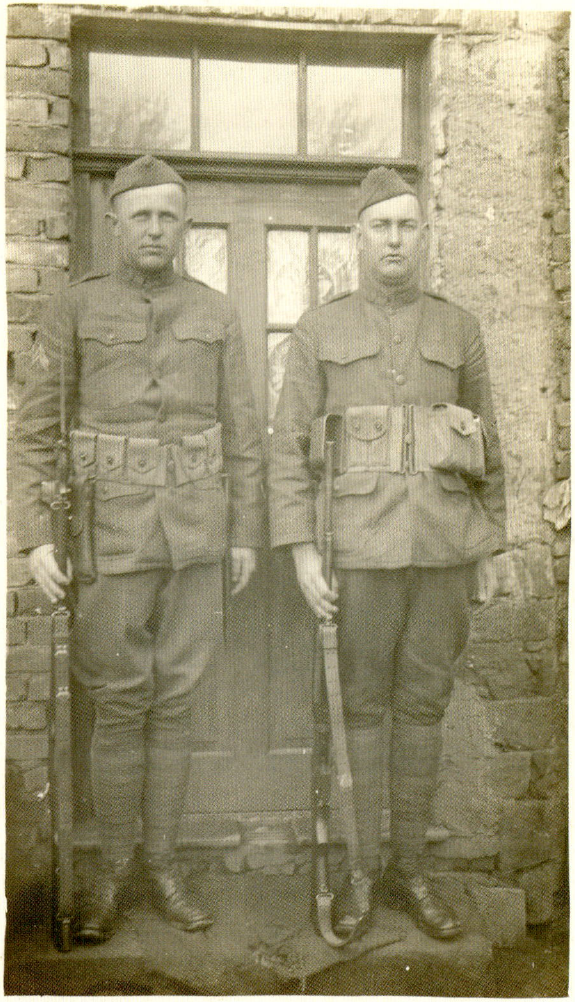

A corporal armed with the Model 1917 US rifle, and M1911 pistol, and private armed with the newly issued Browning Automatic Rifle, (BAR). Most AEF units did not receive the BAR until the early weeks after arrival in the Army of Occupation. The exceptions were the 79th Division and 89th Division, which brought the BAR with them to France, and were the first units to use it in combat during the Meuse-Argonne offensive. The gunner wears the BAR gunner's belt with the steel cup designed to hold the butt of the automatic rifle when used in the "Marching Fire" mode.

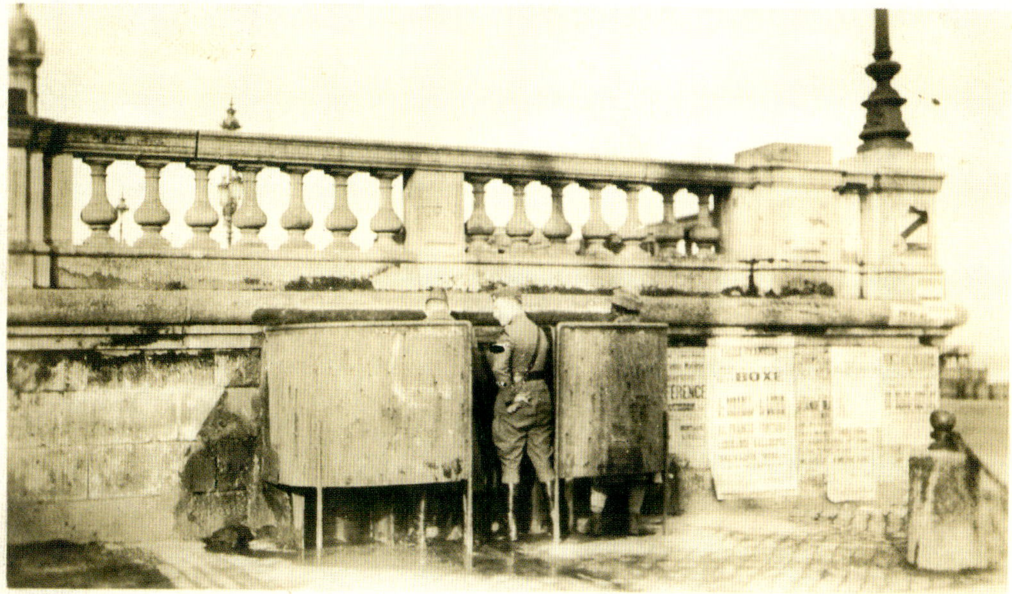

"The French they have the customs rare, Parley vous!" The semi-private urinal known as the "pissoir" found in Paris and other major French cities was frequently commented on and photographed by Doughboys. Here we see two officers relieving themselves in one of these unique (at least to Americans) facilities. No "Jim Crow" separate facilities rules here either . . . the French enlisted man using the pissoir appears to be a French African colonial!

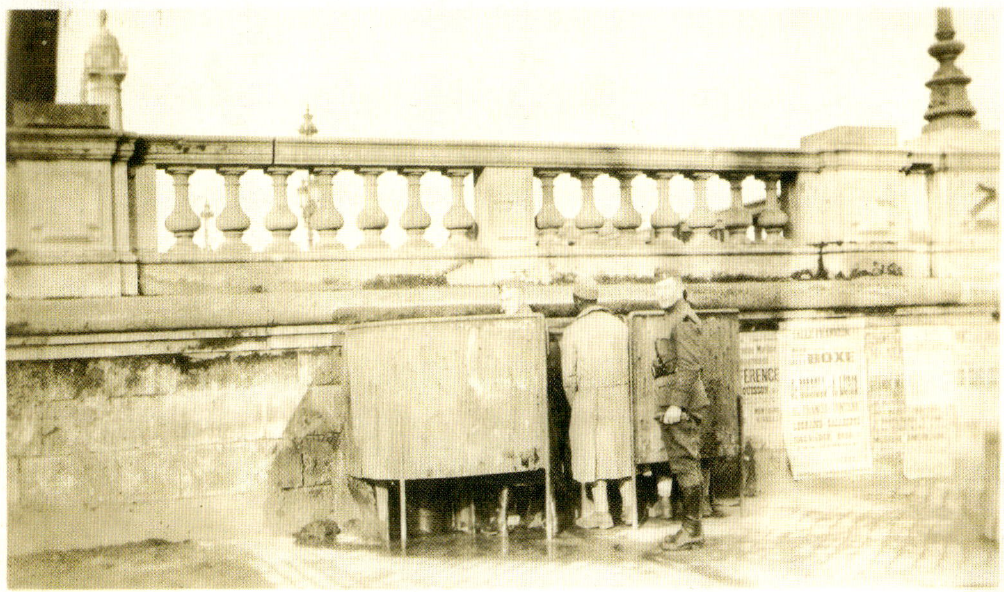

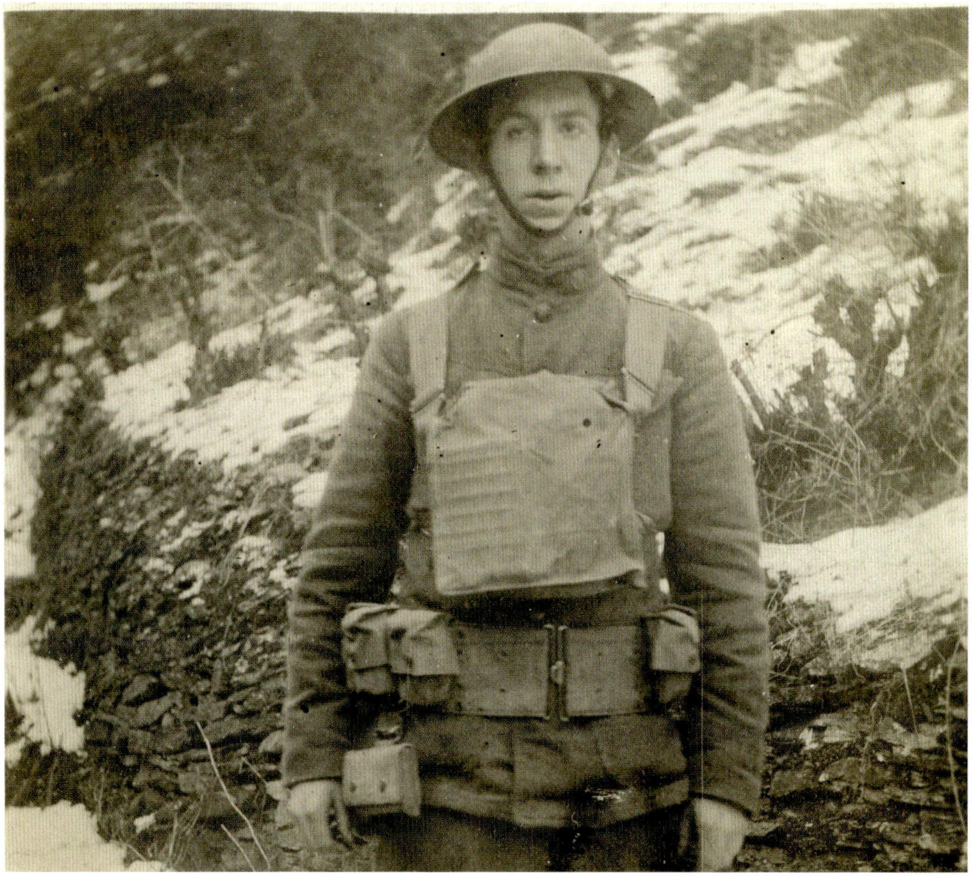

A Doughboy medic, although not wearing a red cross brassard, the enlisted medical belt this soldier is wearing clearly marks him as a medic. The belt is one of the earlier "eagle snap" variety. Interestingly, his diagnostic tag pouch is suspended from one of the extender tabs usually used to attach either the soldiers' canteen or hand axe carrier. His respirator is correctly worn in the alert position on his chest. Absence of shoulder sleeve insignia or overseas service chevrons may indicate this image was taken in late winter or early spring 1918.

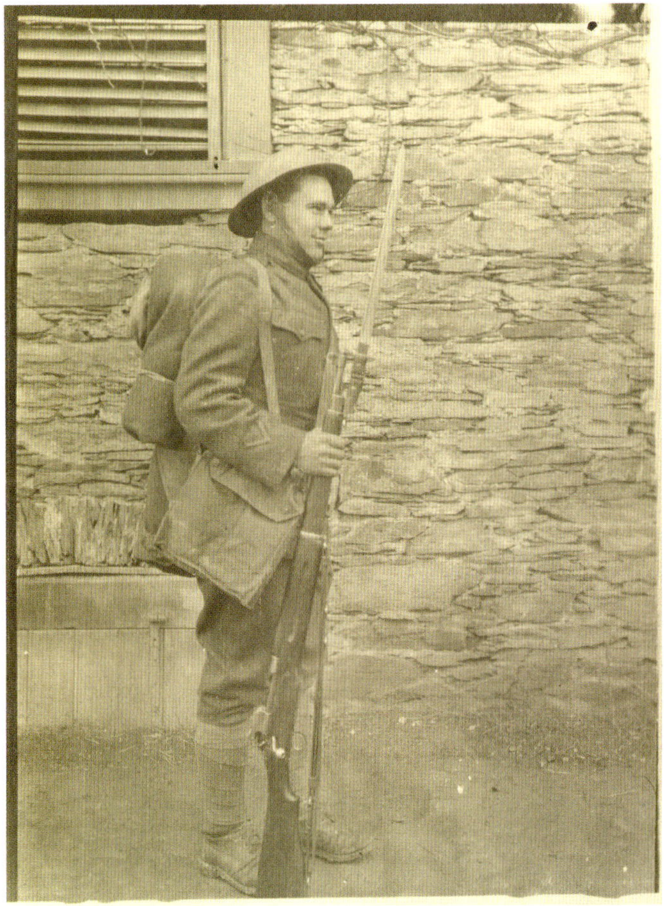

Doughboy in full pack complete with horseshoe roll and fixed bayonet. He sports a single wound stripe, and it appears the horseshoe roll is affixed to the pack with a shelter half guy rope.

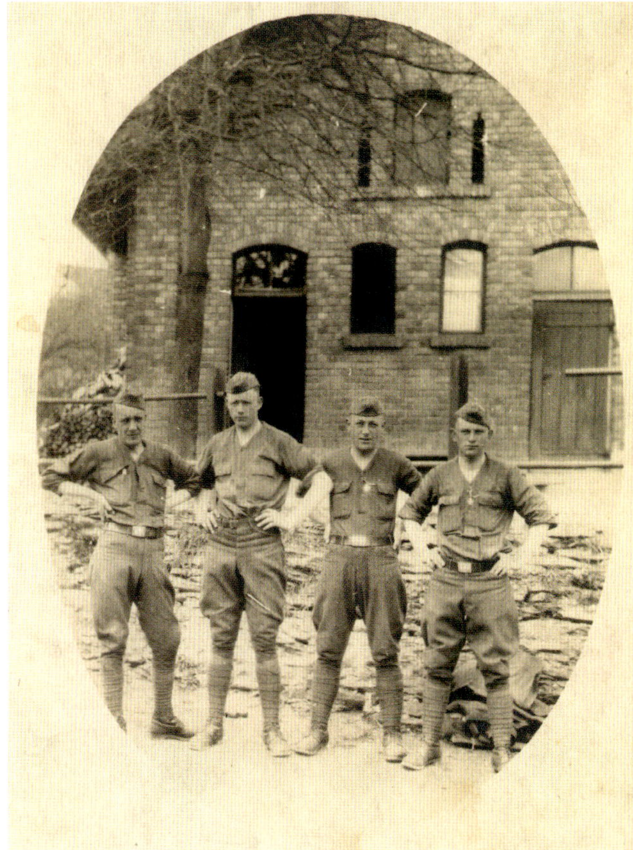

Four tough-looking Doughboys, three of whom are using liberated German equipment belts as trouser waistbelts. Interestingly all four are wearing the shirt collar rolled inside, perhaps so the service coat could be worn without any shirt collar visible, or maybe they have just come off a review or inspection. Behind the far right Doughboy on-grounded equipment can barely be discerned. Two sport chains with small iron cross fobs, from top shirt button to left breast shirt pockets, perhaps securing pocket watches.

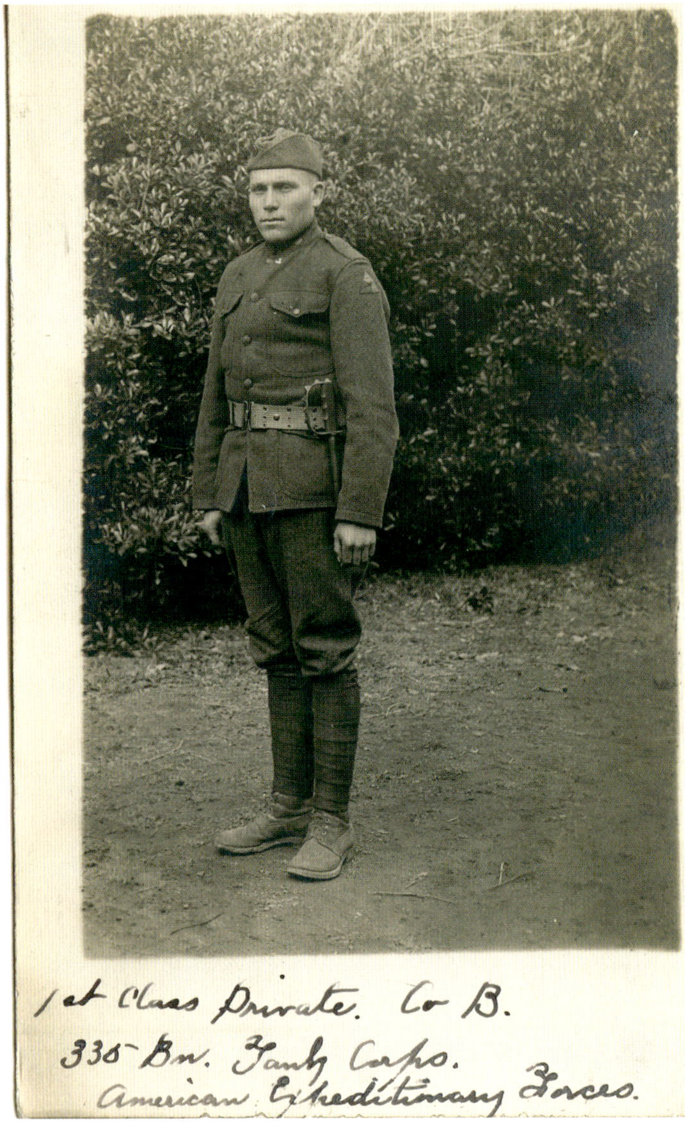

Identified only by rank and unit, a tanker of Company B, 335th Tank Battalion proudly poses for the camera, armed only with a Model 1917 trench knife, most likely of Landers, Frary, and Clark manufacture as evidenced by the stamped pyramid studs.

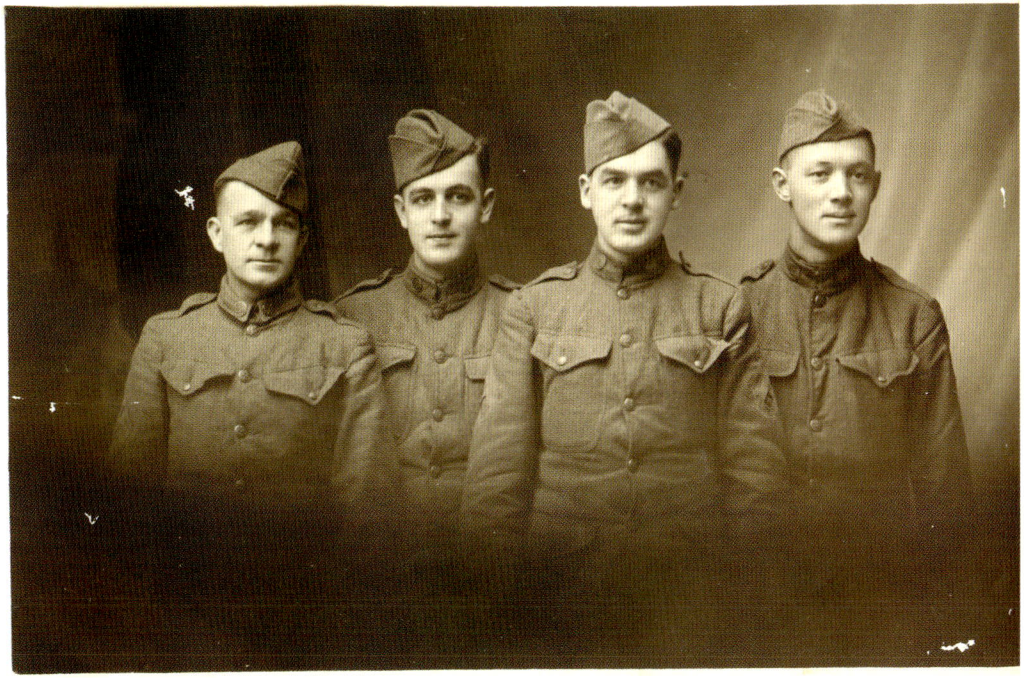

At first glance, a rather common image. The NCO on the far left wears his shirt collar over the coat collar with appropriate collar insignia, and he sports an English style overseas cap with folded-up bill and front buttons to secure the caps' curtain. More interesting is the NCO third from the left. He wears chevrons on both sleeves, the mark of "old salt" pre-war NCOs following issuance of GHQ AEF G.O. No. 75 dated May 18, 1918. This regulation transmitted the War Department directive of April 30, 1918, which prescribed wear of NCO chevrons on the right sleeve only "during the present emergency." Even more intriguing is the fact that his chevrons appear to be those of a sergeant first class grade with the branch identifying symbol between the rocker and the chevron angle neatly excised! This may indicate a change in his assigned specialty, or perhaps more likely issuance of a salvaged uniform issued in a clothing exchange and bath which had the wrong specialty on them and was promptly removed.

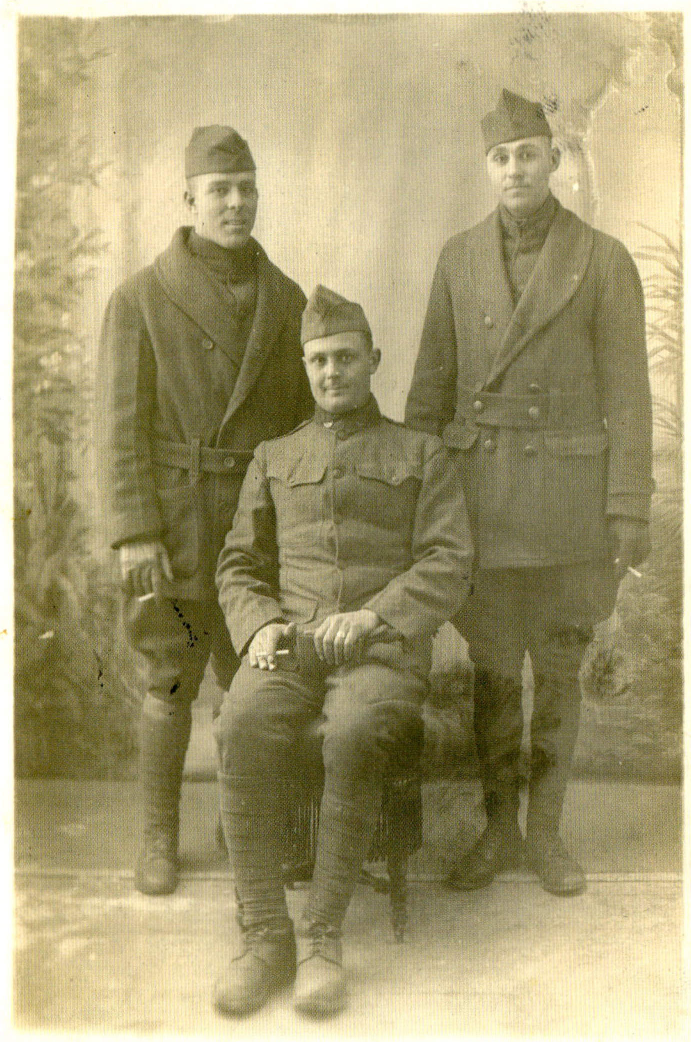

Three Doughboys, cigarette smokers all! Two wear French style overseas caps and the two standing soldiers are wearing the short mackinaw style overcoat. This particular garment is perhaps the least documented of any World War I–era US Army uniform items. Photographic evidence shows them to be fairly common from fall 1918 forward, but the author has never found any specification or official documentation for them. Beyond the common features of double-breasted construction and the distinctive roll collar, they appear in a bewildering array of style details. Some are full belted, others with only a half belt in the rear. Buttons are either plain vegetable ivory or coat size regular service coat buttons. The lower pockets appear in both open and flapped patch pocket variations. Extant examples are generally unlined with the exception of the pocket flaps, and several examples have (unfortunately illegible) tags in the pockets which appear to be similar to standard issue garment tags seen in other garments.

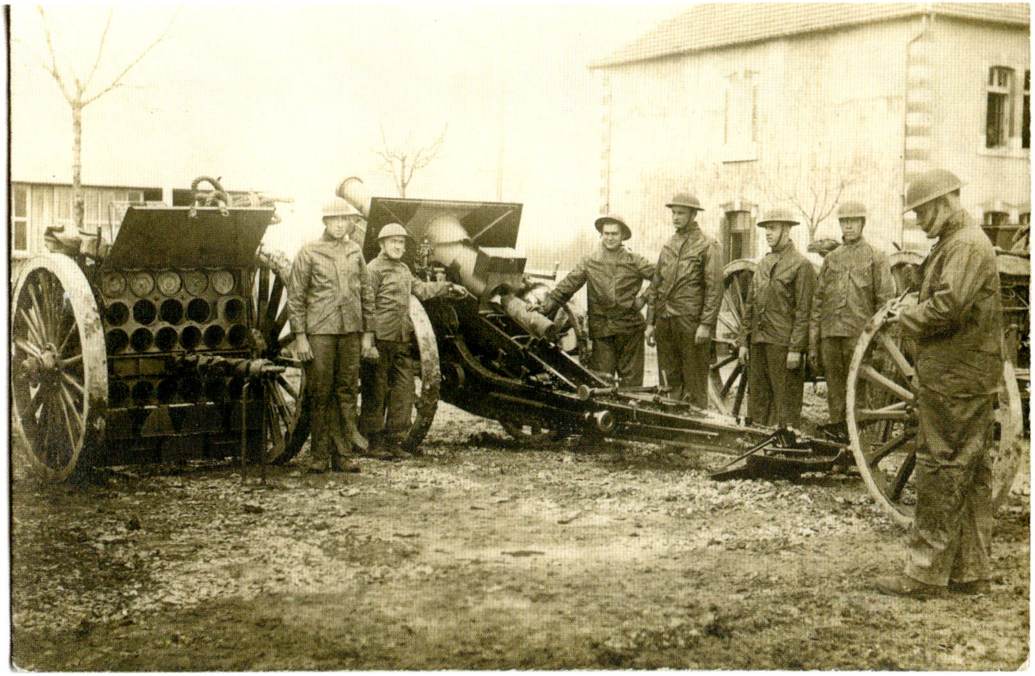

What joy! A section doing gun drill in the Army of Occupation. A nicely camouflage-painted 155 mm Schneider howitzer and crew. The crew are all wearing the oilskin gas protective overgarments, commonly worn by artillerymen when firing shell gas rounds in order to protect them from any leaking mustard gas projectiles. The image is annotated as being "1st section" and is dated April 15, 1919.

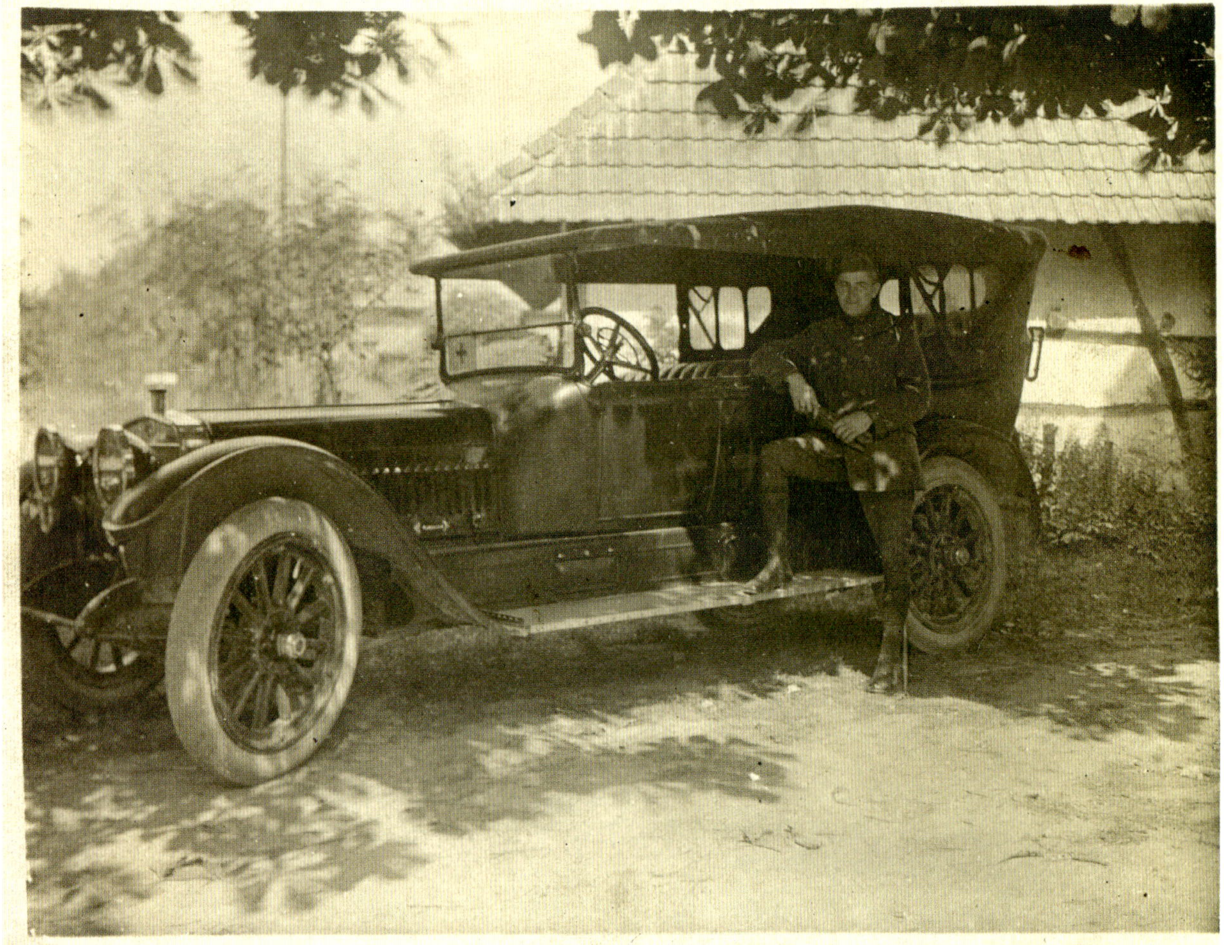

Perhaps an American Red Cross worker. The vehicle is devoid of any standard markings, except for the Geneva Cross placard in the windshield. The automobile is a Winton Six, series 48 (horsepower) with the touring body. The lack of any USA registration markings may indicate this is a very early image. This was one of the higher end cars brought to the AEF. Though a bit indistinct the gentleman with the car wears a mackinaw style overcoat with no distinguishing insignia.

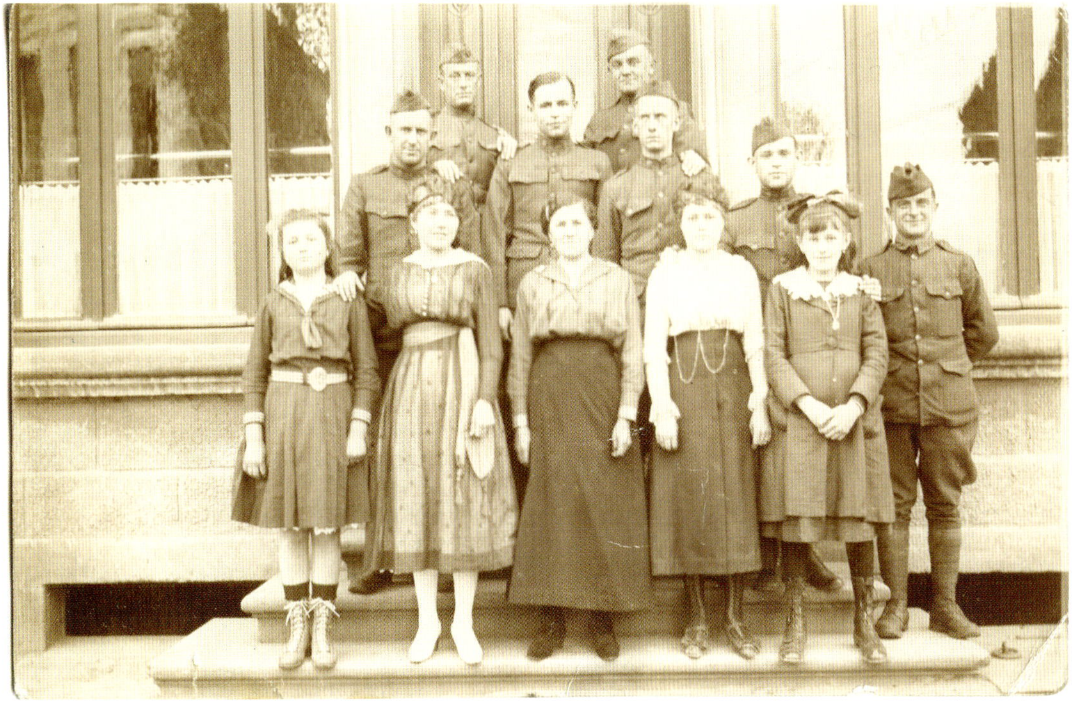

Doughboys with local mademoiselles, possibly three generations of the same family. Given the familiarity of the pose the image was most likely taken in France. Shoulder sleeve insignia can be discerned but are impossible to identify. The right front Doughboy wears his shirt collar over his coat collar.

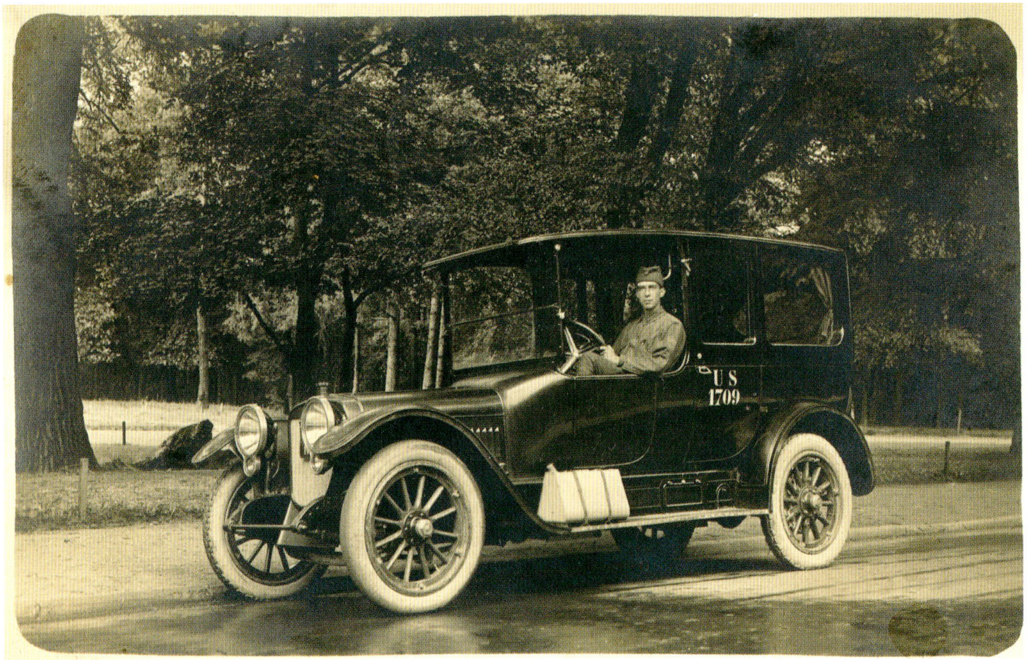

Identified as "Kenneth" and taken in France. Kenneth appears to have sergeant chevrons with, possibly, an engineer castle beneath. Driving such a magnificent machine in shirtsleeve order seems a bit incongruous. Again, a Winton Six series 48, this staff car is the four-door limousine model typical of cars used by higher grade staff officers and associated headquarters. Maj. Gen. Andre Brewster, inspector general of the AEF, used an identical machine as his staff car. The USA registration number "1709" indicates it was the 709th passenger car registered in the AEF. There is a placard barely visible on the radiator, unfortunately unreadable.

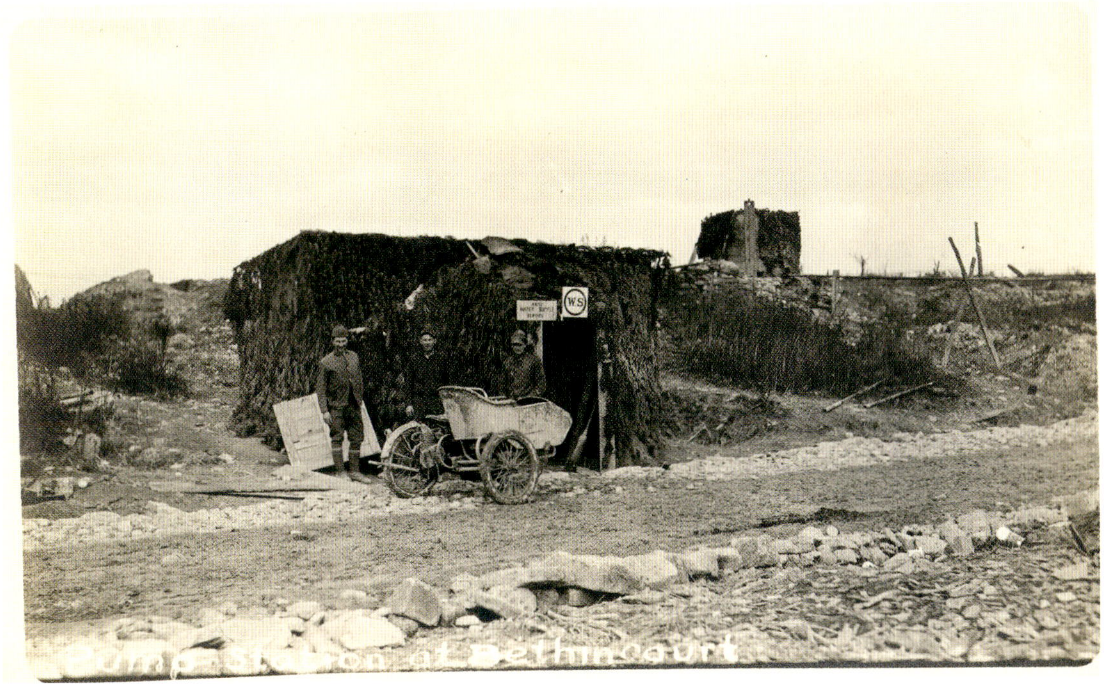

Captioned "Pump Station at Bethincourt," this a most interesting image. The "WS" sign is the unofficial insignia of the 26th Engineer Regiment (Water Supply). An additional sign reads "Army Water Supply Service." The Bethincourt water point was one of the first two established in Meuse-Argonne to support the attack. It was established by Company D, 26th Engineers in the US III Corps zone of advance, with work commencing September 26, 1918, the day after the jump-off. When completed it used gasoline engine-driven pumps, elevated steel tanks, and automatic chlorinators, which fed treated, potable water into cart filling stations and horse-watering troughs. For more than a month the Bethincourt water point furnished a daily average of 20,000 gallons of water a day! To the right of the pump station one of the elevated tanks can be seen, with overhead supported piping crossing the road. This most likely fed the overhead water cart filling station. Also of note in this image is the heavy covering of cloth camouflage on the pump station, and an incongruous sculpted bust attached to the door frame. The motorcycle with side car sports a pair of Model 1904 saddlebags draped over the rear fender. During the Meuse-Argonne operation, the 26th Engineers suffered ten casualties from high explosive shell and gas. Two of the wounded subsequently succumbed to their wounds.

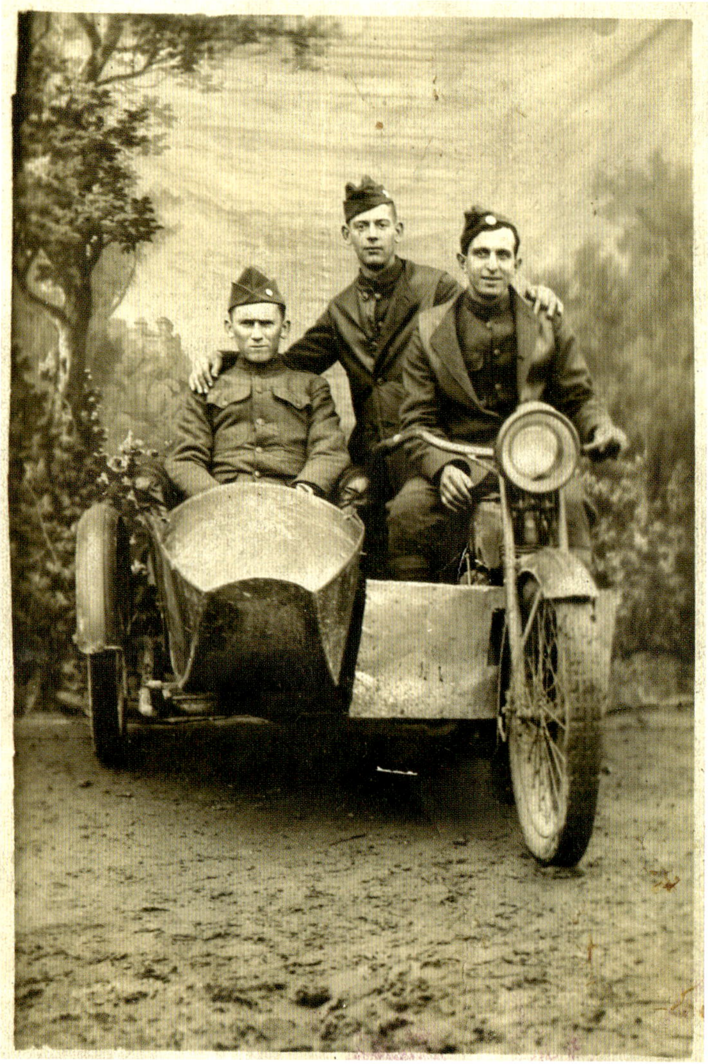

Three pards with their motorcycle with side car. Two of the Doughboys wear the leather jerkin. Though clearly an image taken outdoors note the use of the painted canvas backdrop. The sheet metal splash guard added between bike and sidecar is an interesting field modification.

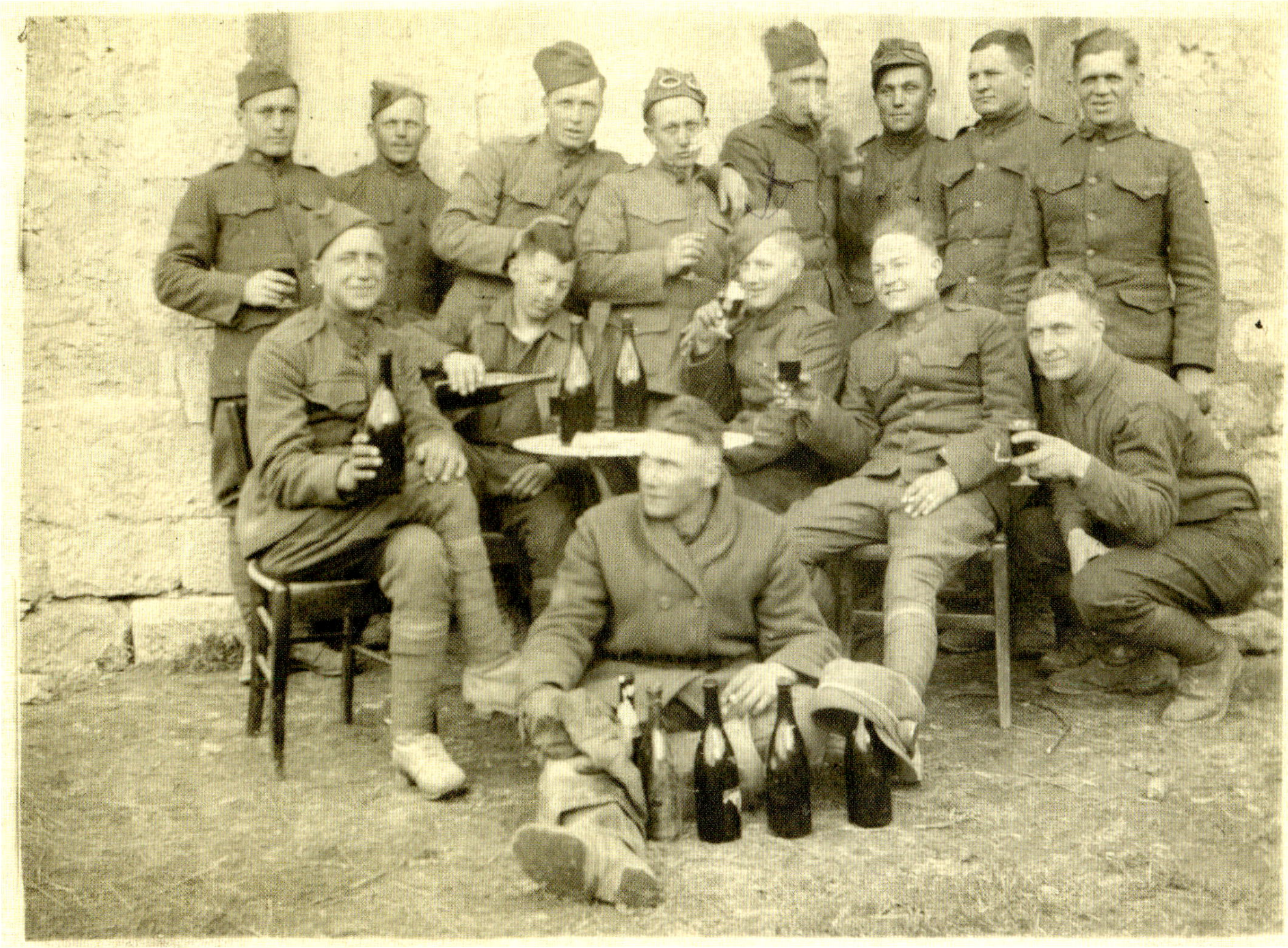

Doughboys and Vin Rouge . . . a common combination. These may be drivers as evidenced by several sets of goggles and Model 1907 winter hats. One hopes they didn't get behind the wheel after this session.

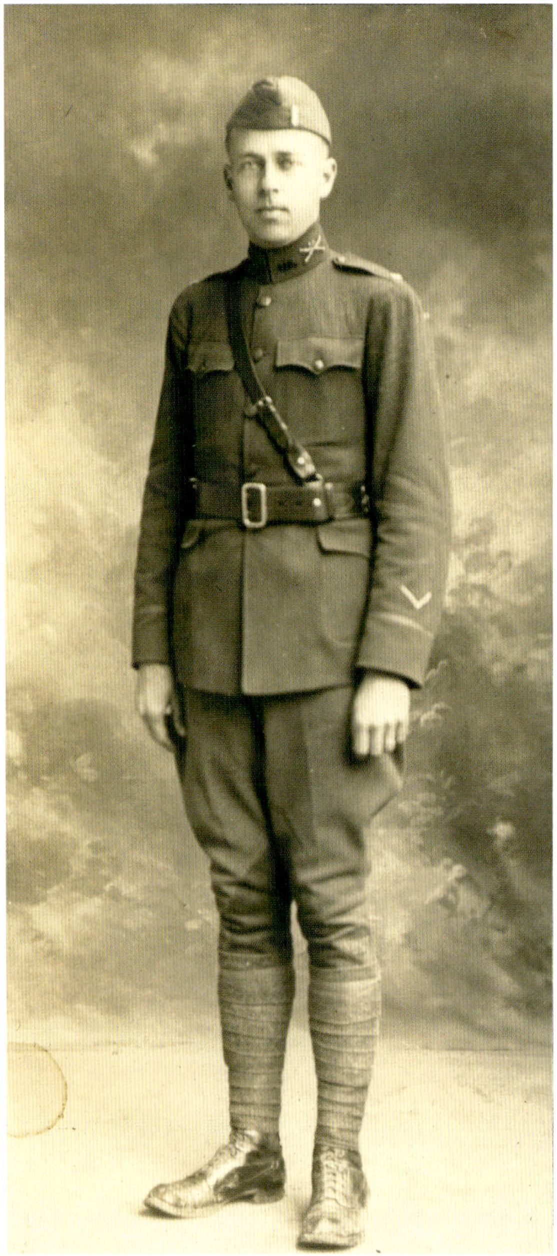

A dapper young infantry lieutenant, complete with Sam Browne belt and chevron signifying six months overseas service. Although his infantry crossed rifles are numbered, they are illegible except to say they display a two-digit number. With no visible shoulder sleeve insignia it is impossible to determine his unit. While his US collar ornaments are blackened bronze his infantry branch insignia appears to be bright brass. As with many junior officers he wears wrap puttees in lieu of leather leggings.

A senior officer with suitably stern visage, complete with half-smoked cigar and well trimmed moustache. He is alas unidentified and rank unknown, but clearly an officer as denoted by the barely visible cuff braid and Sam Browne belt. He wears three ribbons, one of which appears to be the Mexican Service Ribbon, the others may be for Spanish-American or Philippine service. Thus, by age and length of service he is most likely a field grade officer. Like many Doughboys, officer and enlisted alike, he wears the shirt collar over his coat collar, effectively obscuring his branch insignia. This practice was authorized in GHQ AEF G.O. No. 122 dated July 26, 1918. His overseas cap is clearly French style and seems devoid of either rank insignia or branch of service piping. A wristwatch can be barely made out in his left sleeve. Finally, he wears riding boots and affects a swagger stick, perhaps an old Army cavalryman. The setting appears to be a porch or veranda, and he is seated in an ornately carved chair. With no war service chevrons present this may be an early image taken in France.

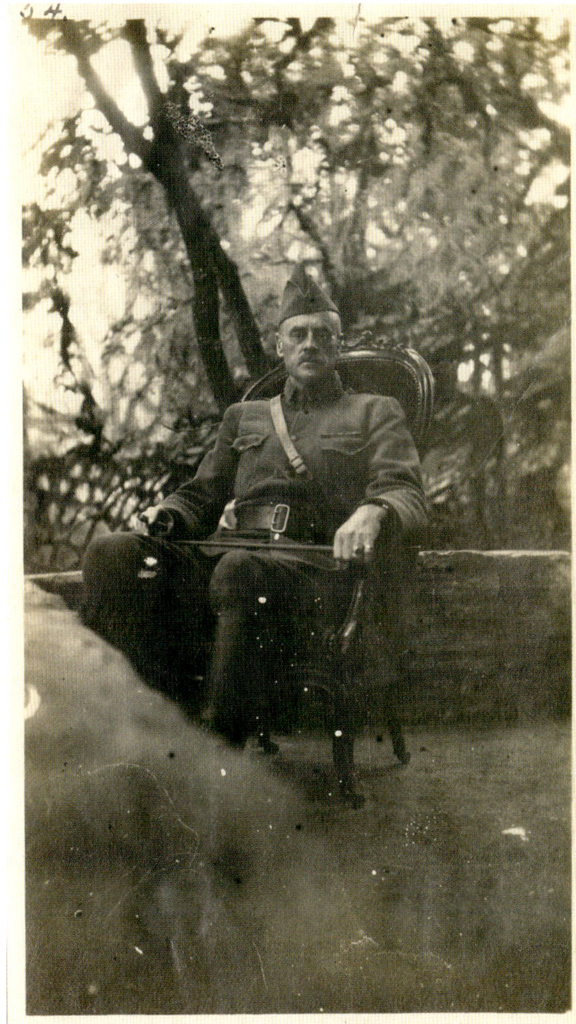

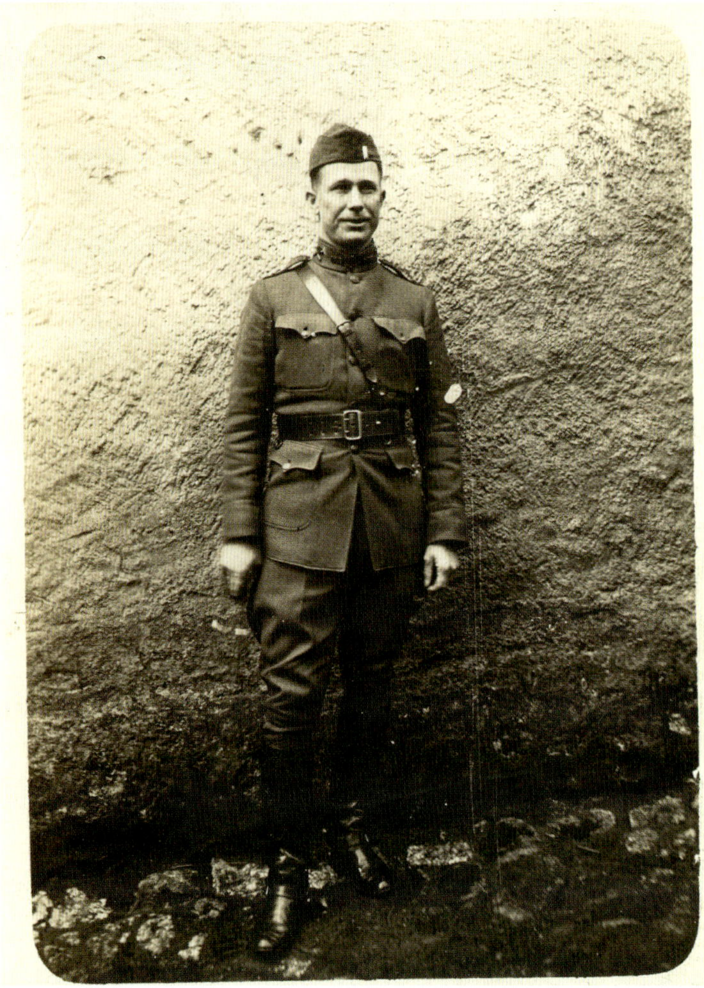

A booted and spurred artillery lieutenant strikes the pose. Though numbered, his artillery insignia is unreadable. His overseas cap displays narrow red piping denoting field artillery. The inclusion of branch color piping on officers overseas caps was initially prescribed by GHQ AEF G.O. No. 7 dated January 9, 1918, and later expanded in GHQ AEF G.O. No. 146 dated September 4, 1918.

The kitchen crew seems a favorite subject in AEF photography. The mess sergeant on the right sports a single war service chevron and a British-style overseas cap with two front buttons securing the curtain of the cap. His cap bears a US ornament. His one visible collar ornament is not clear enough to read. In the center, with a white cap and apron, a young cook holds a substantial ham, apparently well cured by its dark color. At left the corporal wears a home-knit sweater, typical of those produced by the American Red Cross and other organizations stateside and provided to members of the AEF. Additionally, he wears straight-leg trousers. These may be British issue trousers procured by the AEF in France or possibly the US straight-leg trousers which made their appearance in late fall 1918, and issued in lieu of breeches, which were not only difficult to manufacture but were produced in an inefficiently large number of sizes accounting for minute variation in waist and inseam.

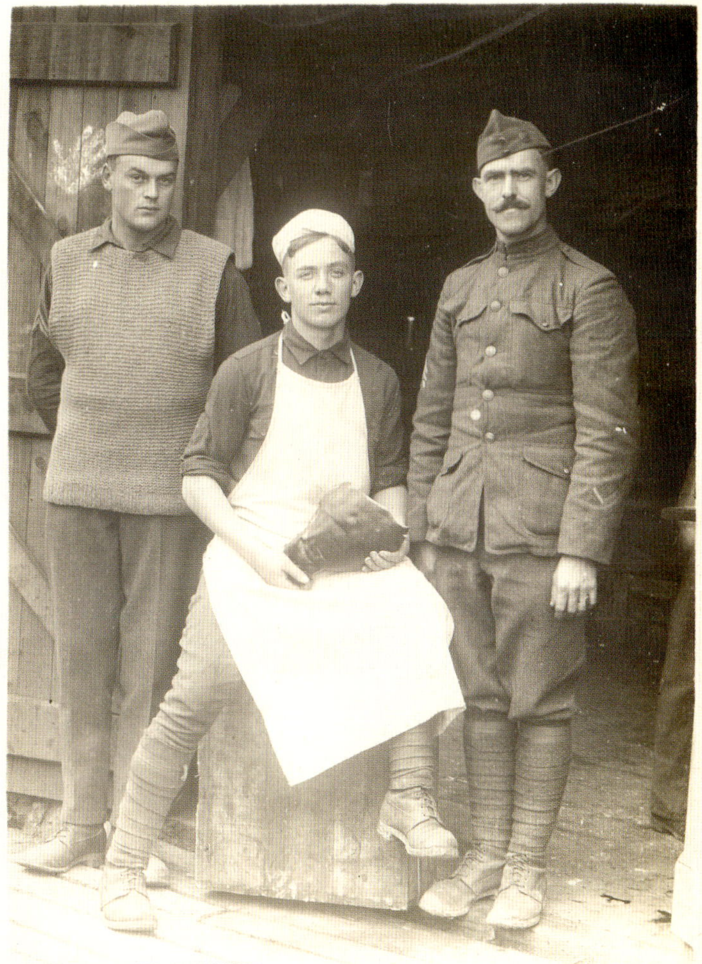

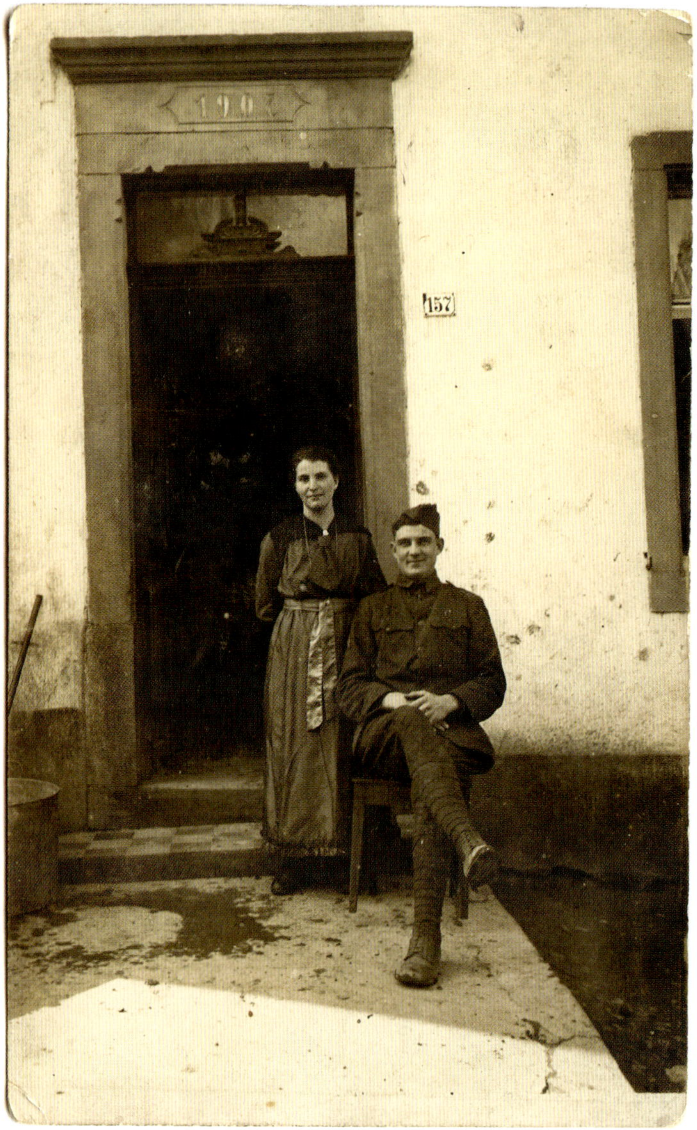

A Doughboy in his billet or possibly at the residence of a fraulein of his acquaintance. Given the style of lettering on the house number and on the doorway lintel (1907) this image as almost certainly taken in the Army of Occupation. His uniform is unremarkable save the often-seen shirt collar rolled over his standing coat "dog collar."

A Doughboy of the 32nd "Red Arrow" Division armed with Model 1917 revolver and appropriate pocket for carrying .45 rounds in half-moon clips. He proudly displays both a wound chevron and a single war service chevron. Both his collar and cap are devoid of prescribed disks.

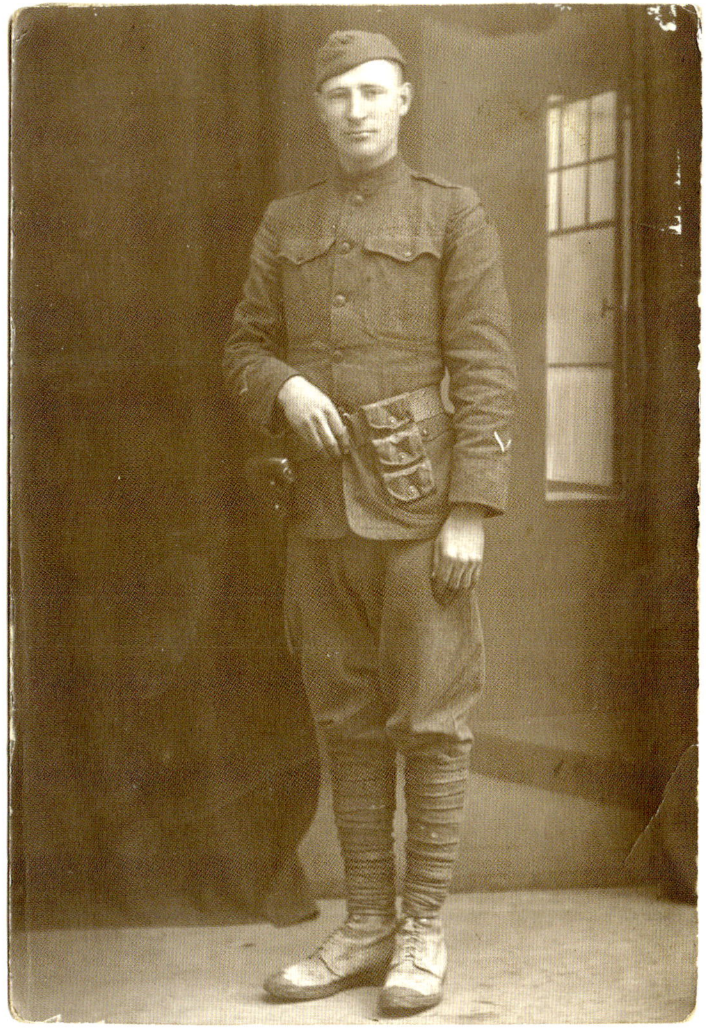

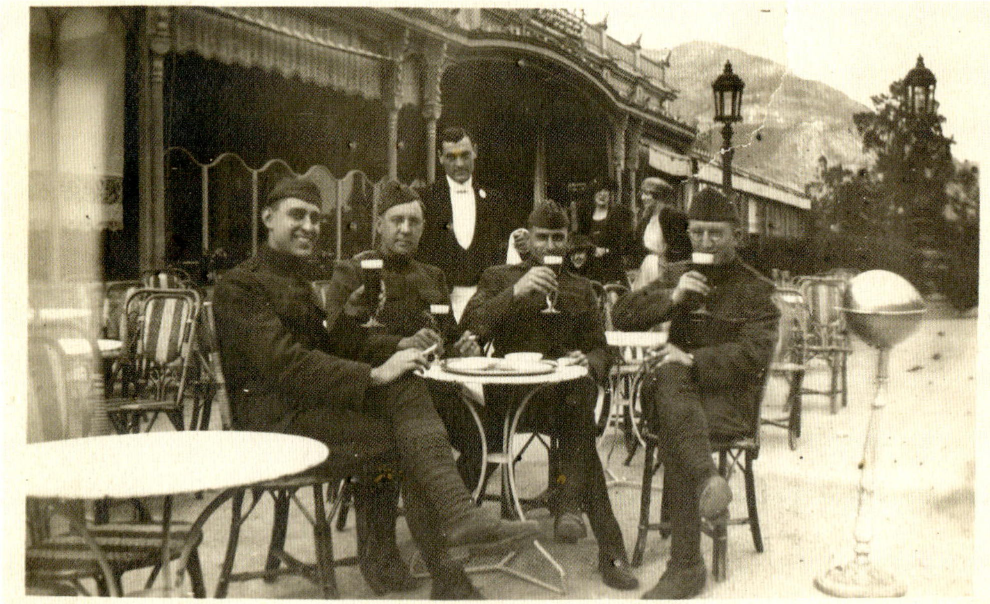

Four Doughboys of Mechanical Repair Shop Unit No. 309 Dijon, France, taken at the AEF leave area in Monte Carlo. The handwritten caption on the reverse identifies the place as the Café de Paris. Images of adult beverage-drinking are quite common in AEF photos, particularly in the post-Armistice period. Looming prohibition in the United States is thus commented on, often quite directly.

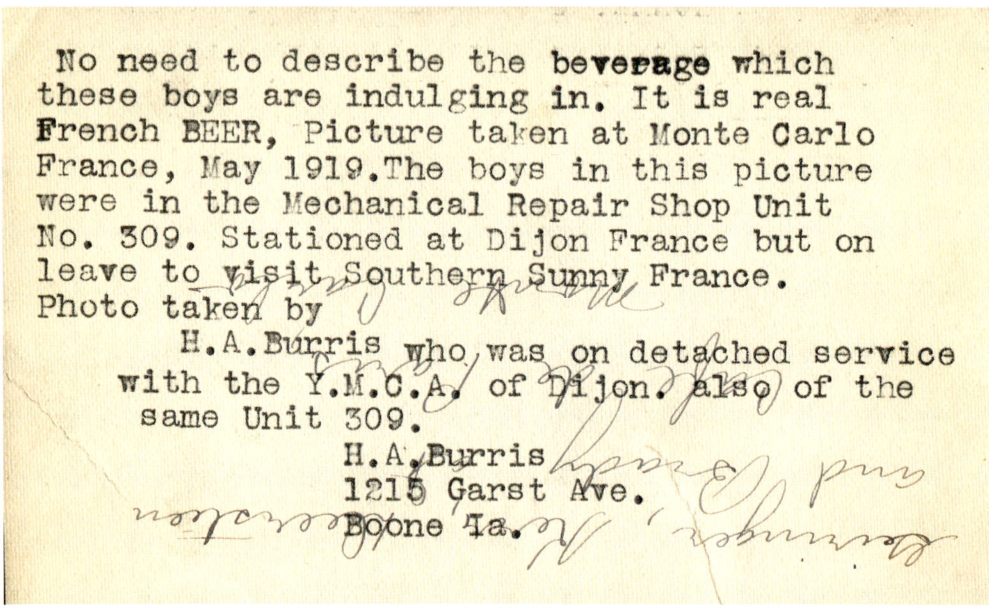

No need to describe the beverage which these boys are indulging in. It is real French BEER, Picture taken at Monte Carlo France, May 1919.The boys in this picture were in the Mechanical Repair Shop Unit No. 309. Stationed at Dijon France but on leave to visit Southern Sunny France.
Photo taken by
H.A.Burris who was on detached service with the Y.M.C.A. of Dijon. also of the same Unit 309.
H.A.Burris
1215 Garst Ave.
Boone Ia.

Reverse: a rare complete caption, and since typewritten, it is legible to boot!

A typical clown-around-and-have-a-smoke pose. The background in this exterior shot looks to be a tar paper and batten barracks or outbuilding. The cigar-chomping Doughboy on the left is armed with a Model 1917 revolver (of either Colt or Smith & Wesson manufacture). He also wears rubber trench boots. The Doughboy on the right wears a French-cut overseas cap which appears to have a cloth insignia sewn onto it. In addition, he wears long trousers versus breeches. These may be either British-purchased trousers or the late-appearing American long trousers. These generally appear only in post-Armistice images taken in the Army of Occupation.

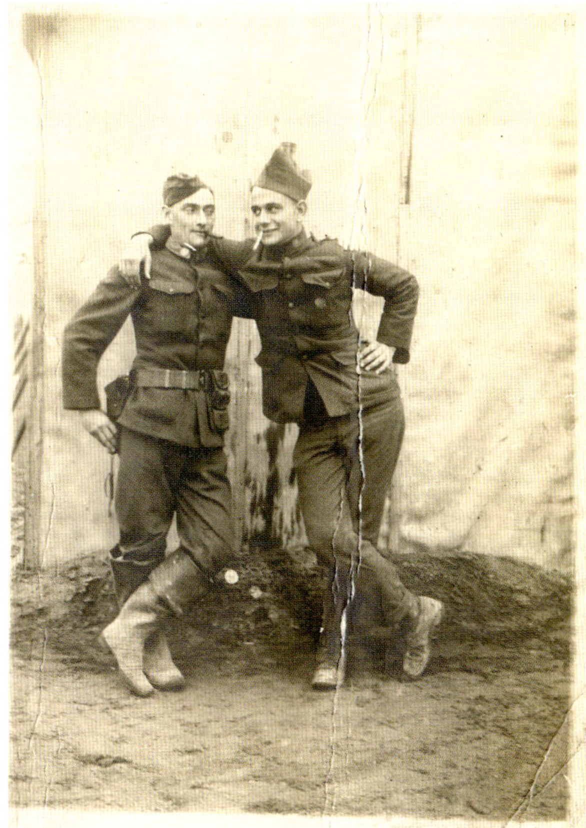

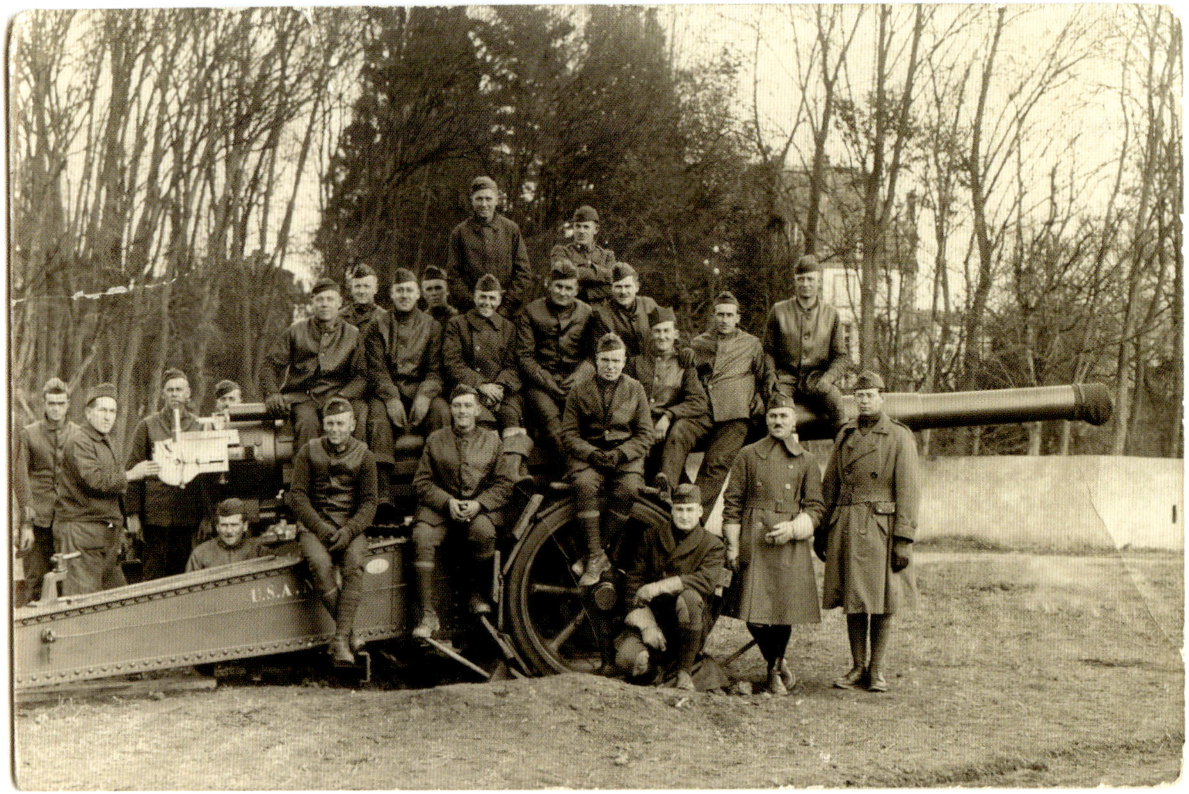

A fine portrait of the gun crew of a 155 mm GPF (*Grande Puissance Filloux*) gun-lovingly polished, washed, and ready for inspection. The gun is set up in position ready for loading, wheels with so-called caterpillar bands in place, wheels chocked, and breech open. The 66th Field Artillery Brigade, consisting of the 146th and 148th Field Artillery Regiments adopted the moniker "The Long Range Snipers" based on the range and accuracy of the 155 mm GPF. The GPF gun could hurl a ninety-nine-pound projectile to a range of 21,000 yards. These guns were retained by the US after the Armistice and remained in the US Army inventory well into the 1930s, when they were used as mobile coastal artillery guns. Nearly all other French-provided mobile artillery pieces (155 mm Schneider Howitzers, and the French Model 1897 75 mm guns) were returned to the French before AEF units returned to the States. The wartime unit newspaper and later the 66th FA Brigade Veteran's newsletter were entitled *The Long Range Sniper*. The three lieutenants at the right front display a variety of overcoat and trench coat patterns and a mix of spiral puttees and leather officer-style leggings. Leather trigger finger-style gauntlet/mittens are in evidence among both the officers and men, as are olive drab woolen gloves. The majority of the men wear the leather jerkin as an outer garment. Also in evidence are jumpers and long trousers which are most likely the brown denim fatigue clothing. One clearly obvious French-cut overseas cap is in evidence.

Inscribed "Somewhere in France" this young Doughboy is armed with the US Model 1903 Springfield rifle. He wears the earlier pattern cartridge belt with "Eagle Snap" pocket closures. His coat is the earlier 1912 pattern evidenced by the two barely visible seams several inches from the sleeve cuff.

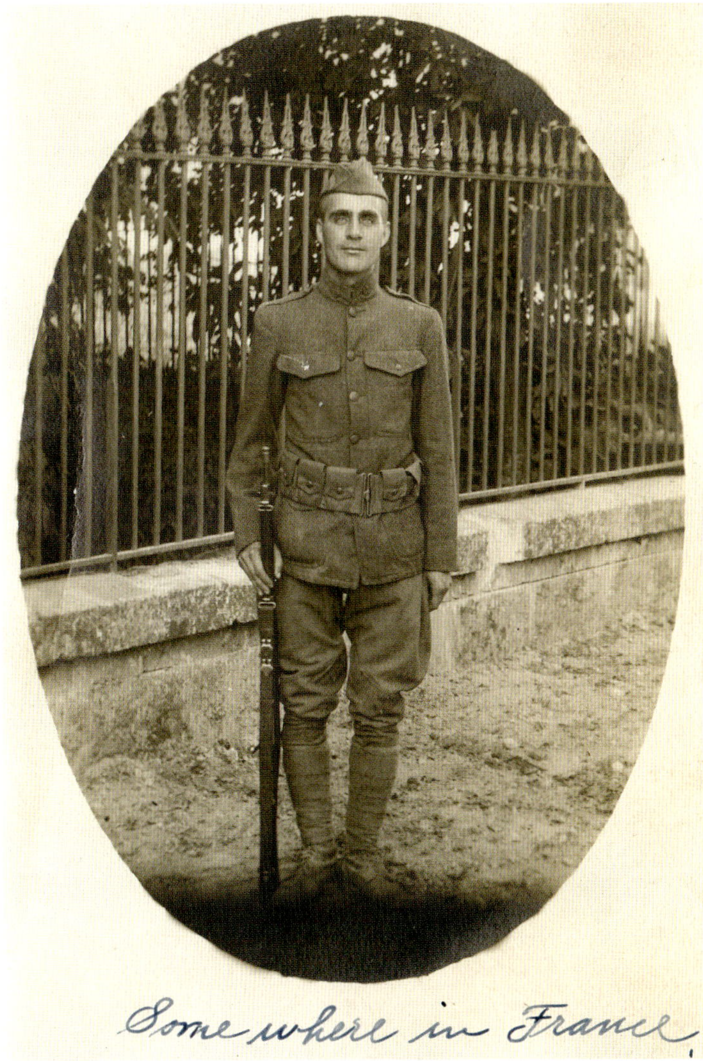

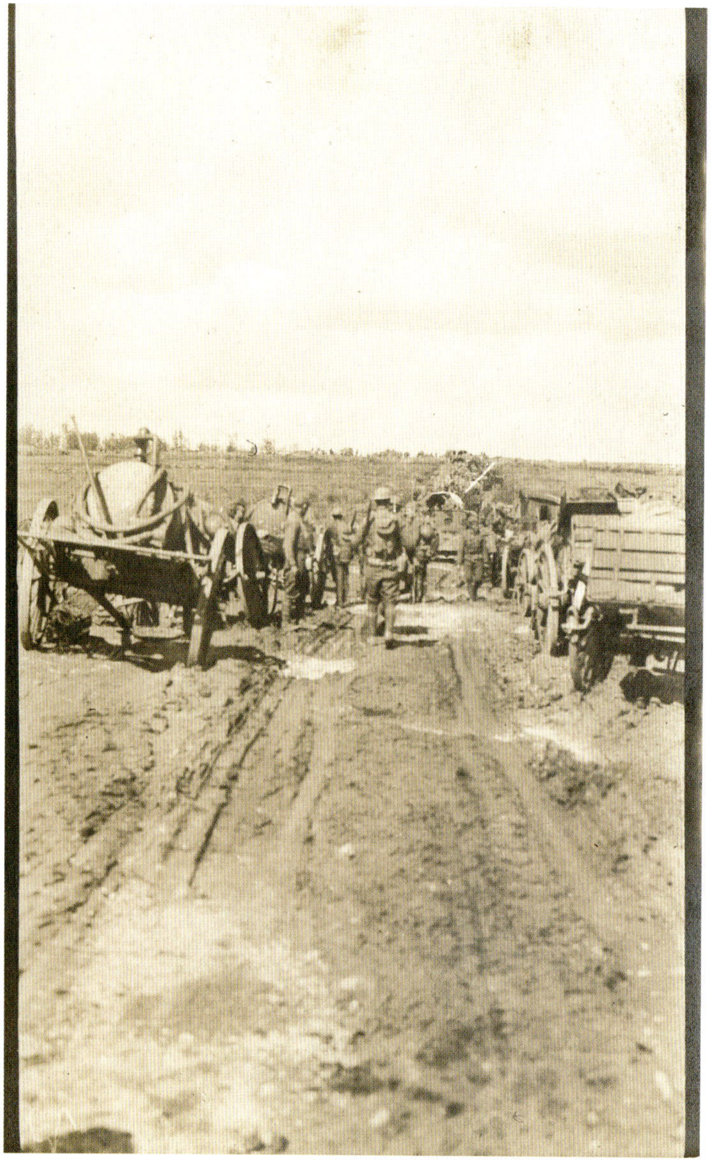

A column on the move, perhaps in the Meuse-Argonne region. This is likely a real snapshot made by a Doughboy while in active service. Water carts are visible on the left side of the road. On the right are a variety of other wagons and carts. All visible soldiers are wearing gas masks in the "carry" position versus the on-the-chest "Alert" position—an indication they are within five miles or less of the front, but not in imminent danger of gas attack.

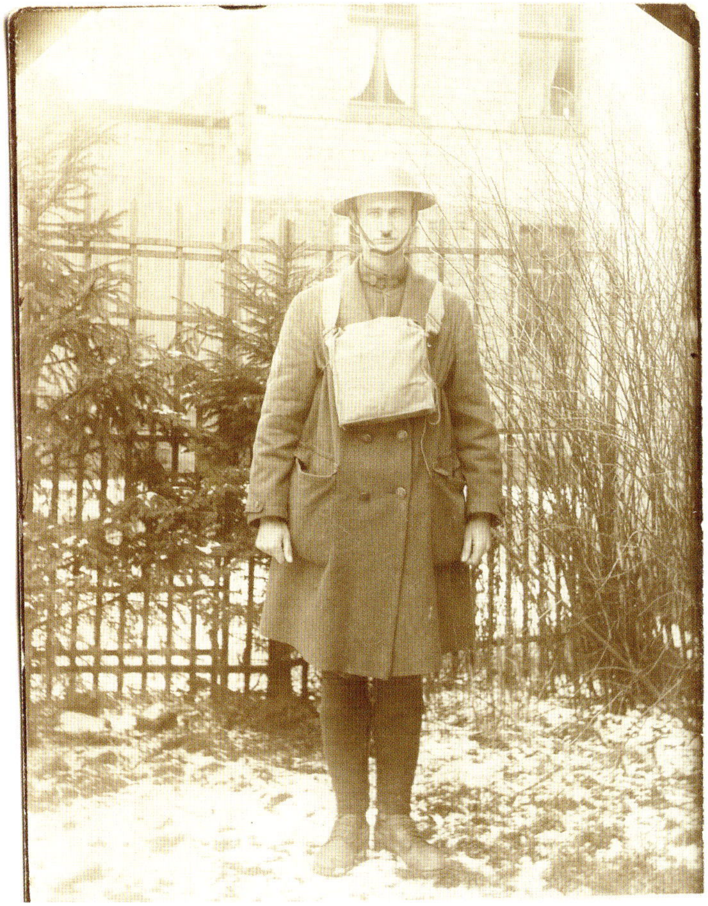

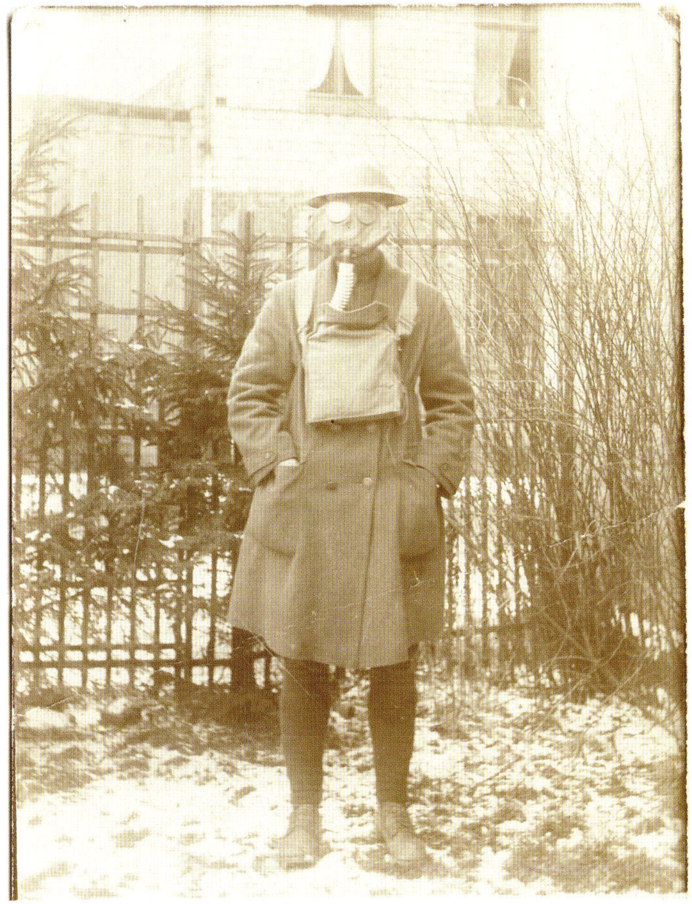

One of the most obligatory of Doughboy poses. Given the novelty of gas warfare, a very high number of Doughboys had their pictures taken wearing the mask and often simply carrying it as well. Since Doughboys were allowed to retain both their steel helmets and gas masks as souvenirs of service many of these images were taken after arrival back in the USA. This Doughboy wears an interesting variation of the roll collar-style overcoat with patch pockets and cuff tabs, the latter rarely seen in this pattern of overcoat.

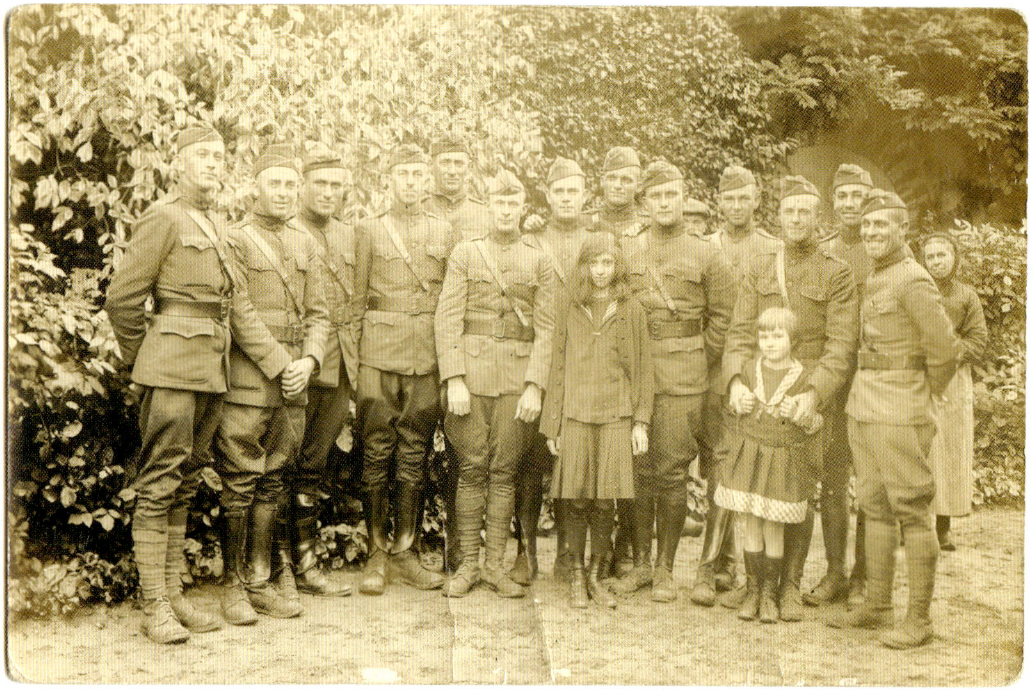

A charming exterior photo of a "bakers dozen" of infantry lieutenants, including a presumably French family. The young daughters are prominent in the foreground, mother in the right rear. The father can barely be seen over the shoulder of the fifth lieutenant from the right. Given the absolute lack of any decorations, wound or service chevrons this image was likely taken early in this particular unit's tenure in France. Notably, all have branch color piping on their overseas caps. Also typical is the mixture of officer's leather puttees made in various patterns, and spiral wool wrap puttees. Half of the group display whistle chains attached either to an epaulette button or a coat button. All are wearing the universal designator of officers overseas, the Sam Browne Belt.

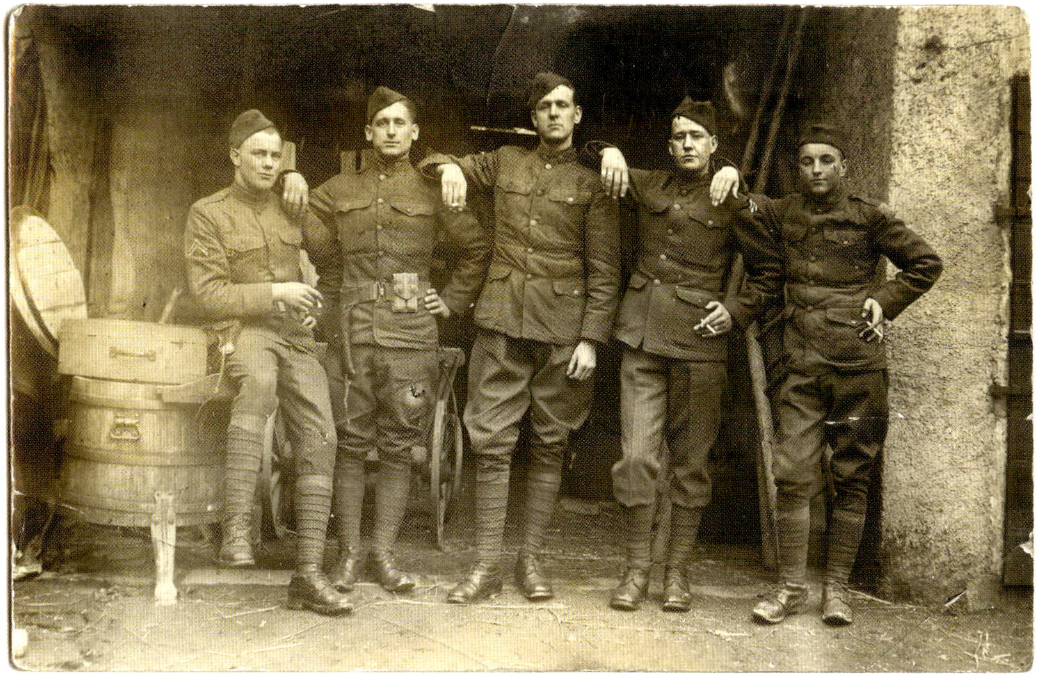

A corporal and four of his squad mates doing their best to look tough. The corporal sits on a laundry tub, most likely in the courtyard of their billet. Third Division shoulder sleeve insignia indicate this is an Army of Occupation image. None appear to have any ornaments on their caps. The corporal and the fourth man from the left are wearing straight-leg trousers, vice breeches.

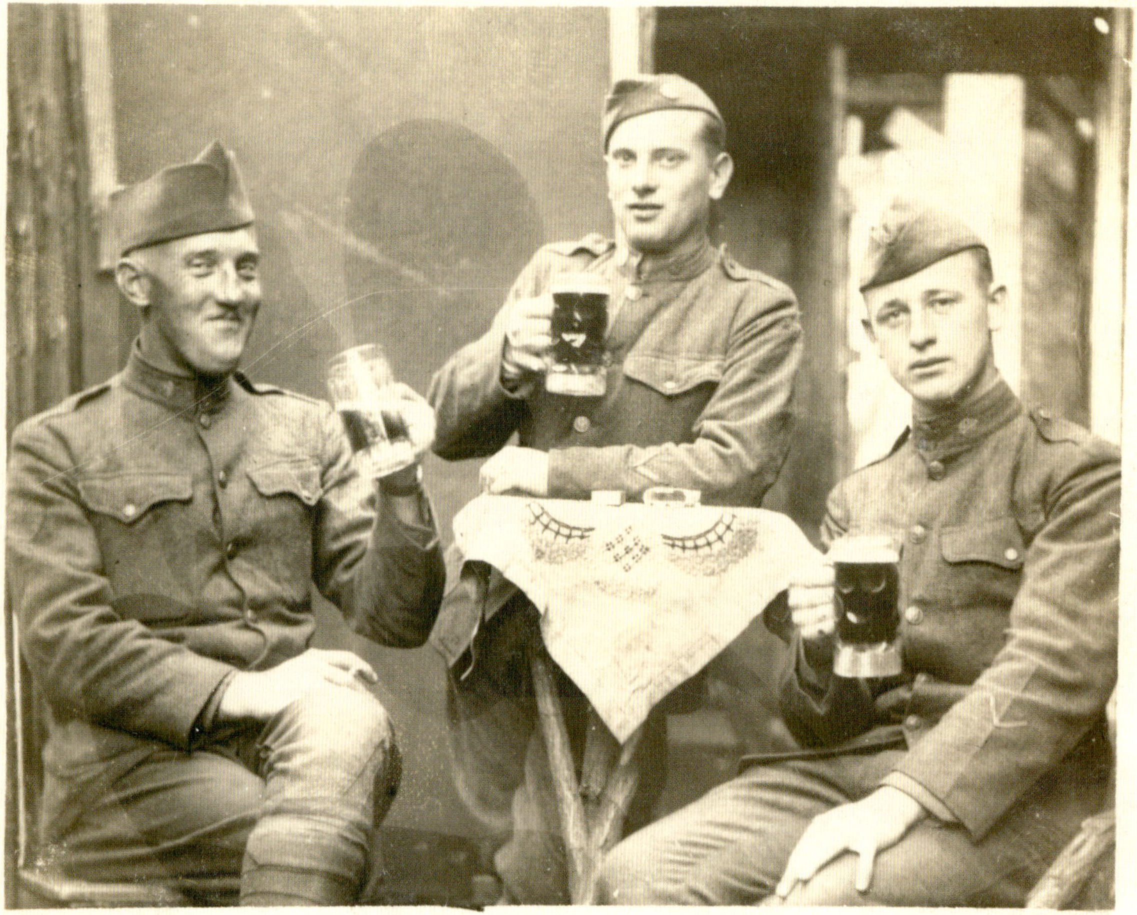

Three Doughboys enjoying the products of the local brewery. Two of the three exhibit six months overseas service chevrons. The smiling Doughboy on the left wears a distinctively French-style overseas cap. On the rustic table there seems to be a box of matches and an empty cigarette pack.

Two Doughboys photographed in an impressively wrecked building. The Doughboy on the right wears an empty revolver holster. His partner on the left wears the Model 1916 for the .45 caliber automatic pistol Model of 1911. Both, however, wear the cartridge pouch for the revolver designed to hold cartridges in three-round half-moon-shaped clips.

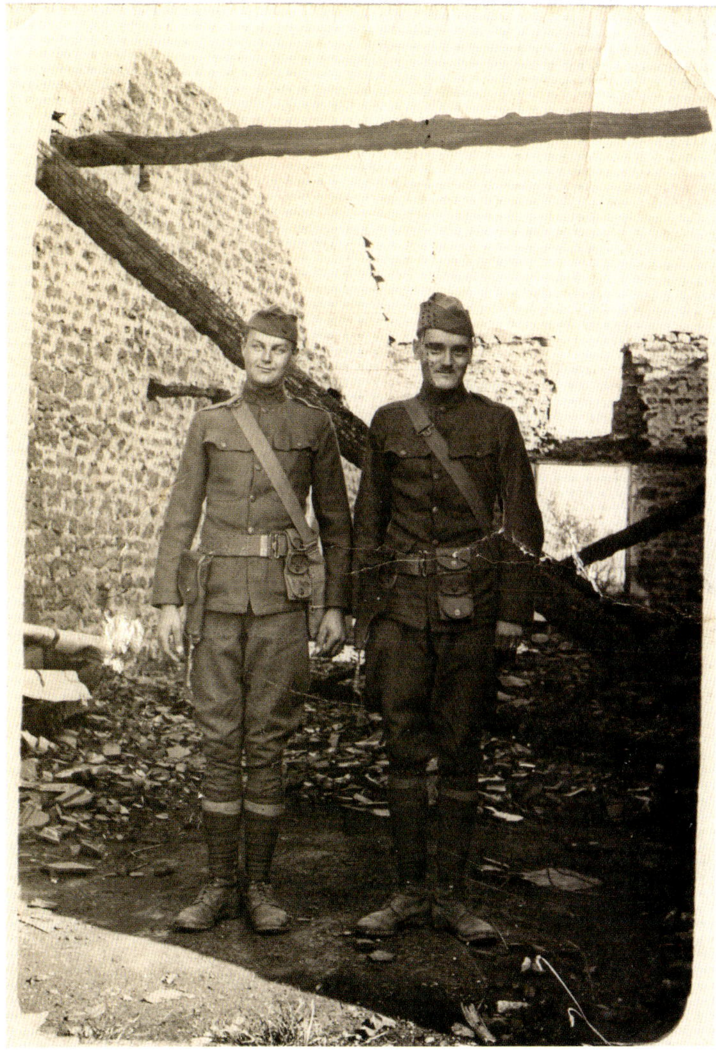

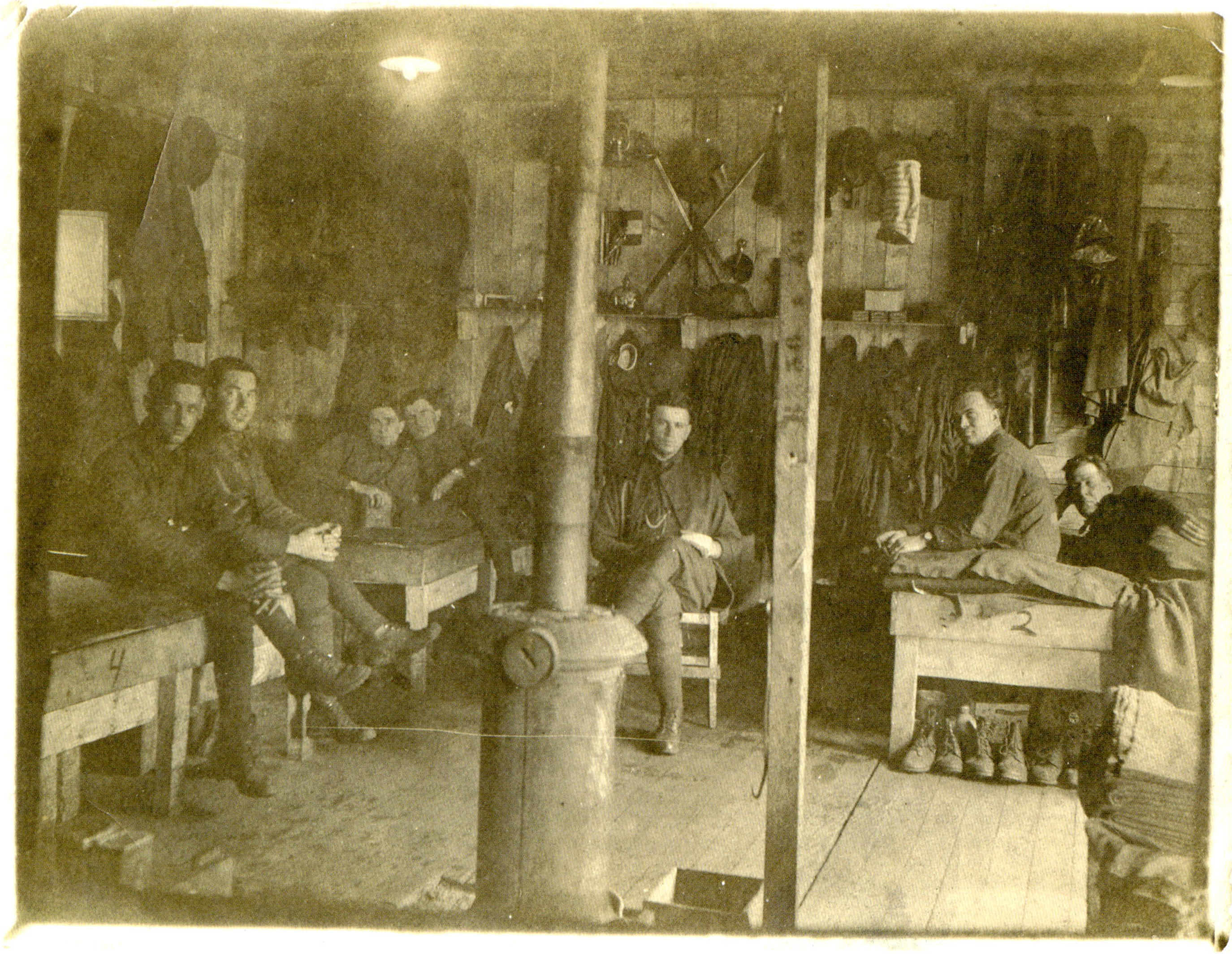

An interior billet photograph. The walls, electric lights, and purpose-built bunks indicate this is a purpose-built barracks building and not a French civilian building utilized as billets. The bunks are prominently numbered, likely to identify occupants for guard duty relief. An impressive array of issue US gear hangs on the walls and the shelves and walls also display captured trophies including swords, bayonets, a stahlhelm (German steel helmet), pickelhaube (German spiked helmet), and at least three cartons of Camel cigarettes.

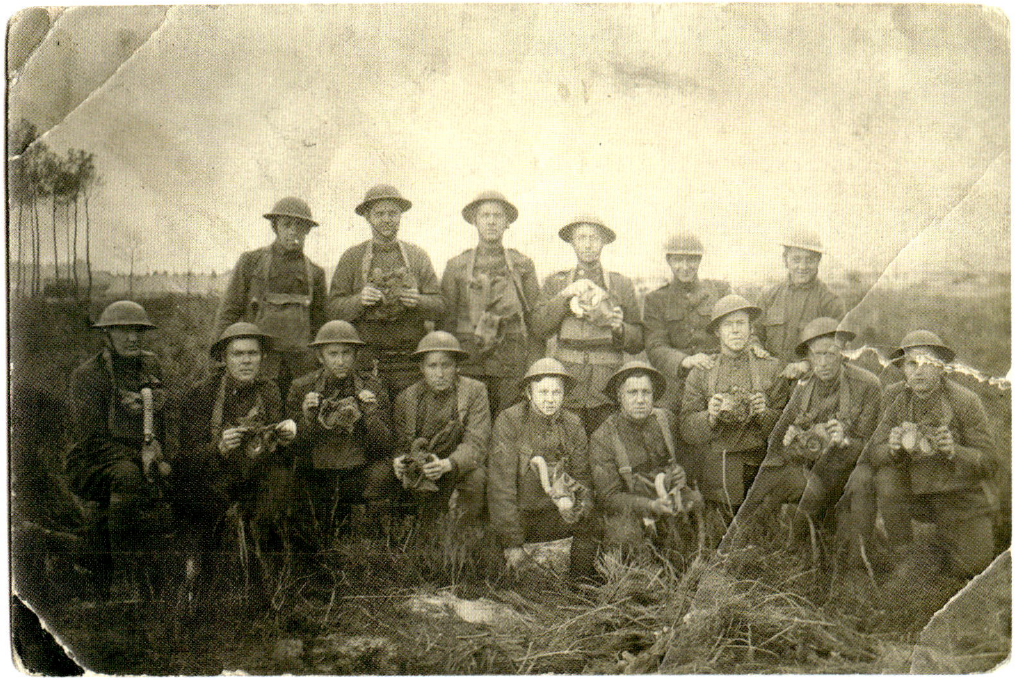

Gas school or simply a bunch of Doughboys posing with their masks. All but two of them are carrying masks, and none are conspicuously armed.

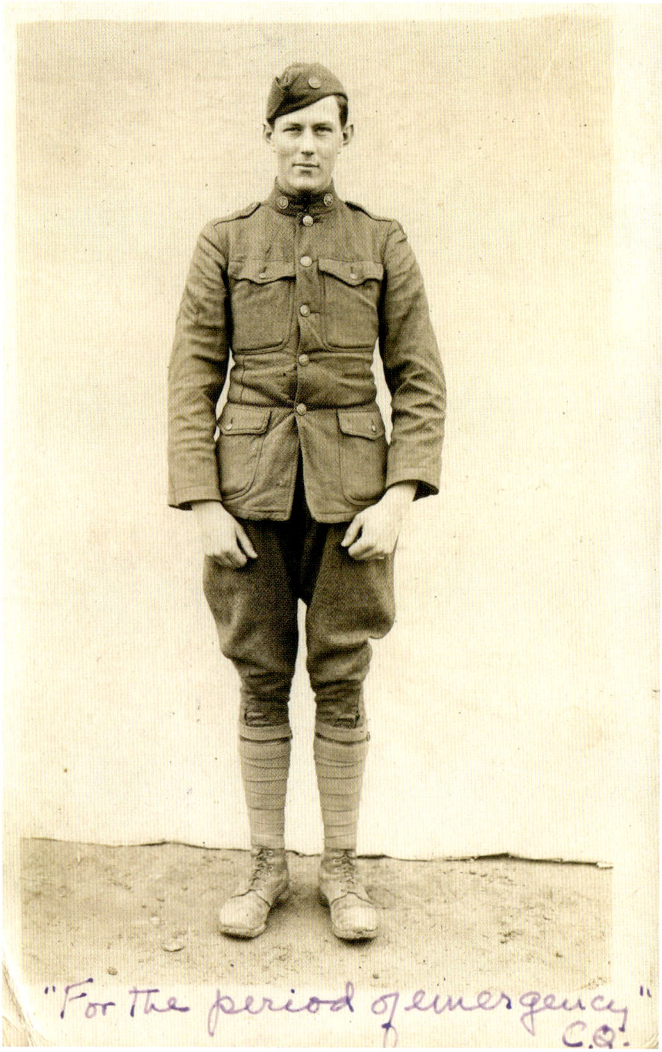

An infantry corporal in a rather ill-fitting coat, perhaps the effect of a recent de-lousing. The hook portion of a hook-and-eye fastening is visible below the bottom button of his coat.

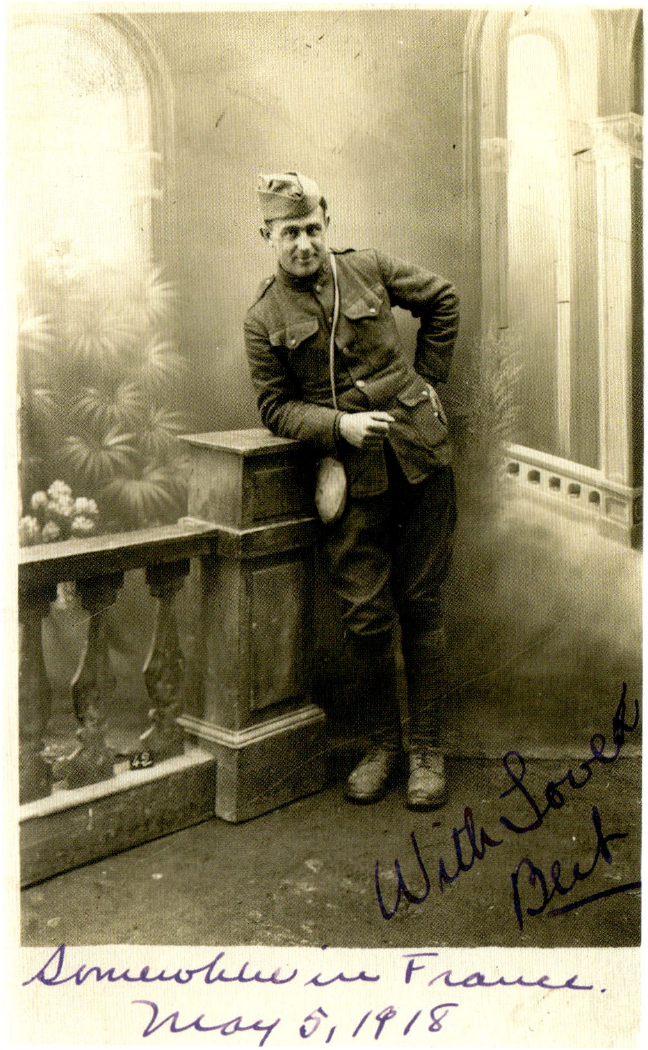

Somewhere in France—a nice indoor portrait of a Doughboy carrying a French M-2 gas mask. The fairly ineffective M-2 was banned from general use in the AEF in June 1918. This can serve as a general indicator of early AEF photographs, as the M-2 is rarely observed in use in the AEF after that date.

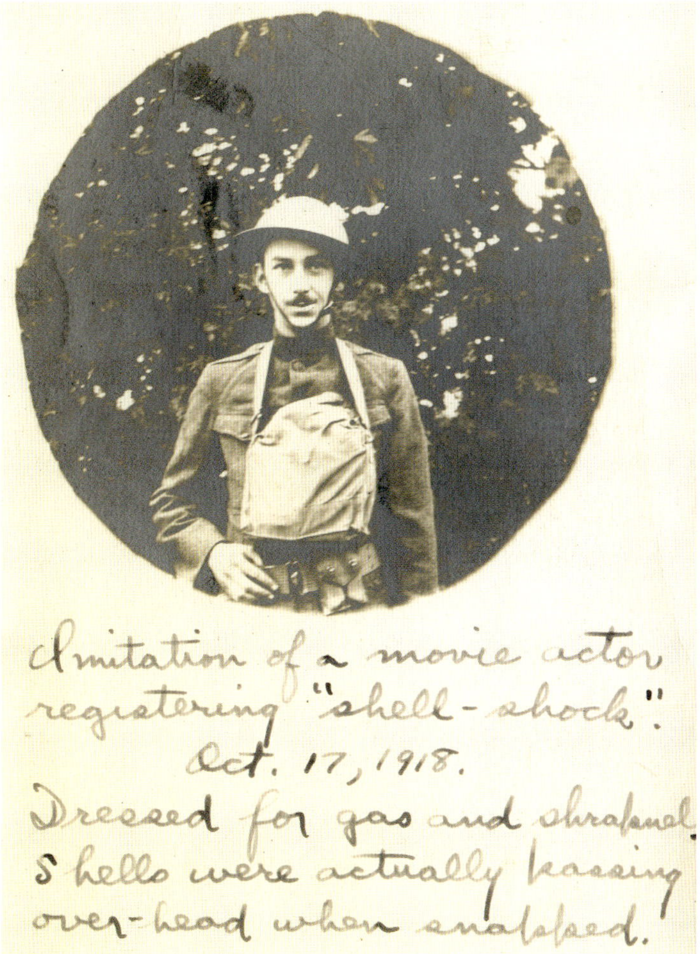

A photograph with a most amusing caption. While not looking particularly worried the subject asserts shells were passing overhead whilst the image was taken. The image is not clear enough to discern anything from his collar insignia. It does appear he is wearing sergeant chevrons on his right sleeve.

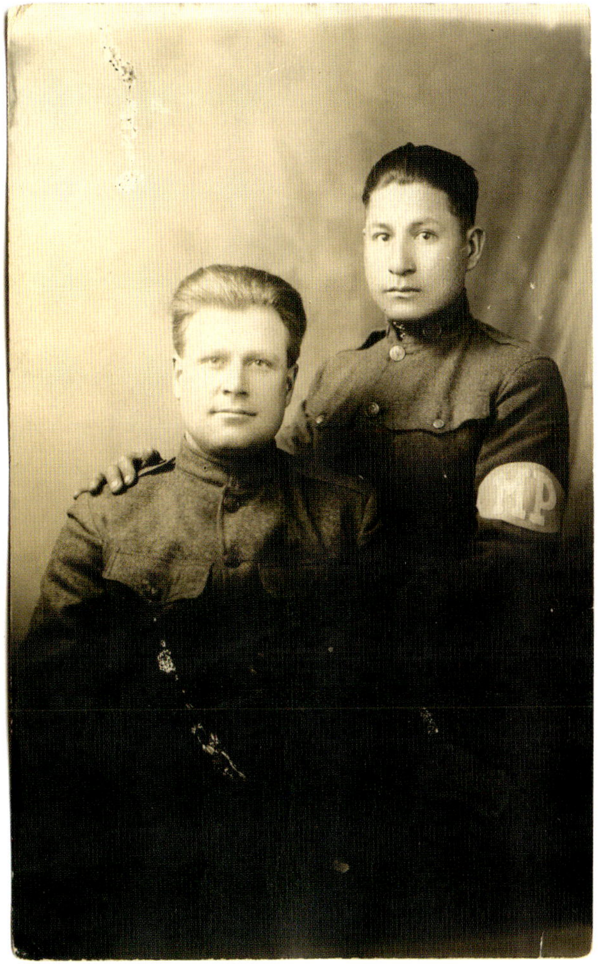

Two Doughboys in studio setting. The Doughboy at right is wearing an unusually shaped MP brassard. He is identified on the reverse as Lawrence Dog . . . undoubtedly a Native American. By some estimates, as many as 10,000 Native Americans served in World War I.

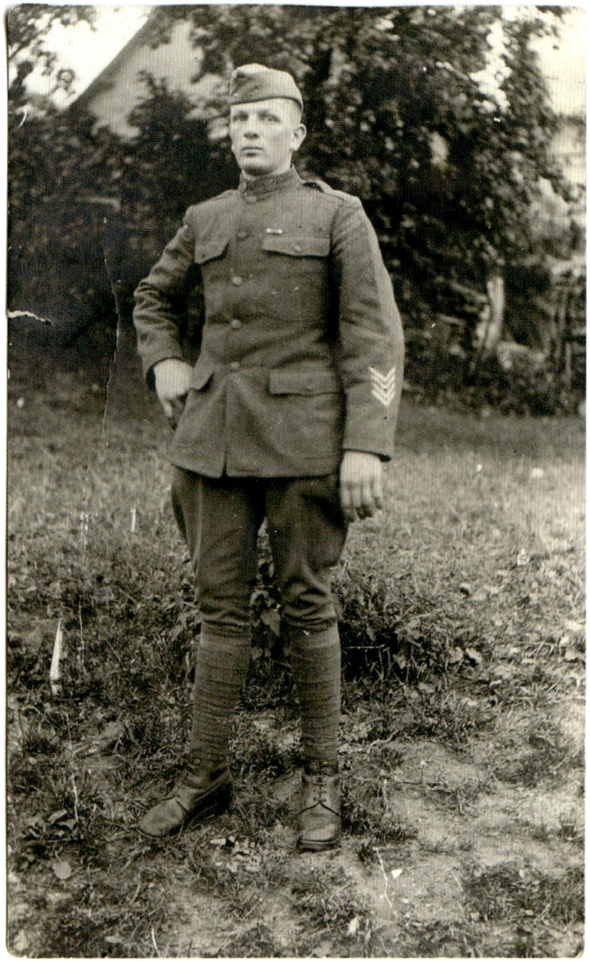

A young Doughboy with the full complement of overseas service chevrons denoting twenty-four months overseas. A barely visible shoulder sleeve insignia may be that of the 1st Division, certainly one of the longest-serving divisions in the AEF. He also wears some type of pin through the front of his overseas cap for reasons unknown. His well-greased boots are laced in the British straight or ladder laced fashion popular in British and Dominion forces.

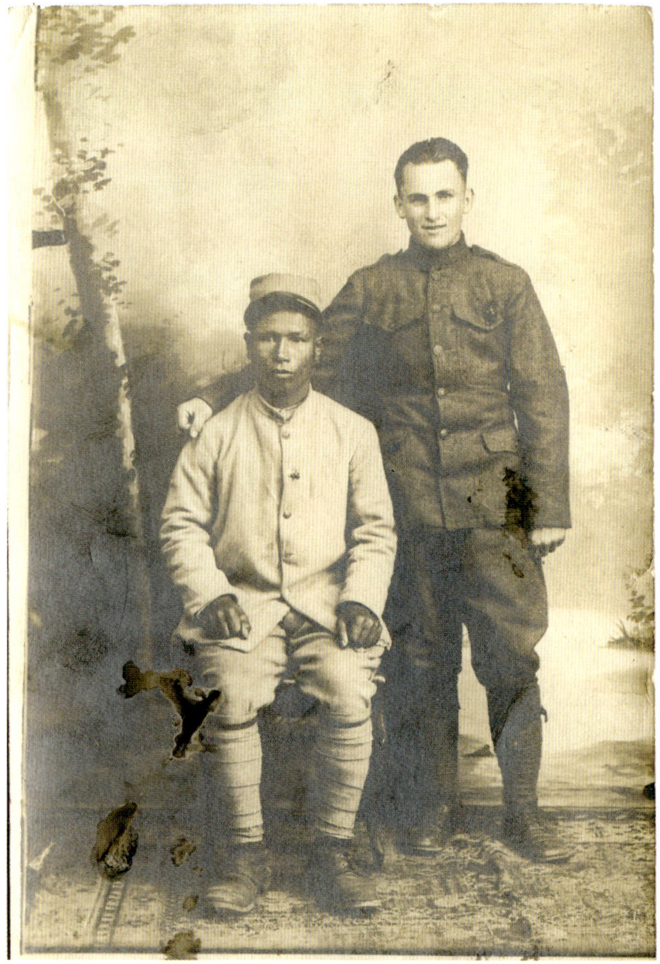

A Doughboy in unremarkable uniform who chose to have an image made with one of the more exotic varieties of his French comrades in arms: a Tonkinese, or Annamite French colonial. Most were often remembered by AEF members as drivers in the convoys that brought them to the front.

A young Doughboy with at least two souvenirs—a German belt and a German shepherd!

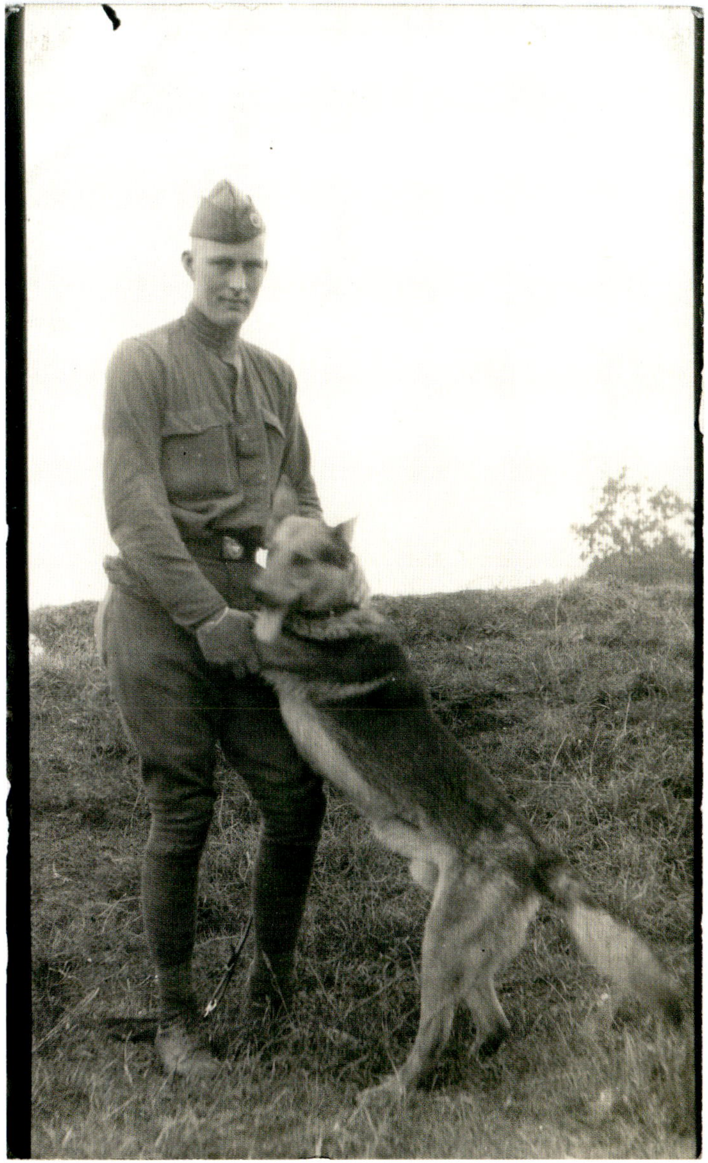

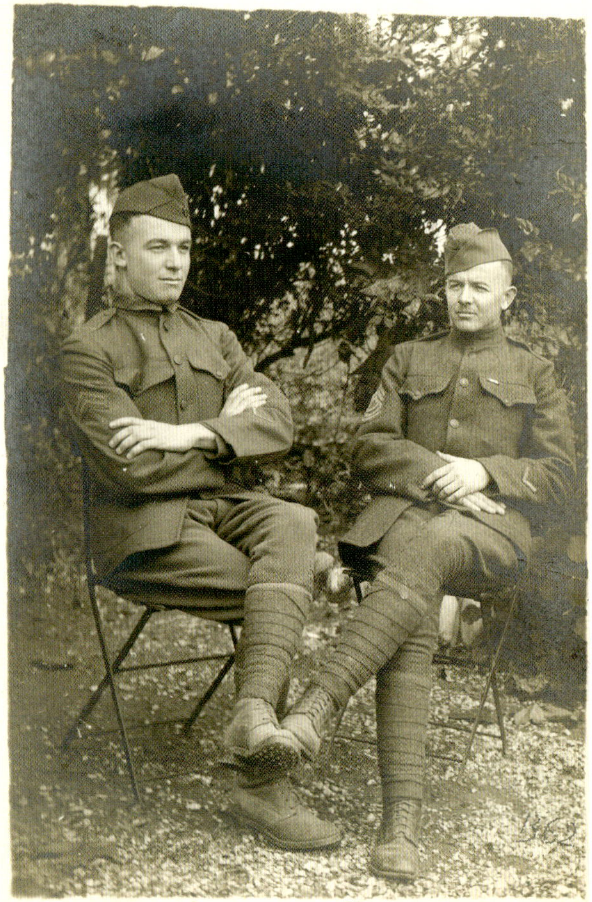

A study in looking "Hard Boiled." A regimental sergeant major and corporal doing their best to look tough. The lack of collar insignia save the one on the corporal's cap makes it impossible to identify the unit. The sergeant major is wearing shoulder sleeve insignia but it cannot be identified. Both wear single overseas service chevrons indicating six months overseas service. The sergeant major wears a single ribbon, which may be for Mexican Border Service. He is wearing the cap toe, smooth side out, russet marching shoes, while the corporal wears rough side out, hobnailed field shoes.

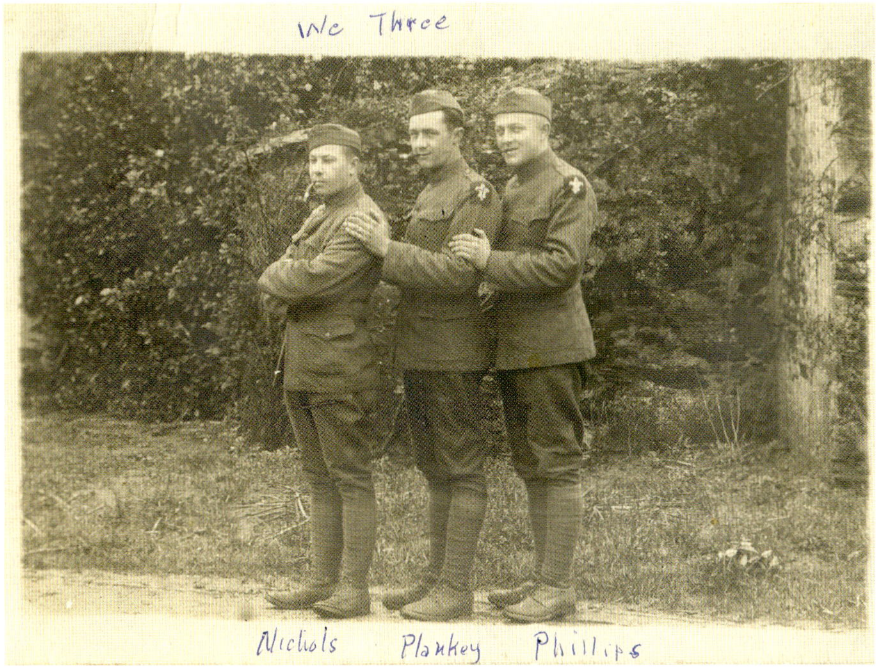

"We Three" . . . two of whom wear what appears to be the District of Paris shoulder sleeve insignia. All sport dashing pipes. There are no discernible collar or cap insignia, and none of the three wear overseas service chevrons.

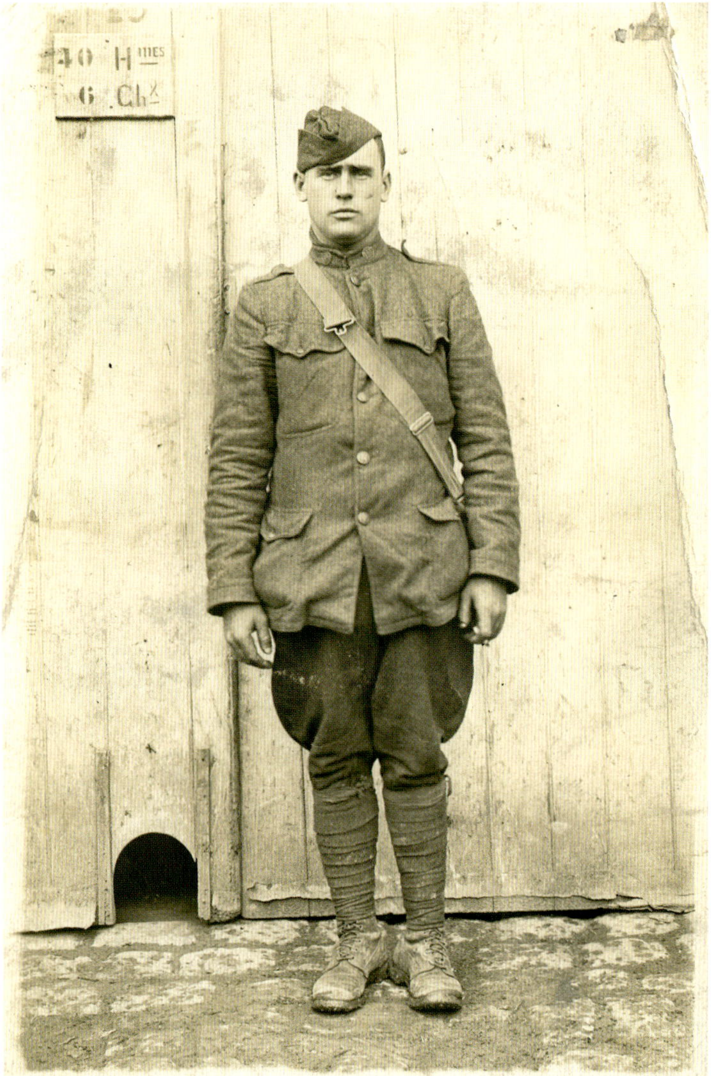

An engineer private in front of his billet, in this case marked as having the capacity to house forty men ("40 hmes"), or six horses ("6 chx").

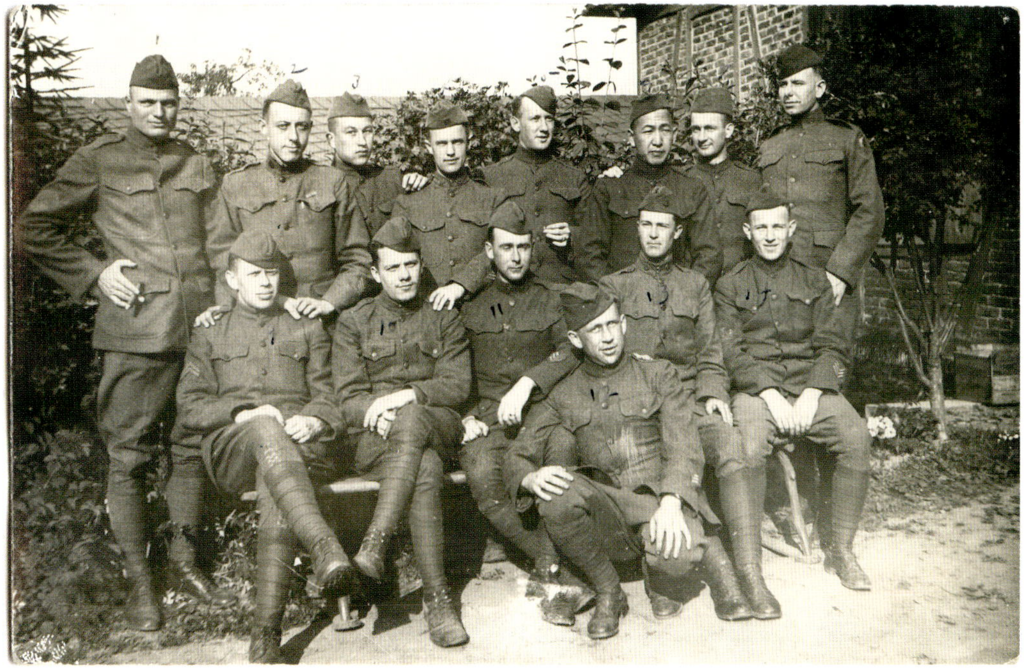

Although unidentified as to unit, each of these Doughboys save one, is named and his hometown given. A Doughboy standing at far right displays a shoulder sleeve insignia which appears to be that of the 42nd "Rainbow Division." Five of the subjects are wearing three overseas service stripes. About half have no collar insignia at all. The rear rank standing Doughboy, third from right is identified as being from Arizona. He is almost certainly a Native American.

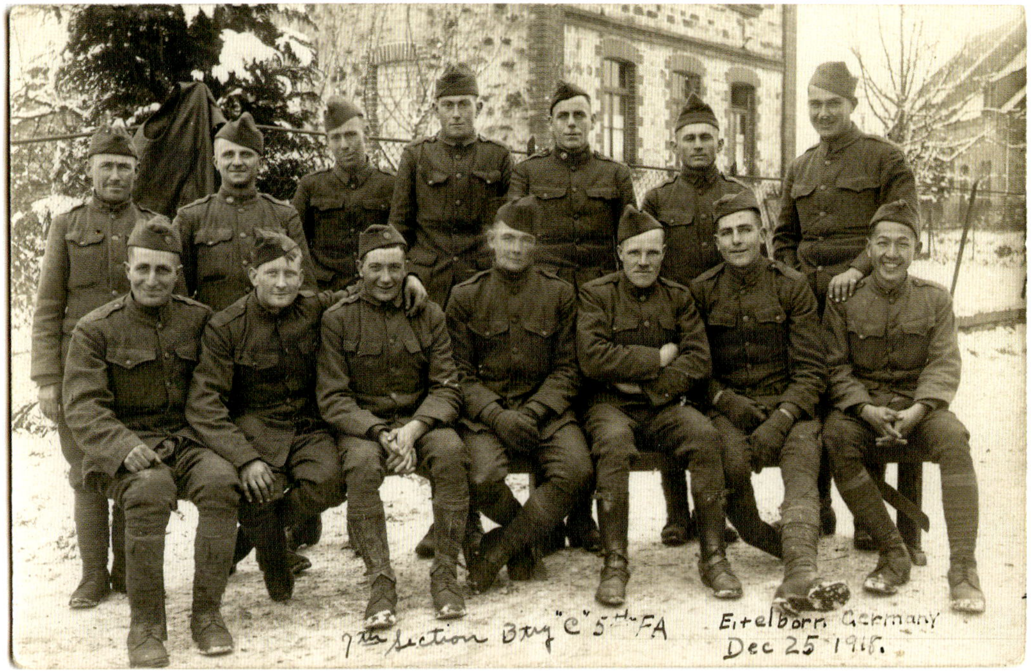

An interesting group shot of a section of the 7th Section, Battery C, 5th Field Artillery, 1st Division, AEF, taken on Christmas Day, 1918! For such a long serving veteran outfit it is notable that only one of the sitters displays any overseas service chevrons. Several front row sitters are wearing officer-style leather puttees, one with spurs. The redleg seated at far right is almost certainly of Asian or Native American descent. In an effort to appear uniform it appears one of the group doffed his jerkin and it can be seen hanging on the chain link fence at the left of the image.

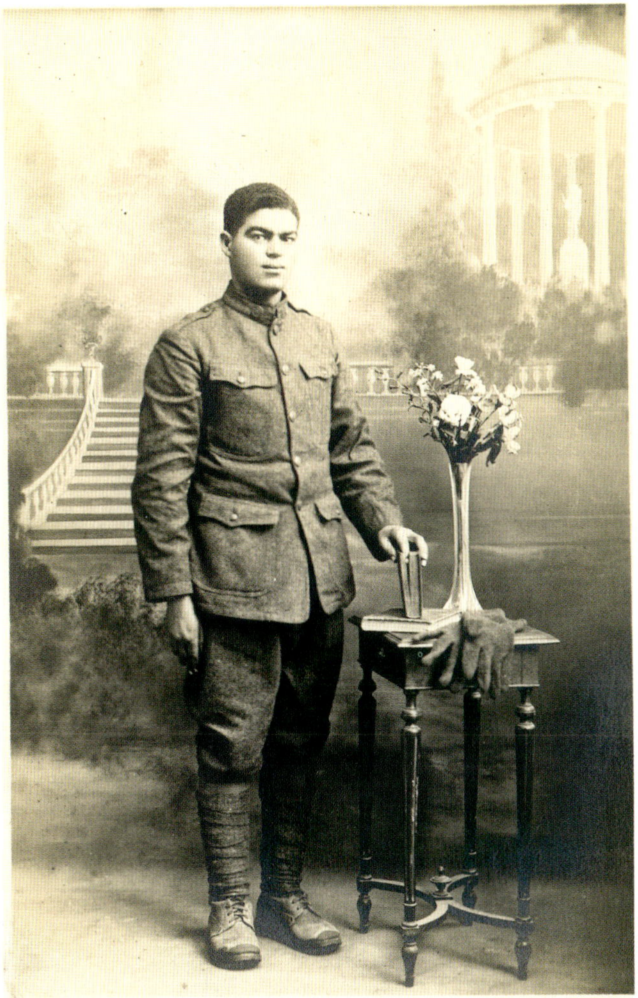

Another unidentified black Doughboy photographed indoors. On the stand to his left a pair of issue olive drab woolen gloves can be seen.

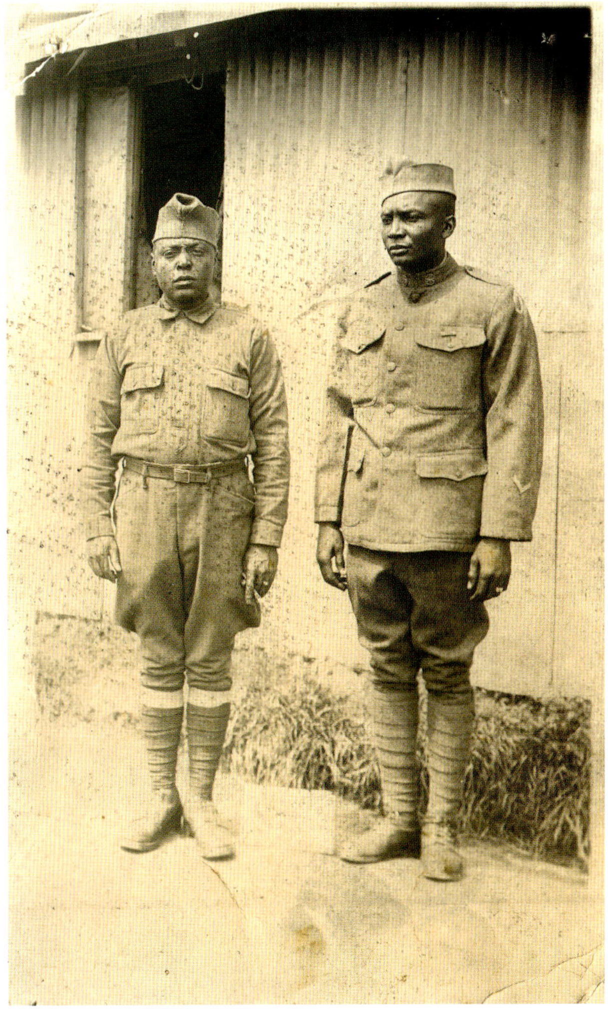

Two black Doughboys, in outdoor setting. The visible shoulder sleeve insignia on the soldier standing at right may be that of Advanced Section, Services of Supply, although his collar ornament looks like a lettered infantry disk. A photographer's identification slate may be seen between their feet.

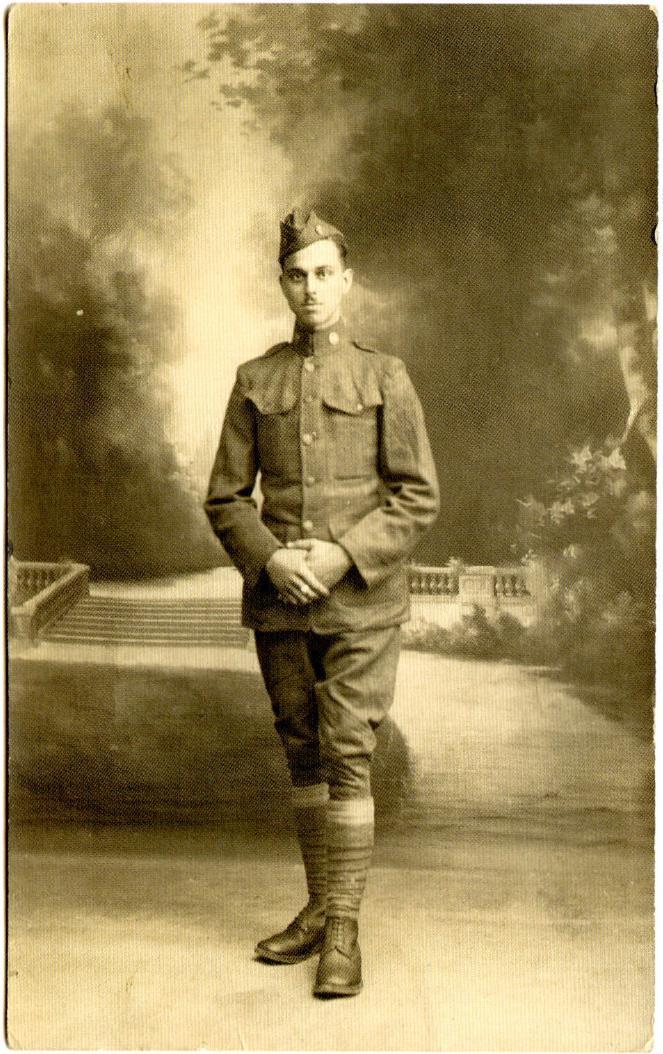

A black Doughboy in an indoor portrait, with painted backdrop. Interestingly, he wears two ornaments on his cap. He also appears to be wearing British issue B-5 "Ammunition Boots," straight laced in British style.

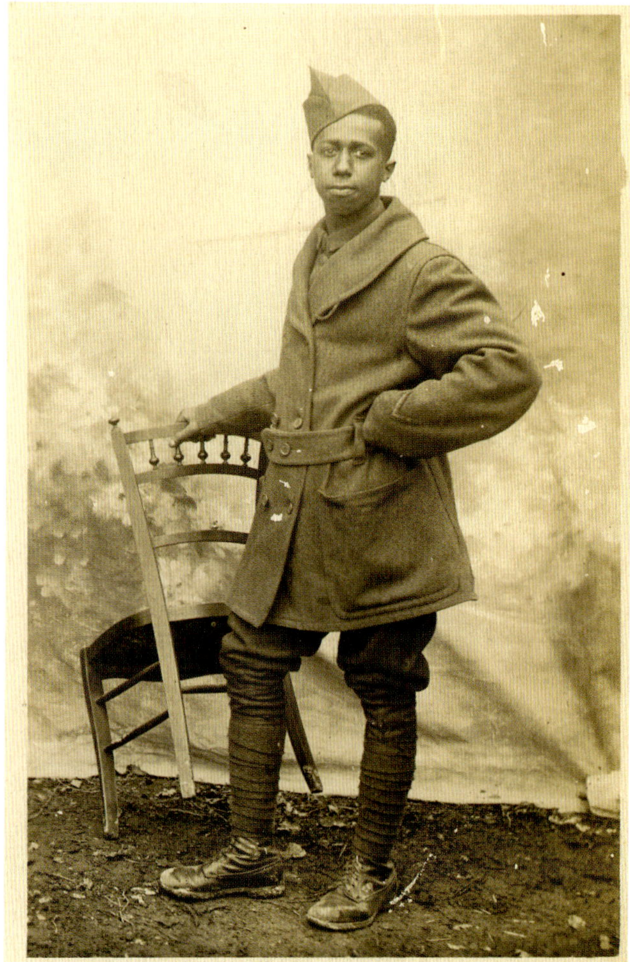

A black Doughboy in an exterior shot against painted background. He wears a French-style overseas cap and one of the myriad variations of short Mackinaw-style overcoats. He proudly displays a single overseas service chevron on his lower left sleeve. His boots appear to be cap toe smooth side out russet marching shoes.

A black Doughboy, "Edward" of Company B, 811th Pioneer Infantry. The 811th did not sail for France until October 1918. It remained in France until July 1919, and primarily performed stevedore work. He wears what appears to be a standard infantry ornament on his cap. In his inscription on the reverse he mentions his shoes being too large. Although muddy, these appear to be the "Metallic Fastened Field Shoe," a.k.a. the "Pershing" boot. This final field shoe pattern used in the AEF included triple layer outsoles, heel horseshoes, heel and sole hobnails, and an iron toe plate. The reverse inscription to his mother reads in part, "do not laugh at my shoes because they are too large."

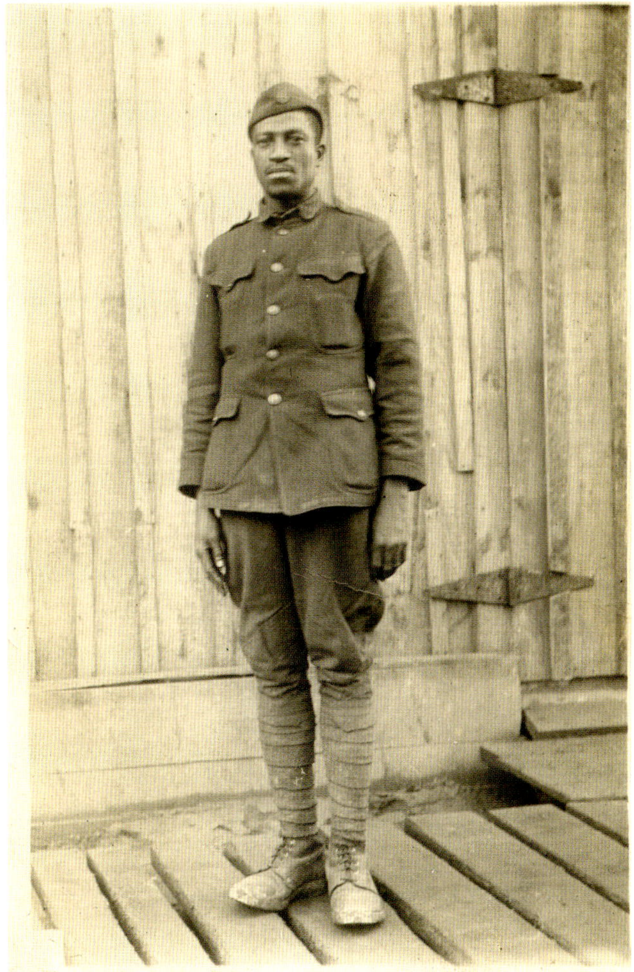

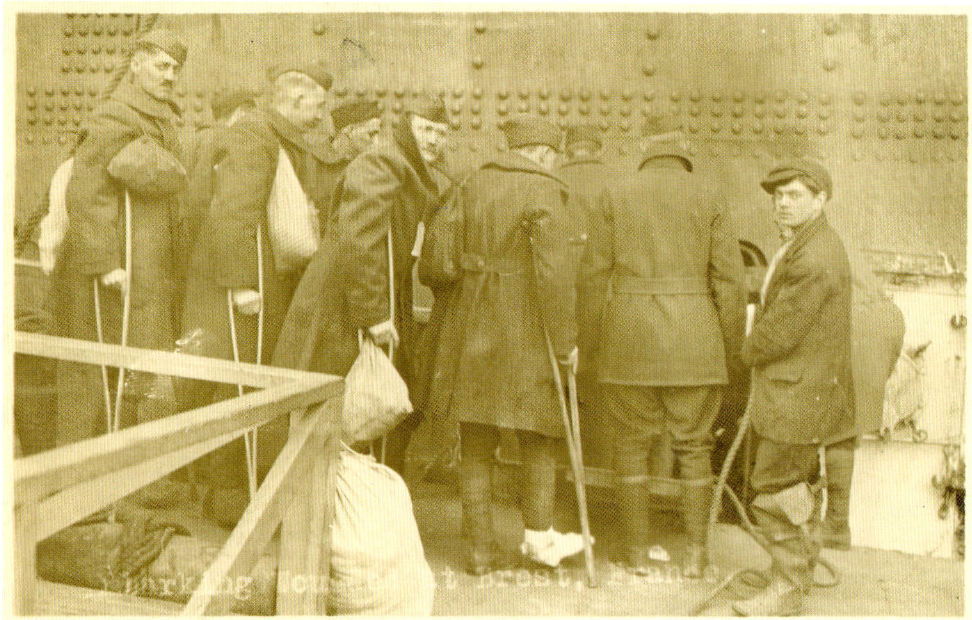

Captioned "Embarking wounded at Brest," the four wounded Doughboys seem to have suffered injuries to their lower extremities, as all are using one and in some cases two crutches. All appear to be wearing freshly issued new uniforms, and interestingly none of them has even had time to sew on their hard-earned wound stripes. All carry small ditty bags which likely contain toilet articles, a mess kit, and any personal items they were able to retain as they traversed the AEF medical evacuation system.

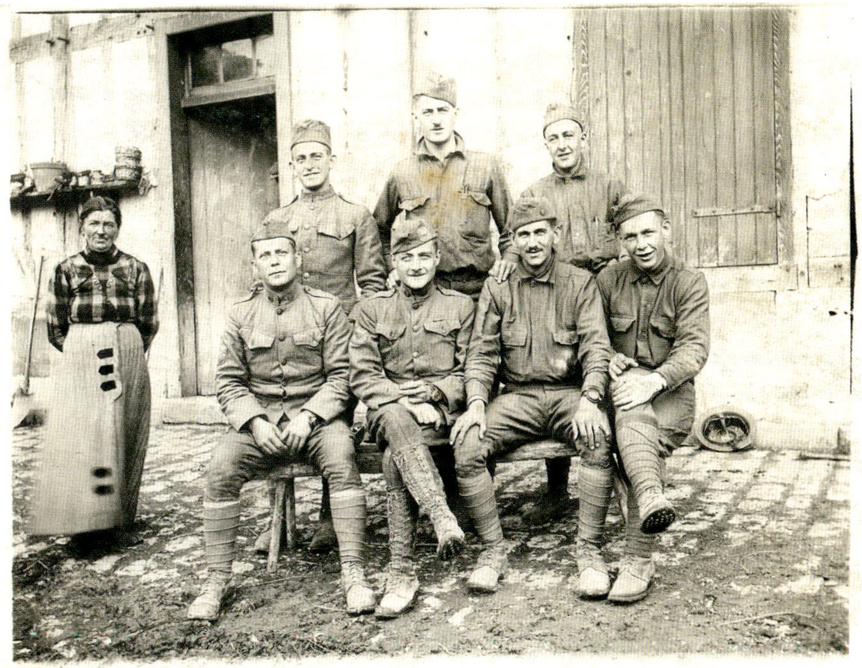

A very interesting image of a group of engineers, no doubt taken outside their billet. Given that none of them wears any overseas service stripes this may well be an image taken in France, before the Armistice. The absence of any gas masks indicates the location is fairly far from the front lines. A steel helmet is noted, however, against the wall of the building. The master engineer, junior grade, seated second from left wears full lace-up leather boots, and in decidedly unauthorized fashion wears his senior engineer, j.g, rank insignia on both sleeve and his overseas cap. In addition, he wears a single ribbon, which appears to be for Mexican Border Service. A notable variety of wristwatches are in evidence. The Doughboy seated to the left of the master engineer wears a very large wristwatch. This is actually a pocket watch placed in a commercially available wrist band designed to convert a pocket watch into a wristwatch.

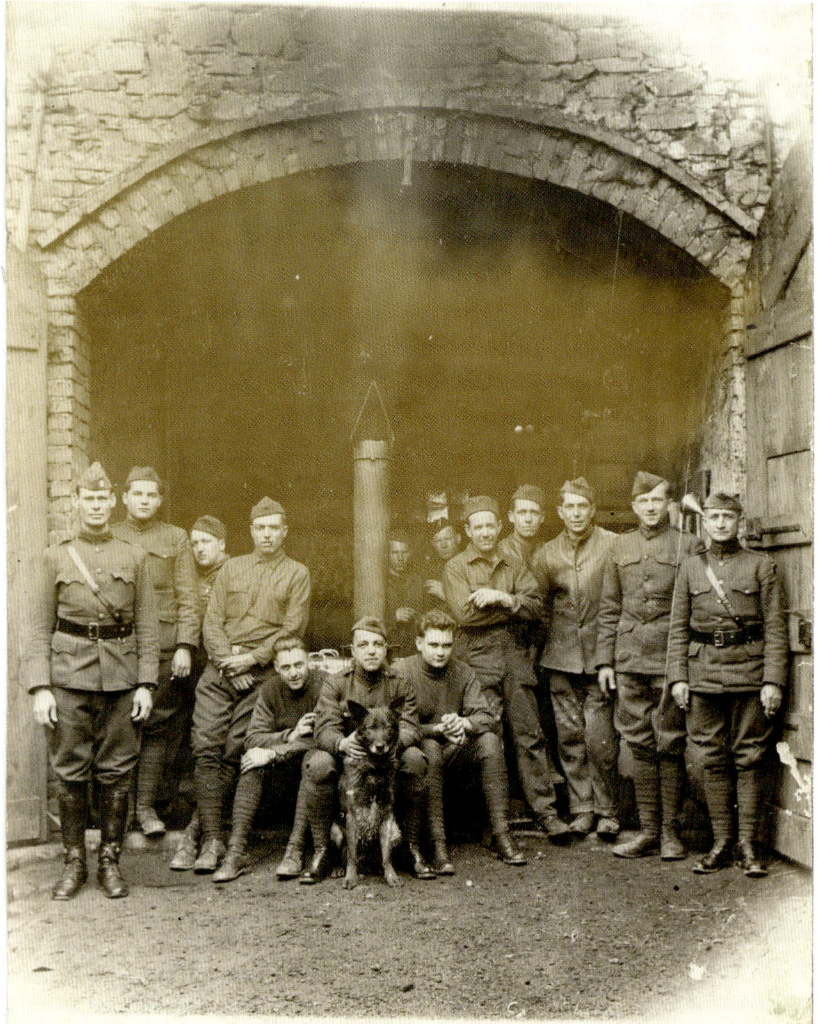

A kitchen crew of the 42nd "Rainbow" Division. Evidenced by the presence of shoulder sleeve insignia this image was taken in the Army of Occupation. The cook stove appears to be a rolling kitchen, perhaps dismounted from its wheels, which would account for its relatively low overall height. Standing at extreme left and right of the photo are the officers, a captain at left, a lieutenant at right. The Doughboys in between exhibit a wide variety of uniform items including the leather jerkins, Red Cross donation sweaters, some apparently brown or blue denim fatigues, and a souvenir German belt. A dark-muzzled shepherd dog rounds out the group. Although indistinct, stacks of crated ration items and canned goods line the back wall of this stall.

An image of a Doughboy with a diminutive ally, a French soldier.

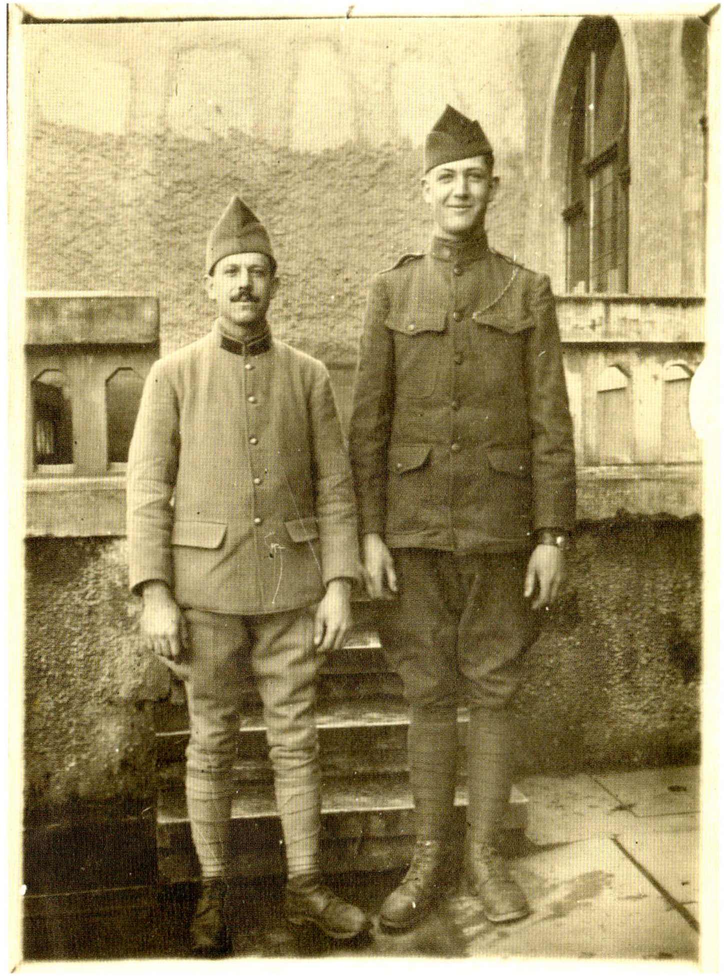

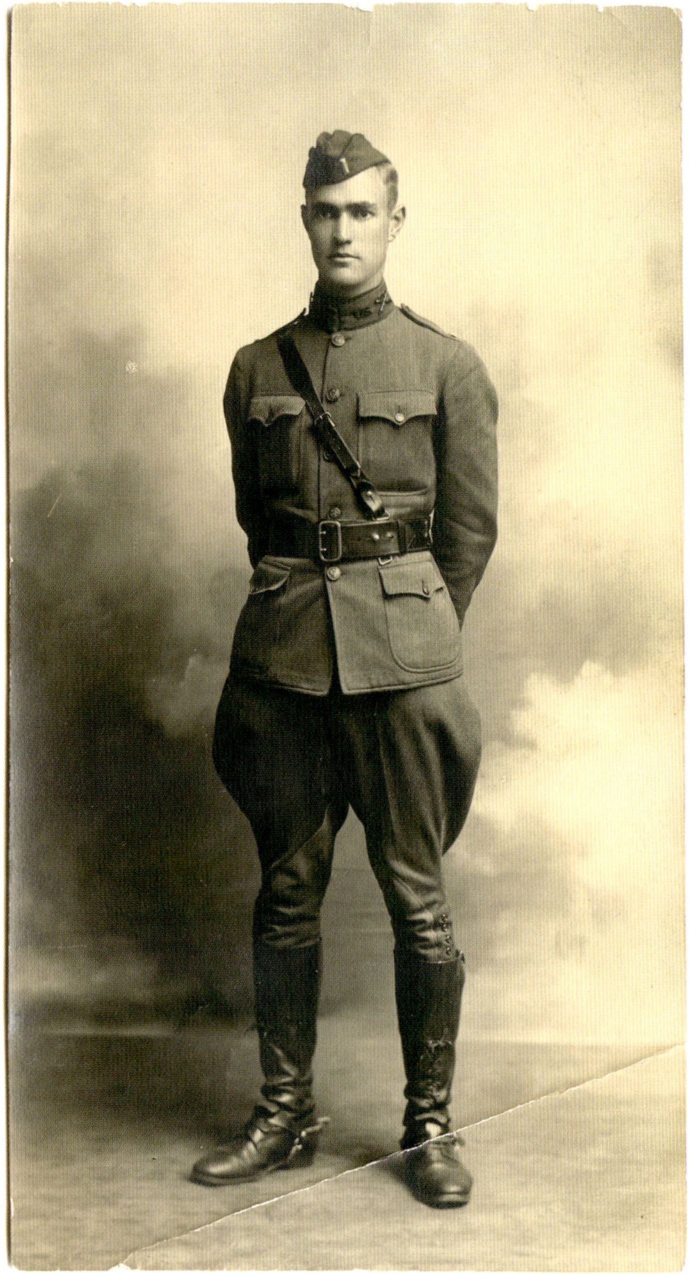

An impeccably attired young field artillery lieutenant resplendent in boots, spurs, Sam Browne belt, chamois reinforced breeches, and overseas cap with artillery red branch-colored piping. The spurs are officer-quality private items as evidenced by the flat chain style instep straps. He could certainly have appeared in the advertisement of any of the myriad outfitters dealing in officers uniforms and findings circa 1918. The numbers on his crossed cannon field artillery insignia cannot be discerned.

A twice-wounded infantry lieutenant photographed in a professional studio setting. His overseas cap displays broad ribbon-style branch trim versus narrow piping. His cap also has what appears to be the "TO" 90th Division insignia on the cap's curtain opposite the lieutenant bar. On his left wrist the chain of an Identification bracelet can be seen with the added appendage of a small charm. White collar and cuffs are also visible. Possibly an image made soon after return to the States.

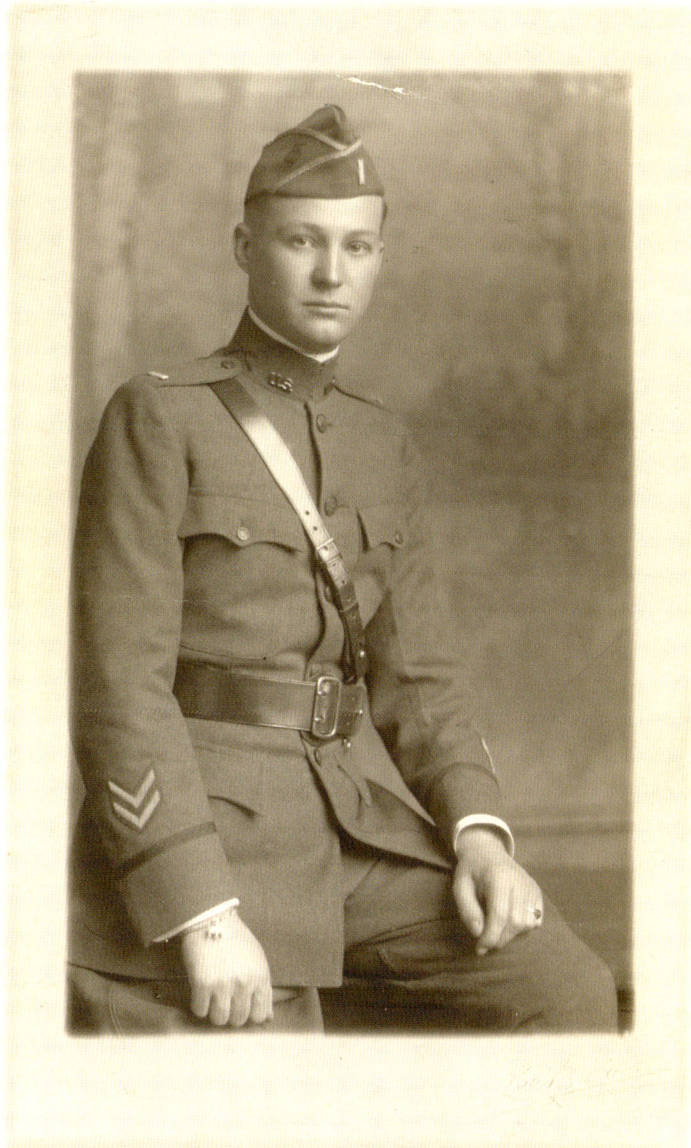

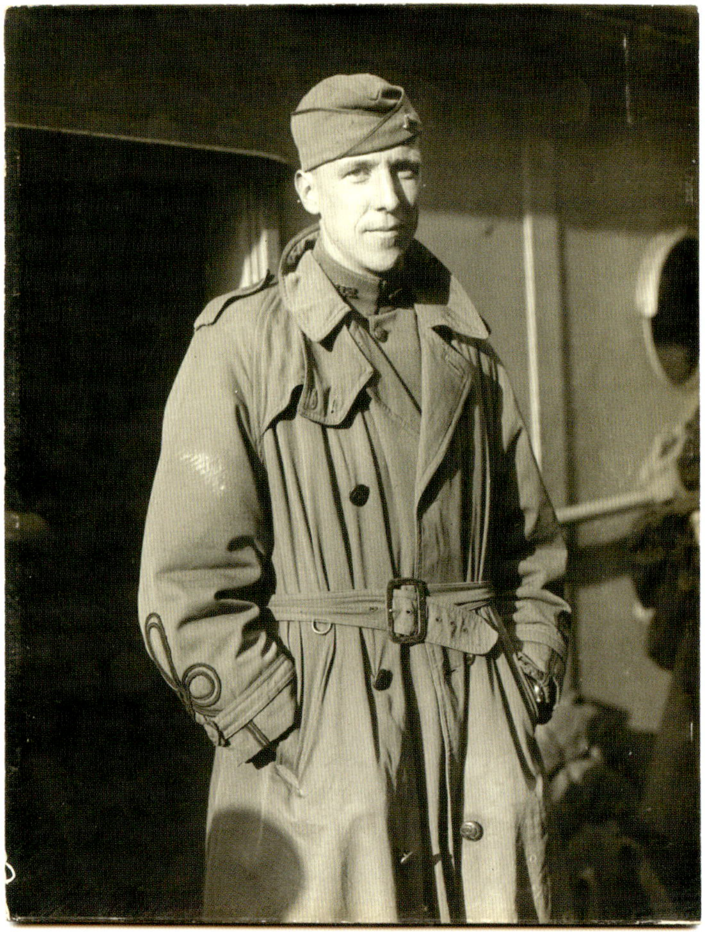

A first lieutenant photographed aboard ship, almost certainly on the trip back home from France. A wristwatch is barely visible in the folds of his left sleeve. Especially unusual is the application of lace sleeve rank insignia on a trench coat. No rank is visible in the more common location, the epaulets. While lace sleeve rank insignia are commonly seen on the wool overcoat and prescribed by regulation, they are most uncommon as a badge of rank on the trench coat. HQ, AEF G.O. No. 7 dated January 9, 1918, authorized officers to wear the "so-called trench coat" with insignia of rank to be worn on the shoulder. His overseas cap displays wide tape or ribbon branch color trim.

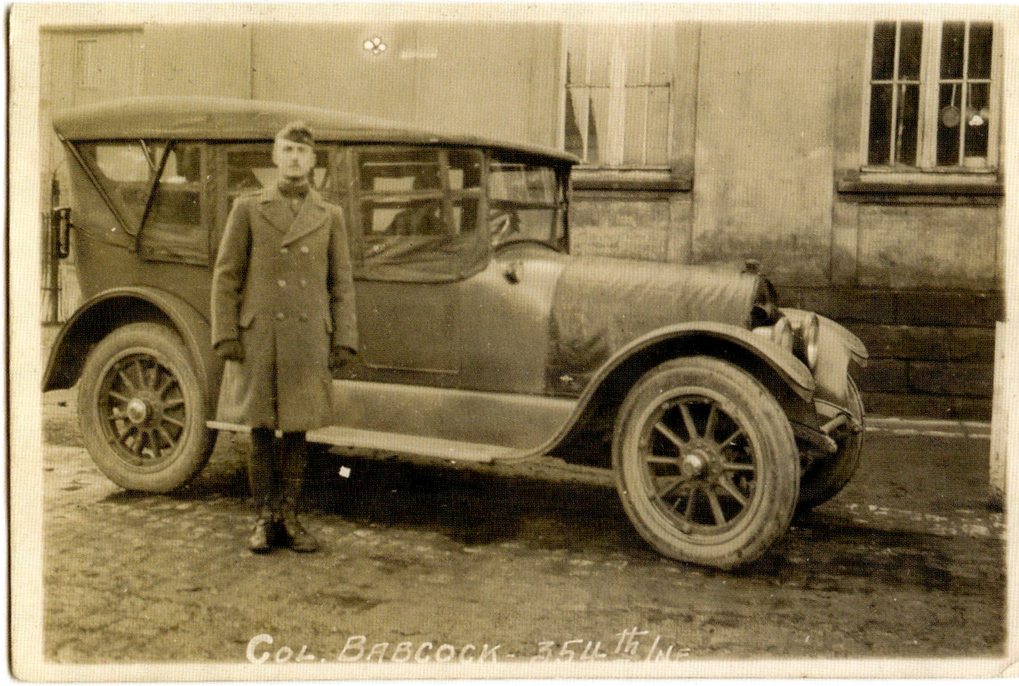

Col. Conrad S. Babcock, commander of the 354th Infantry, in front of his staff car. The car is a Cadillac 57 touring car with complete winter enclosure and hood blanket in place. The Cadillac 57 was a higher end staff car normally the province of regimental and higher level commanders. Babcock was a career officer of the "Old Army" from the West Point class of 1898, a veteran of the Philippine Insurrection, and intervening years in the peacetime army. Assigned to command the 28th Infantry, 1st Division, AEF, in July 1918, within hours of the jump-off for the battle of Soissons, Babcock soon ran afoul of the new division commander, Maj. Gen. Charles P. Summerall. His candor in reporting difficulties, and the impossibility of executing some of his orders based on faulty understanding of actual conditions at the front by Division HQ, branded him (at least in Summerall's eyes) as a commander "prone to see obstacles." In early August 1918, he was relieved of command of the 28th Infantry, a slight from Summerall that Babcock never forgot. His good reputation with peers and willingness to request a court of inquiry regarding his relief paid off. A West Point classmate at GHQ, AEF, saw to it he got another regimental command, in the 353rd Infantry of the 89th Division. He later was reassigned to the 354th Infantry in the same division. By all accounts he rendered excellent service in both outfits. His resentment of Gen. Summerall, nevertheless remained a galling lifelong issue for Babcock.

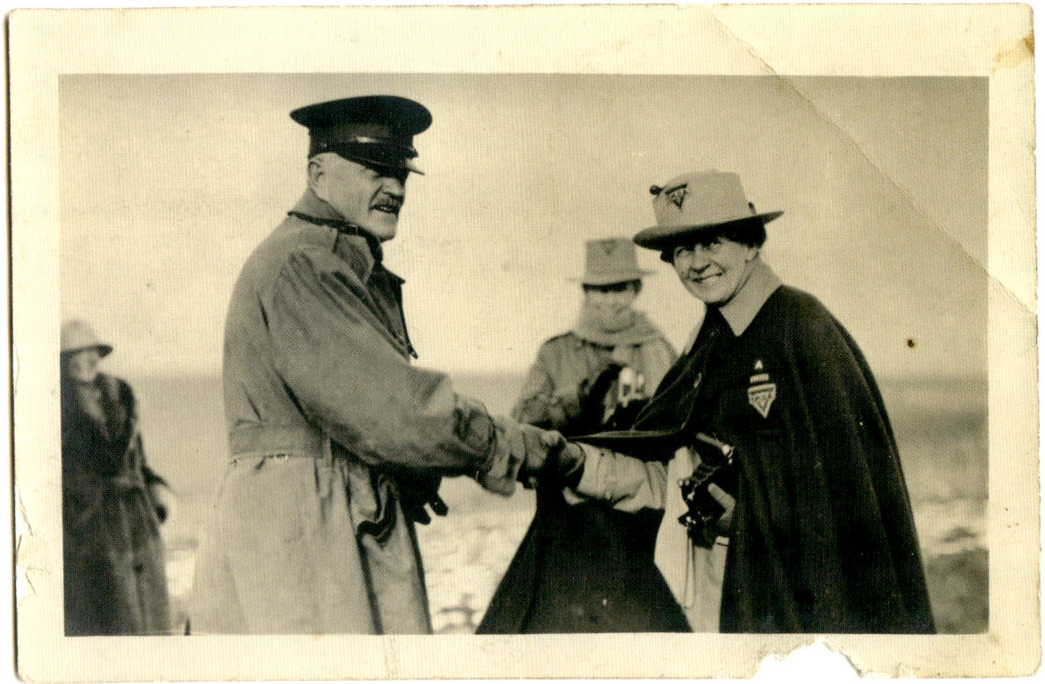

A rare image of a smiling General of the Armies John J. Pershing. The normally dour Pershing was known to be charming with the ladies. In this case it appears he has just had his picture snapped by a woman YMCA worker. Other YMCA ladies look on. The camera is a typical Kodak bellows type camera of the period. She wears the red triangle YMCA insignia on both her cap and cape. In addition, her cape also displays what seems to be a miniature 3rd Army shoulder sleeve insignia, and what may be one of the many unauthorized victory ribbons.

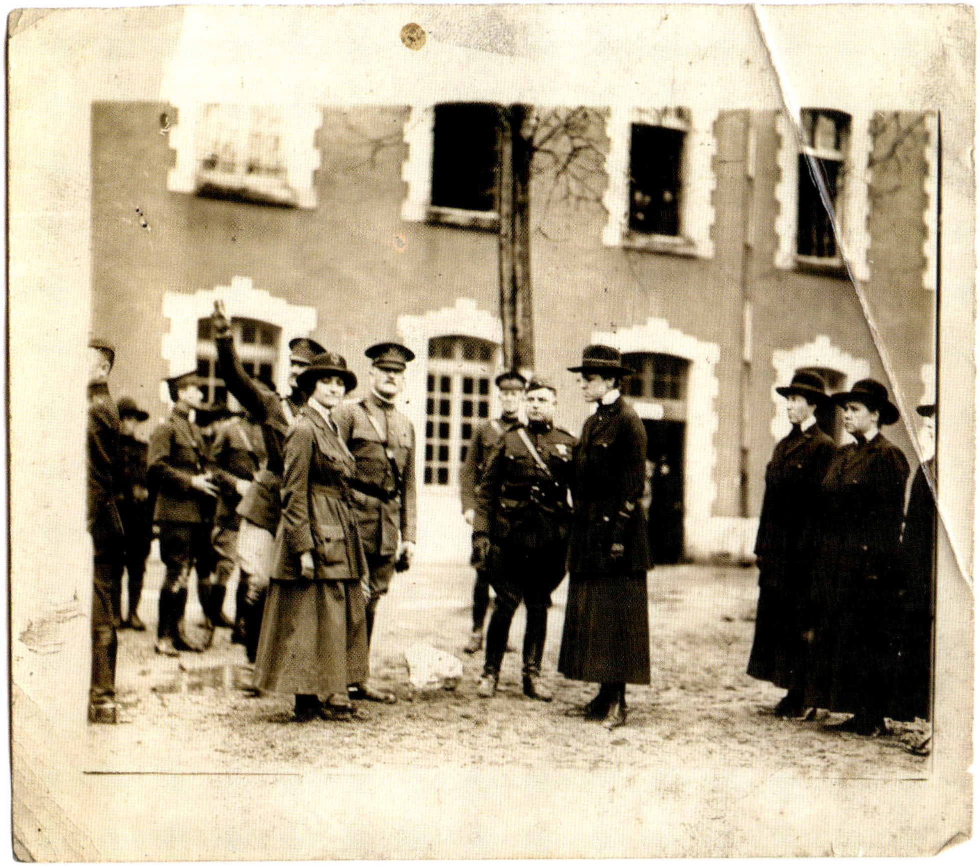

Gen. Pershing at what may be an award ceremony for Army nurses. From other identified photos taken at this location the place is the Caserne Baraguey-de Hilliers in Tours. At right are Army nurses in a formation. Standing in front is Julia C. Stimson, Chief Nurse of the AEF. To her right is a rather portly Marine Corps officer. Pershing, in a characteristic pose, holds a pair of gloves in his left hand. To his right is a woman YMCA worker. Behind both Pershing and the YMCA worker is Pershing's aide, Col. John G. Quekemeyer, who appears to be calling for a vehicle. A noted polo player and equestrian, Quekemeyer is invariably seen in widely flared light-colored riding breeches. Perhaps the most highly regarded of the many officers who served Pershing as an aide de camp, Quekemeyer went on to a very successful Army career. Nominated for duty as the commandant of cadets at USMA in 1926, he died quite suddenly of pneumonia February 28, 1926. The resulting shock was too much for his mother, who died days later. They were both buried in their hometown of Yazoo City, Mississippi, March 3, 1926.

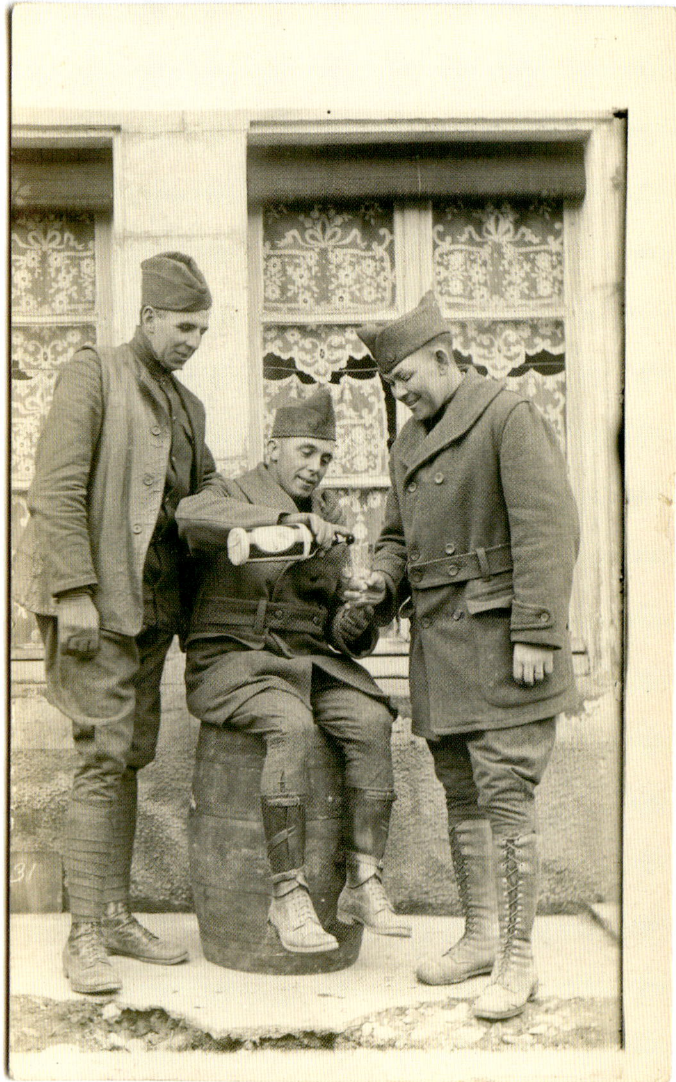

Three Doughboys sampling the fruit of the vine. The seated pourer and his companion on the right wear short roll collared belted Mackinaw-style overcoats. At right the buttons are plain, and at left the buttons appear to be coat size standard eagle buttons. The Doughboy at right wears a medical ornament on his French-cut overseas cap, and has full lace-up leather boots. The seated Doughboy wears smooth cap toe russet shoes and officer-style leather puttees. A US disk adorns his French-style cap. The standing Doughboy at left is the most "regulation" appearing of this threesome of "pill rollers." He wears the wool-lined leather jerkin over his service coat. His shoes also are the smooth toe russet type.

A bugler of the 77th Division photographed outdoors against a painted backdrop. He wears chevrons signifying a single wound and six months overseas service. The rather cockeyed ribbon he wears cannot be identified. As often seen he wears a French-cut overseas cap. He has chosen to wrap his puttees from the top down so the fastening tapes are just above the ankle. This not generally seen in the AEF; however, it became a style affectation among mounted troops and was popular in the interwar era.

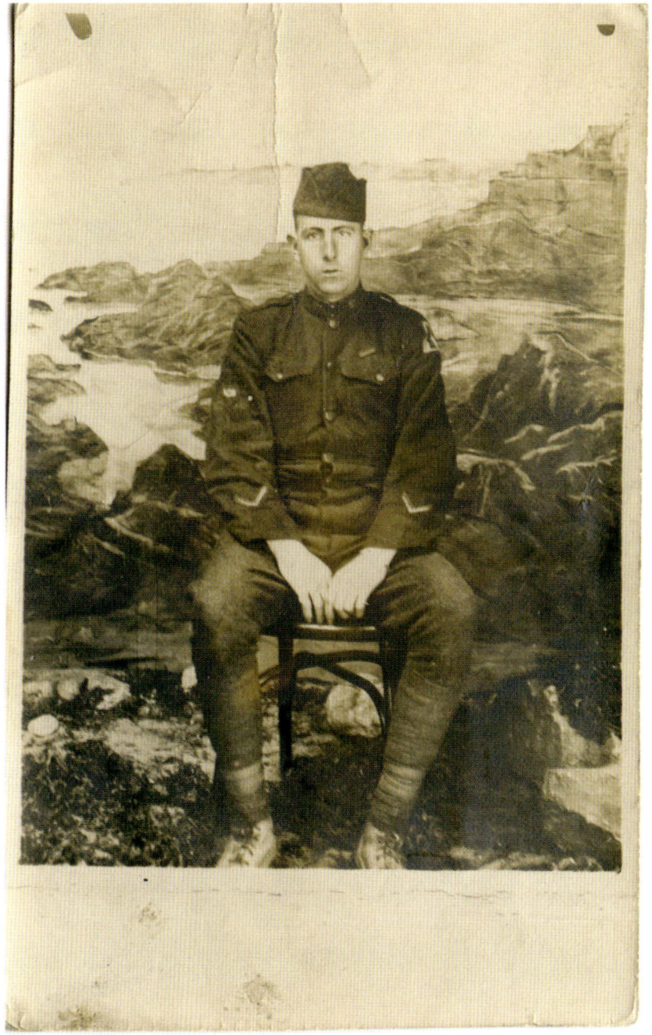

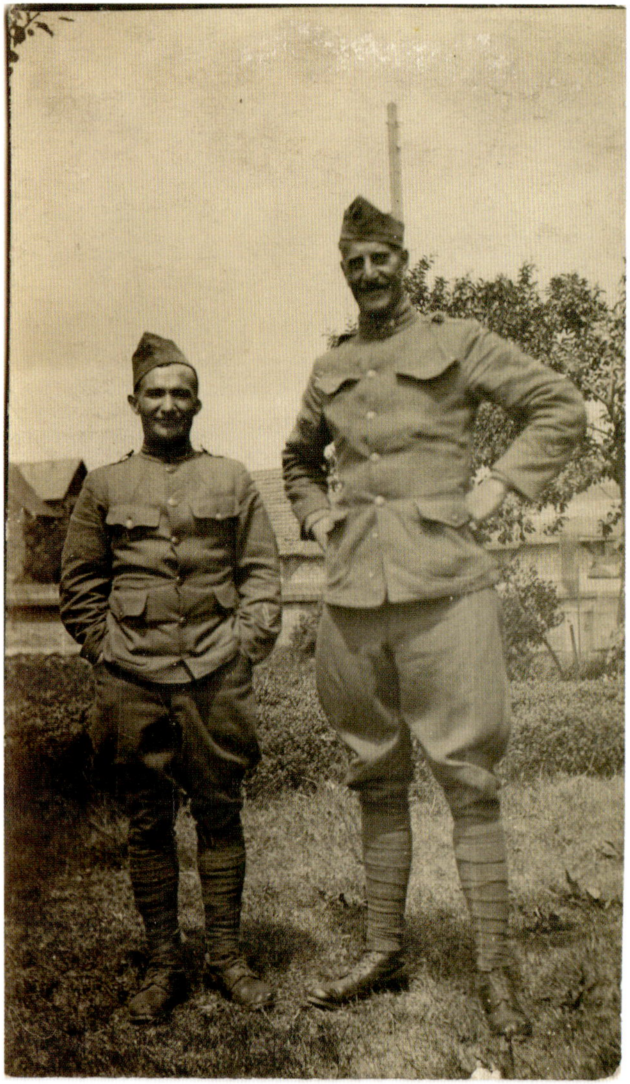

"The long and the short of it," a perennial gag photo in the military pairing the tallest and shortest guys in the outfit. In this case both Doughboys wear French-style overseas caps and wear chevrons signifying a year of overseas service.

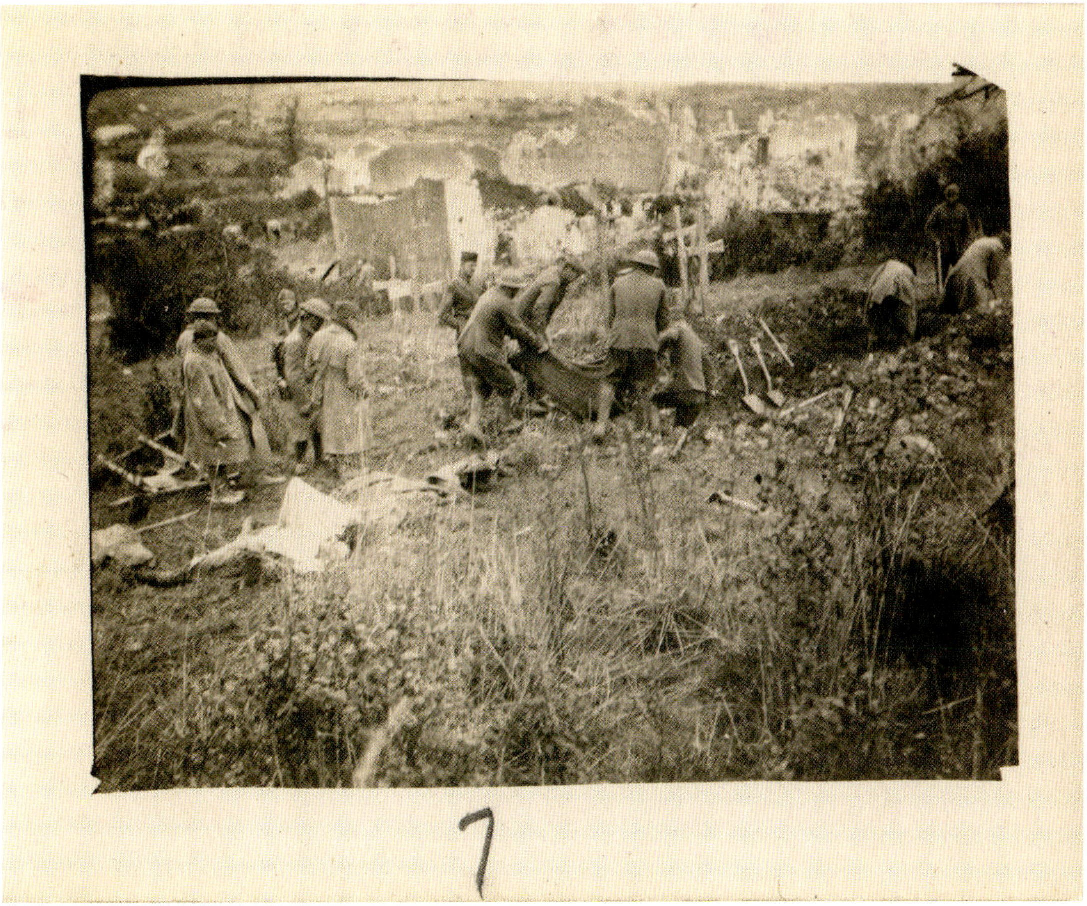

A sobering candid photo of a burial detail at work in the Meuse-Argonne.

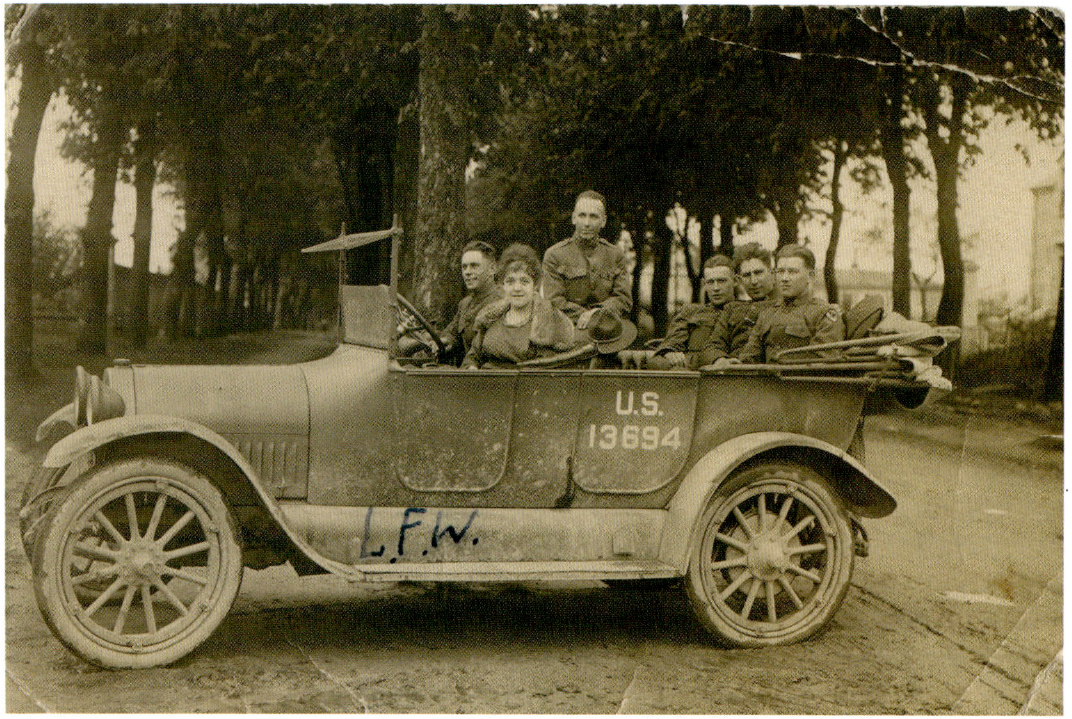

Five Doughboys and one local gal out for a joy ride. The corporal holding his campaign hat wears a single overseas chevron, and the fellow sitting in the backseat wears an unidentifiable shoulder sleeve insignia. The car is likely of English make since it is right-hand drive. Nonetheless, it is clearly marked as an AEF vehicle.

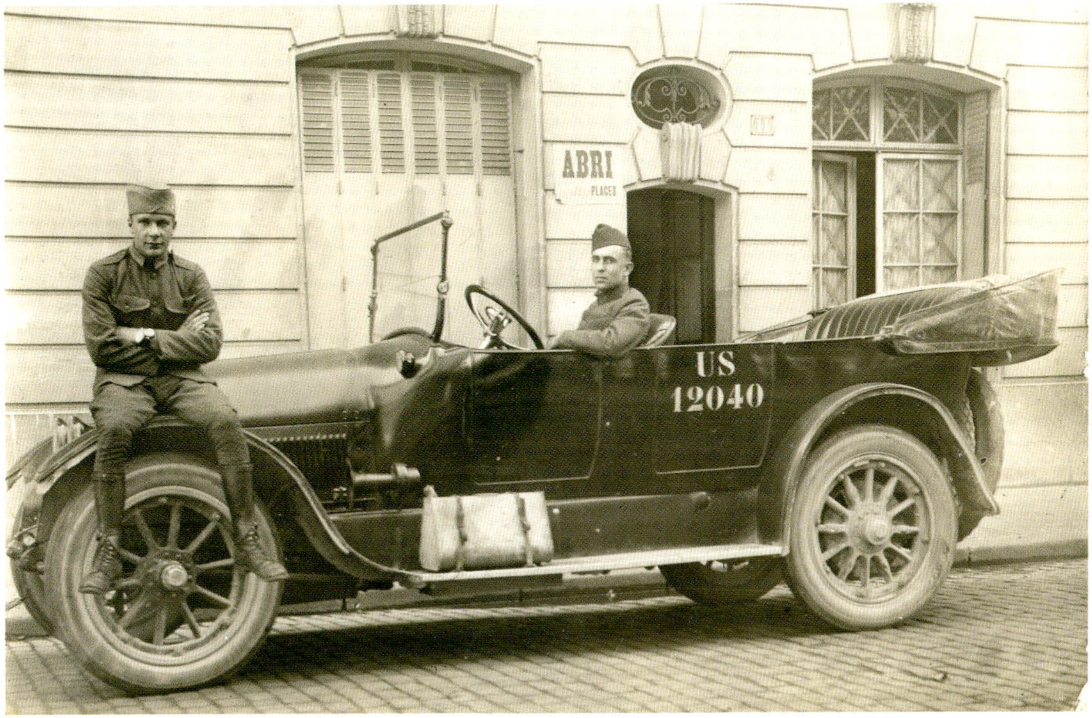

Another Cadillac 57 touring car all shiny and clean. It appears to be in factory black finish, as was fairly common for staff cars not assigned to frontline units. Dual spare tires are mounted on the back of the car. The top is fully folded with tonneau cover neatly in place. The placard on the building in the background reads "ABRI 45 places" a shelter with a forty-five-person capacity. The Doughboy seated on the front fender wears officer-style leather puttees and the driver sports a French-style overseas cap.

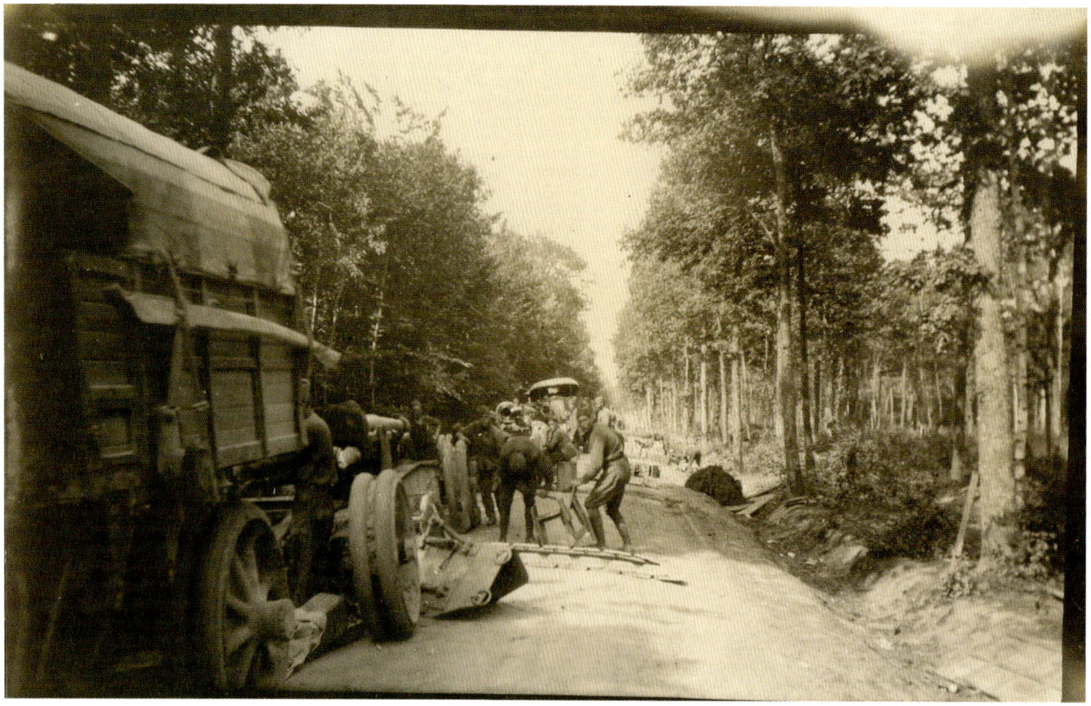

An Artillery unit equipped with 155 mm GPF guns somewhere in France, most likely the 66th Field Artillery Brigade "the Long Range Snipers." The crews are either installing or removing caterpillar bands, which provided the gun carriage with better flotation on soft ground.

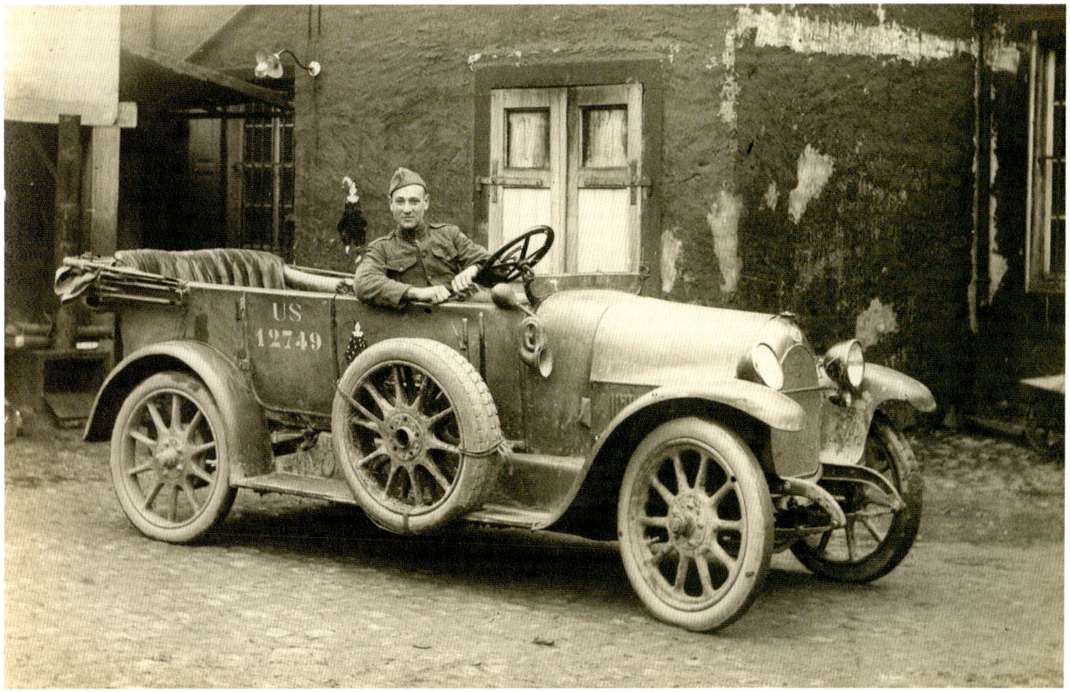

Another interesting staff car with English style right-hand drive. Note the extra spare wheel tied onto the standard spare tire mount on the driver's side. A bulb type horn, missing windshield, and rather out-of-whack headlight add to the rakish look of this hard-used ride. The driver wears an indistinct shoulder sleeve insignia. The standing clown figure appears painted on the building and on the car, but what unit this signifies is unknown.

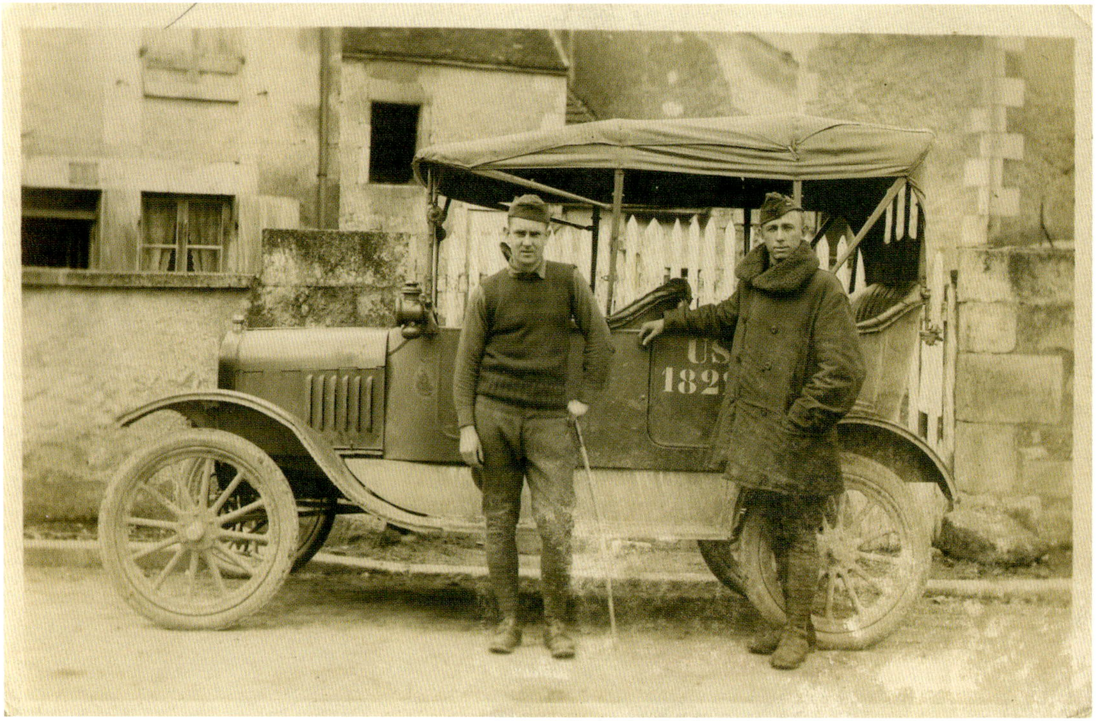

A rough-looking Ford Model T, which appears to have had the addition of at least one shelter half to repair a well-worn top. The Doughboy at left wears a sleeveless sweater typical of those supplied by American Red Cross and other relief organizations to soldiers of the AEF. On the right his partner wears an officer-style canvas Mackinaw coat with Mouton collar. He also sports an English-style overseas cap with two small front buttons. The cap has a small badge attached which is possibly an officer-style shirt size Signal Corps insignia.

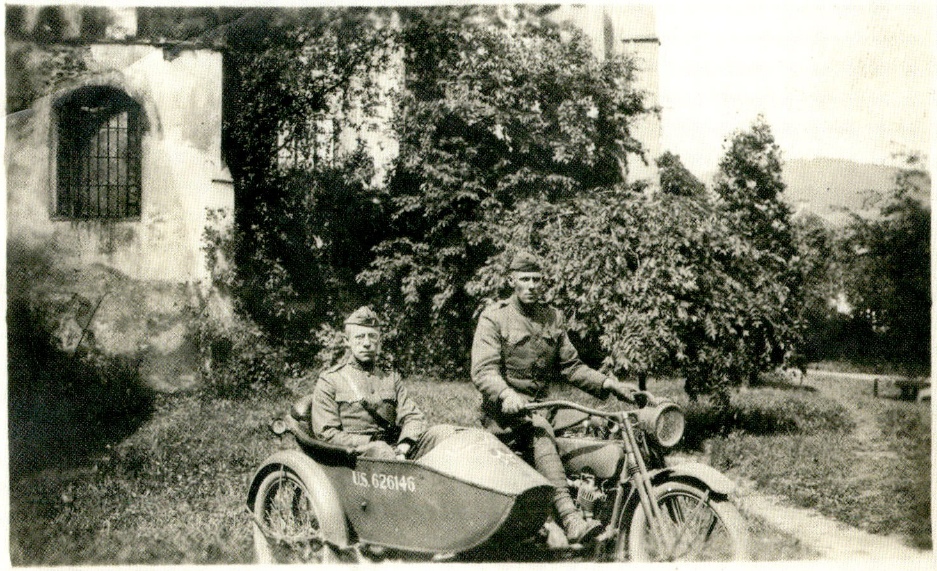

A bespectacled lieutenant and his driver in a Harley-Davidson motorcycle with sidecar. The lieutenant appears to be wearing artillery collar insignia, and the 2nd Division insignia on the sidecar is most likely that of 15th Artillery, which used the Indian head superimposed on various color rectangles to denote subordinate elements in the regiment.

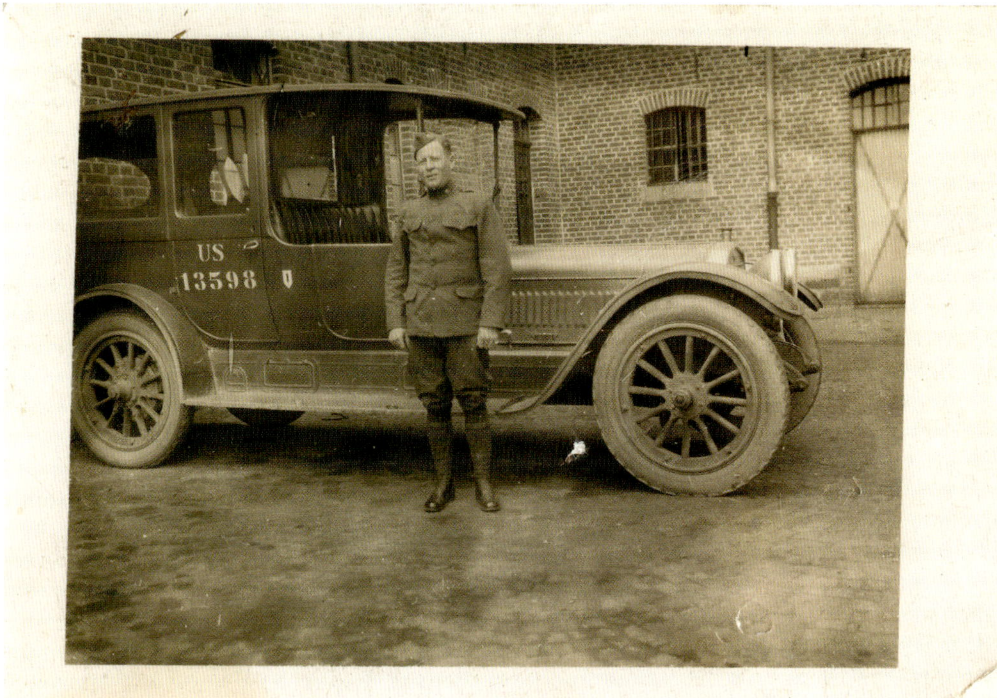

A Winton Six limousine, one of the larger and rarer staff cars in the AEF,with the driver compartment more or less open and a fully enclosed passenger compartment. This is almost certainly the staff car of one of the higher ranking officers in the division. It displays a rather small 1st Division insignia, which differs from the prescribed post-Armistice vehicle insignia that included a laurel wreath surround of the basic division insignia. The driver wears chevrons denoting eighteen months overseas service.

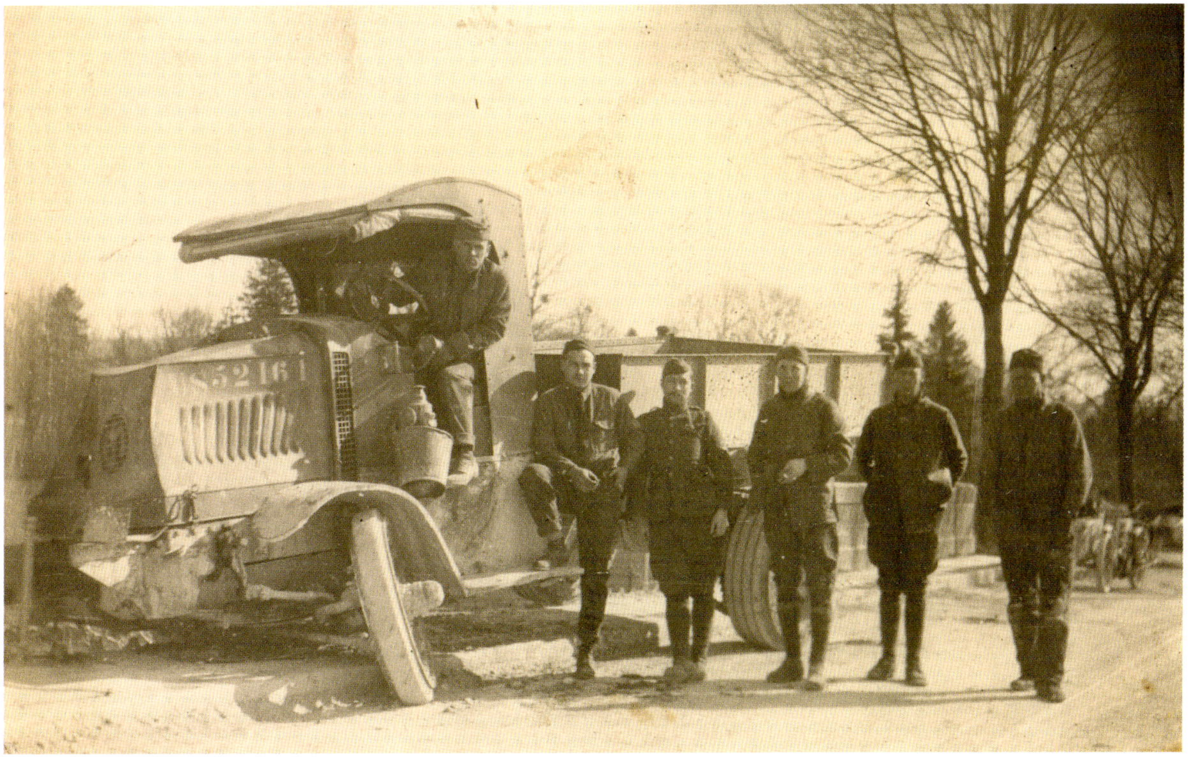

A bad day for this heavy Mack truck. Obviously it has sustained some major front end damage, though the crew seems unconcerned. The "5" prefix in the serial number identifies this as a 5-ton or higher-capacity truck, in accordance with GHQ AEF Bulletin No. 90, dated November 11, 1918. Behind the truck is a motorcycle with side car, most likely either an Indian or Harley-Davidson.

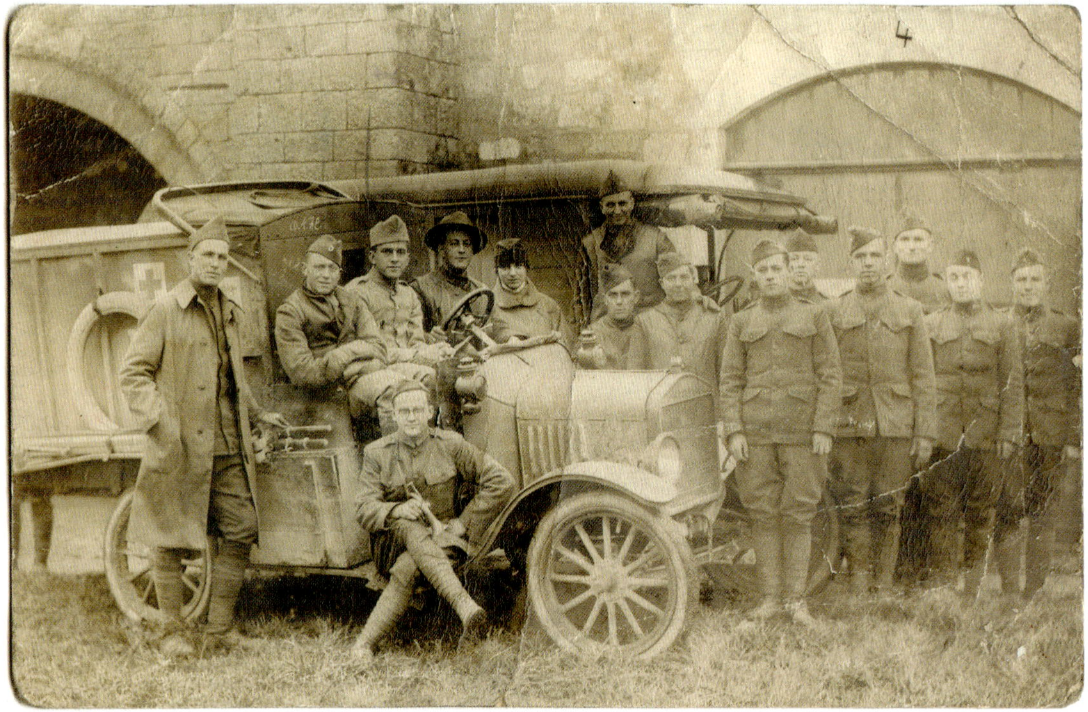

A most interesting image of a pair of ambulances. In the foreground is a light Ford Model T ambulance, with the cab canvas folded back. On the bulkhead one can read the inscription "O.K. FE"—likely the ambulance assembly section's final inspection notation. To the rear of the Model T "Tin Lizzie" is a heavy GMC ambulance. Seated in the model T there appears to be a French soldier, and standing to the rear a female worker whose organization cannot be determined. A bespectacled bugler is seated on the Model T's running board.

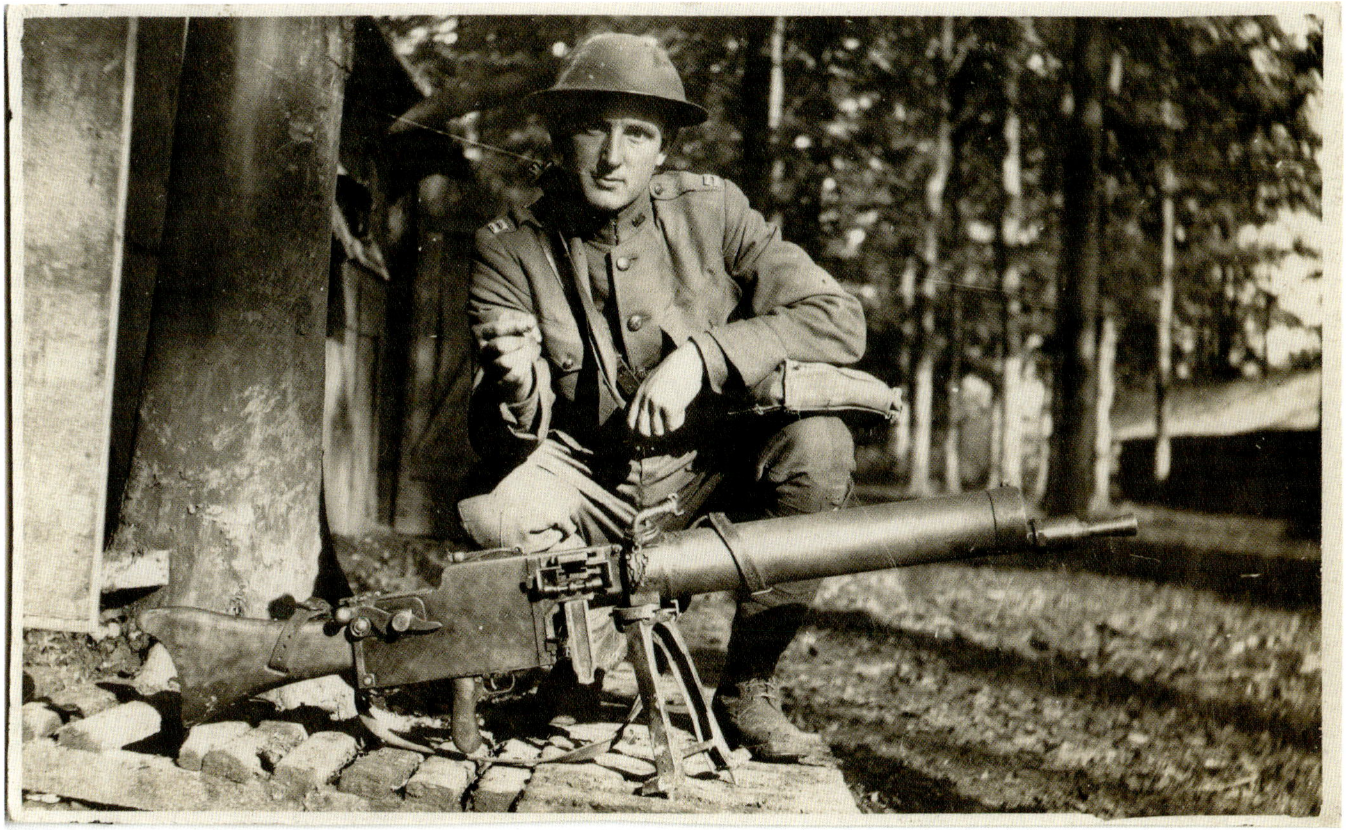

A captain of the AEF photographed with a fairly pristine MG08/15, the most produced light machine gun used by the Germans in World War I.

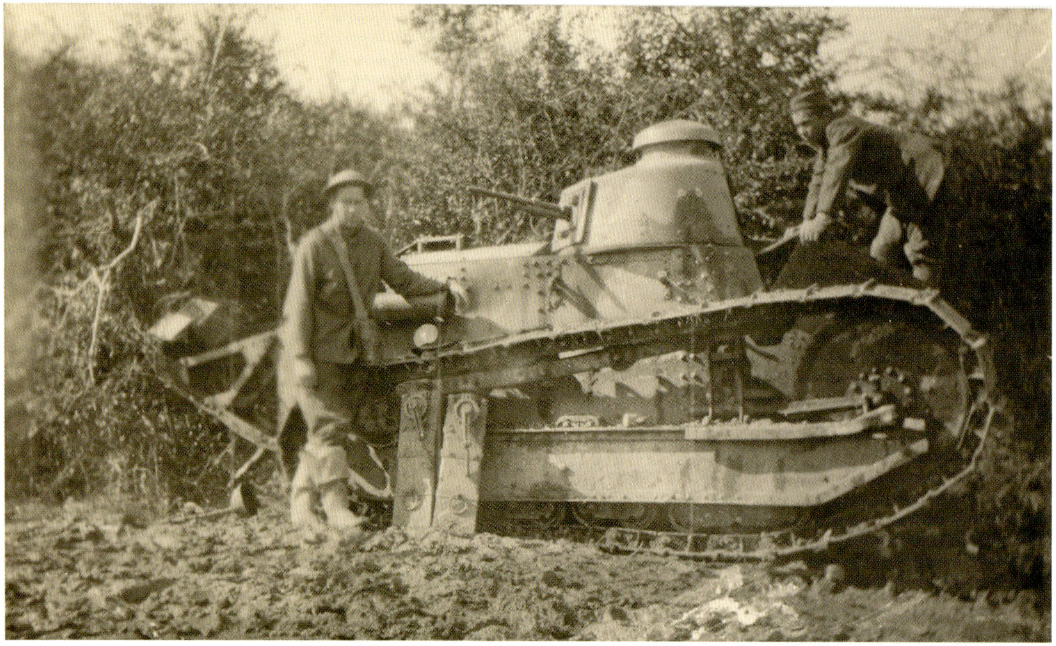

An American tank crew works on their Renault FT-17 light tank. This particular FT-17 variant carries the Hotchkiss machine gun as its main armament. To the left of the standing doughboy are two wagon jacks, a style common in the nineteenth century. This may indicate the crew was recently adjusting track tension on the tank. He wears the standard steel helmet and high rubber boots.

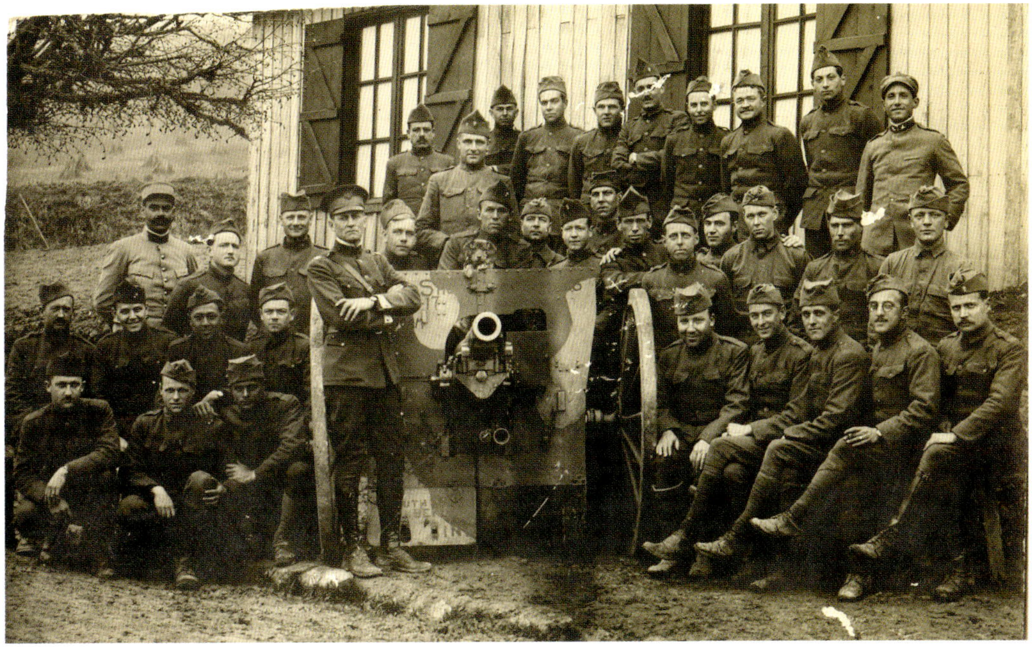

The gun that fired "America's First Shot." This French 75 was assigned to Battery C, 6th Field Artillery, 1st Division, AEF, and is credited as firing the first shot at German forces from a gun position near Luneville, France, October 23, 1917. The gun remained in continuous service with Battery C, until spring 1918. Battery officers requested the gun be returned to the USA as an iconic and historic relic. At that time it was estimated the gun had fired in excess of 20,000 rounds, and was becoming dangerously worn. The request was approved, and the gun was returned to the museum at the US Military Academy, West Point, New York, where it remains on display today. This photo was taken as the gun was being cleaned and prepared for shipment back to the States, at the US Ordnance Depot, Domgermain, France. The gun shield bears the inscription: "First Shot of War, 6:10 am, 10-23-17, Battery C, 6th Field Artillery, near Luneville." The soldiers are men assigned to the Ordnance Depot, and include Capt. R. R. Kennedy, standing next to the gun with arms folded. Seated at far right front row is Pvt. C. H. Platt, who was the unit telephone and office orderly. Interestingly there are two allied soldiers in the photo. The one at extreme right appears to be Italian and at left is a Frenchman, sporting a luxurious moustache. A puppy mascot can be seen directly over the center of the gun shield. The Doughboy seated third from left in the second row is clearly Asian American.

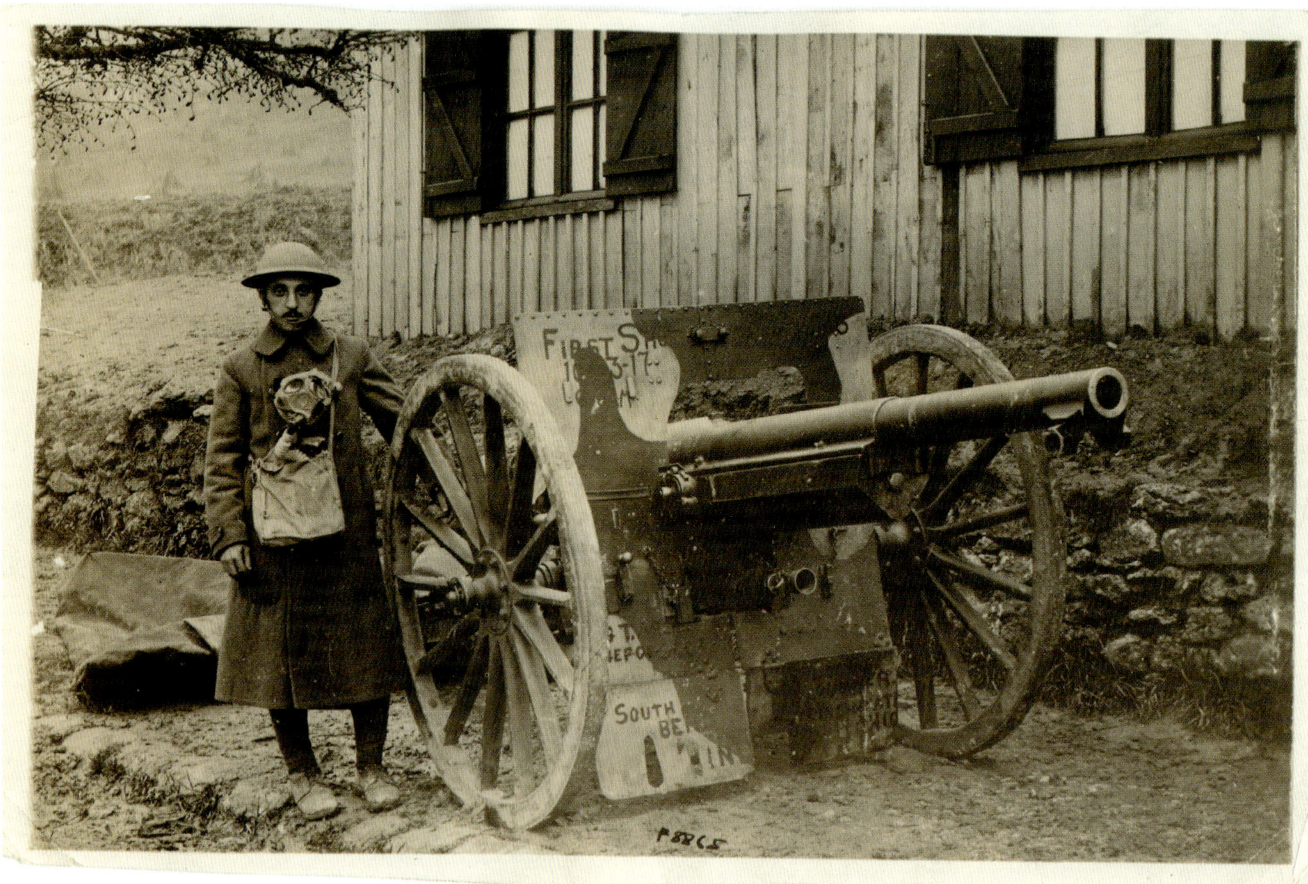

Another image of the "First Shot" gun, at Domgermain, with an unidentified Doughboy.

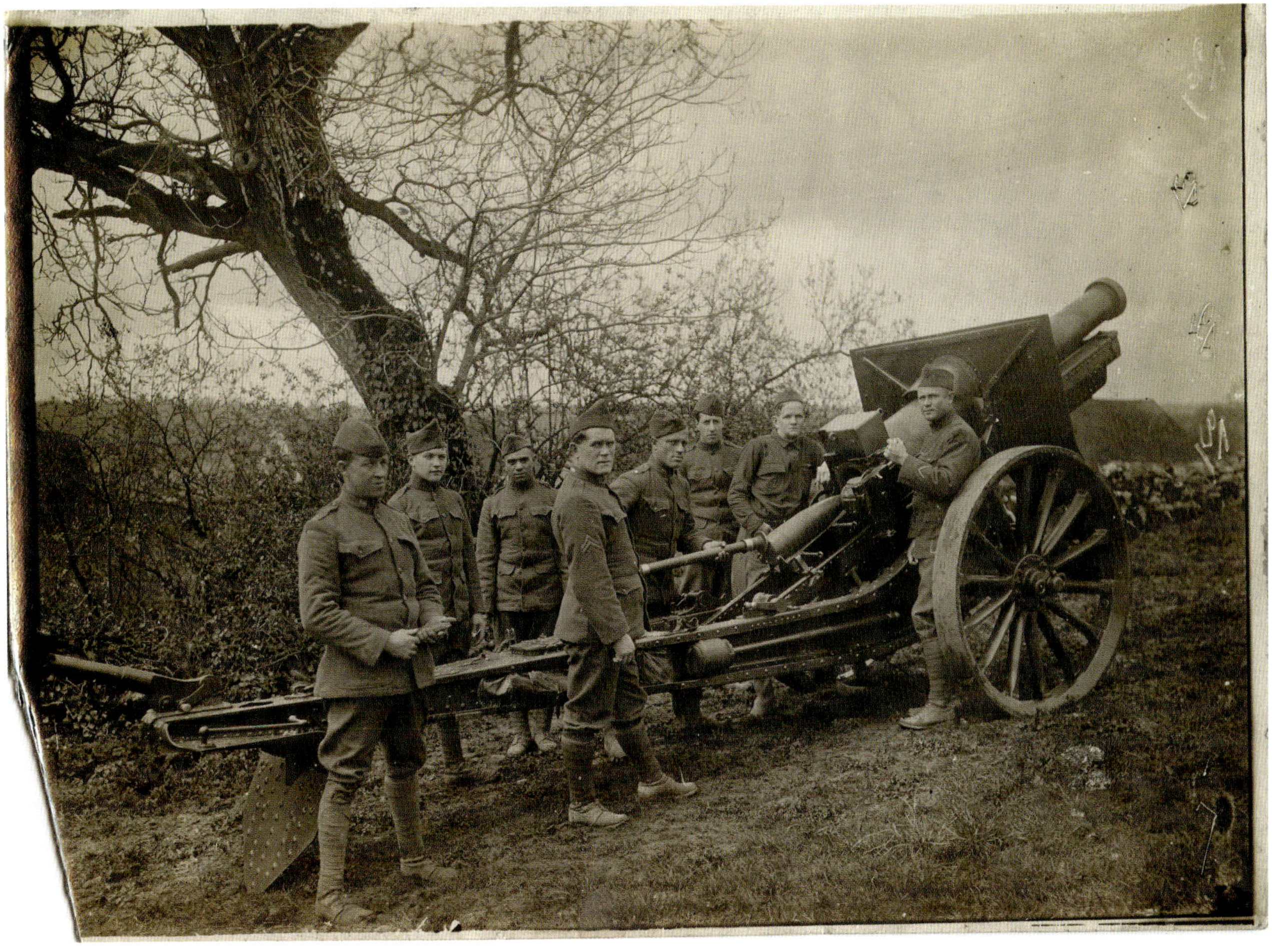

Gun drill in the Army of Occupation with a 155 mm Schneider Model 1916 howitzer. The Doughboy manning the breech of the gun displays the 6th Division shoulder sleeve insignia. Since each division had only one heavy 155 mm howitzer regiment assigned, this must be a gun from the 11th Field Artillery, 6th Division. The 11th Field Artillery was attached to both the 89th and 33rd Divisions during the Meuse-Argonne offensive, and made quite a name for itself, being by many accounts the farthest forward 155 mm howitzer unit of any in the AEF. "Calamity Jane," a 155 mm Schneider gun of the 11th Field Artillery was widely credited as the AEF gun to fire the last shot of the war at 1159 on November 11. A claim made of course by a great many others.

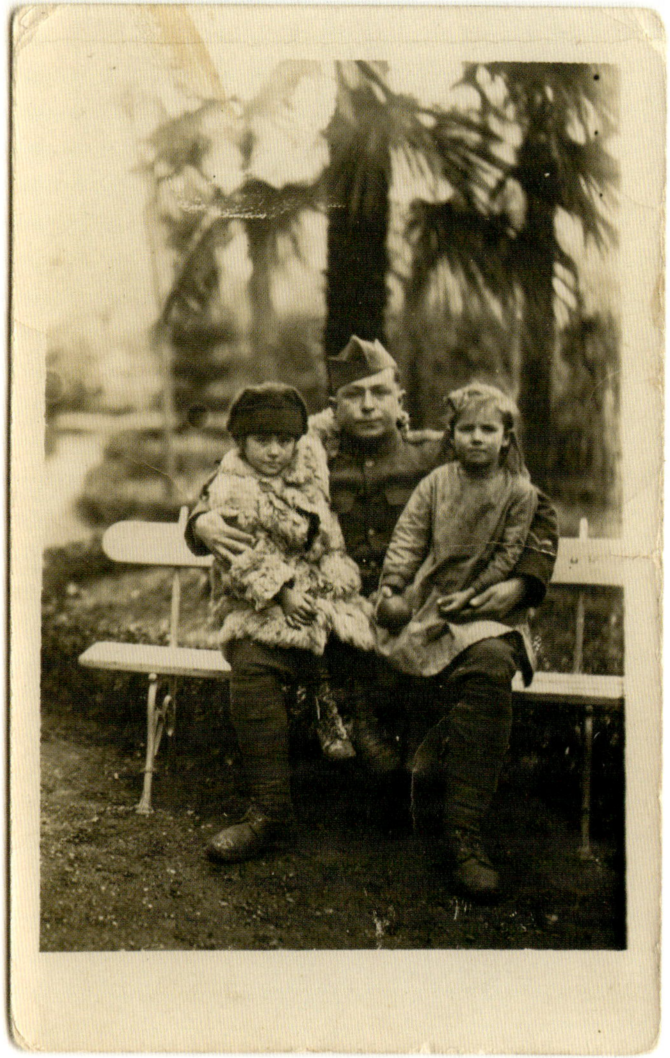

Doughboys and local kids, an often-seen subject in AEF and Army of Occupation photos.

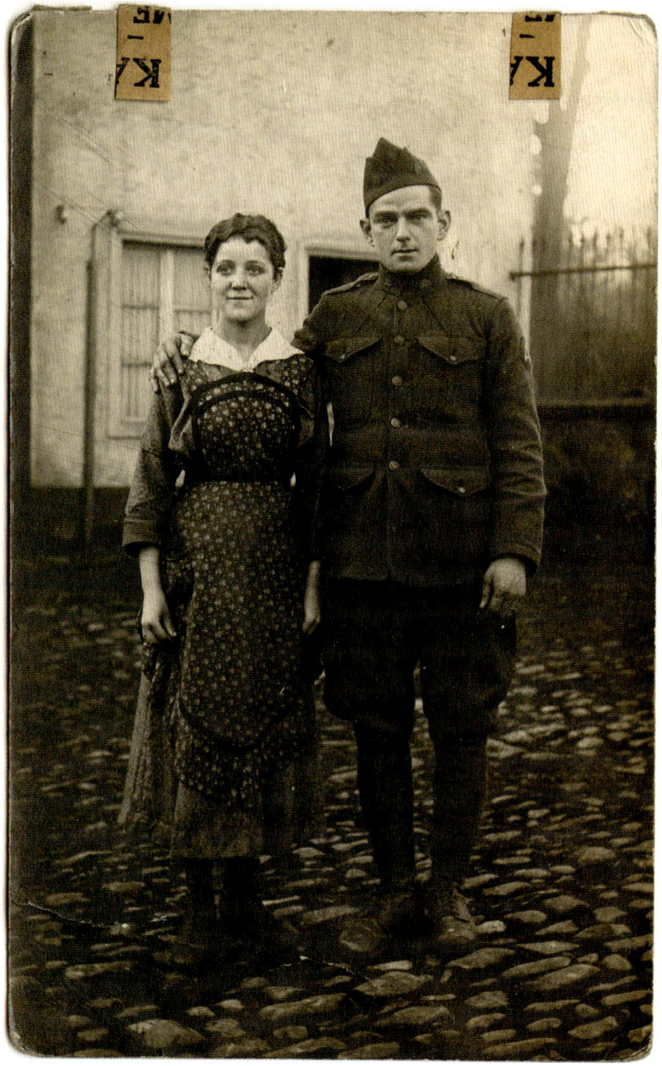

Sporting two insignia on his French-style overseas cap, this artilleryman poses with a local fraulein in the Army of Occupation.

Two Doughboys with local girls. The Doughboy at left wears chevrons denoting a sergeant first class, Signal Corps.

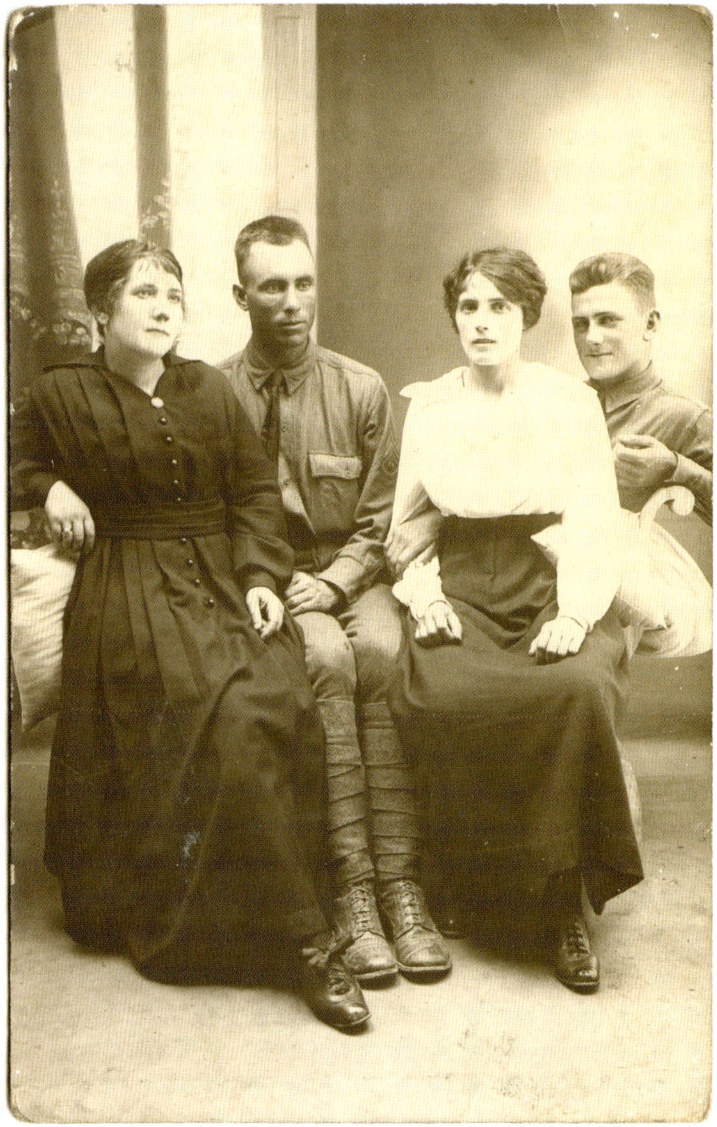

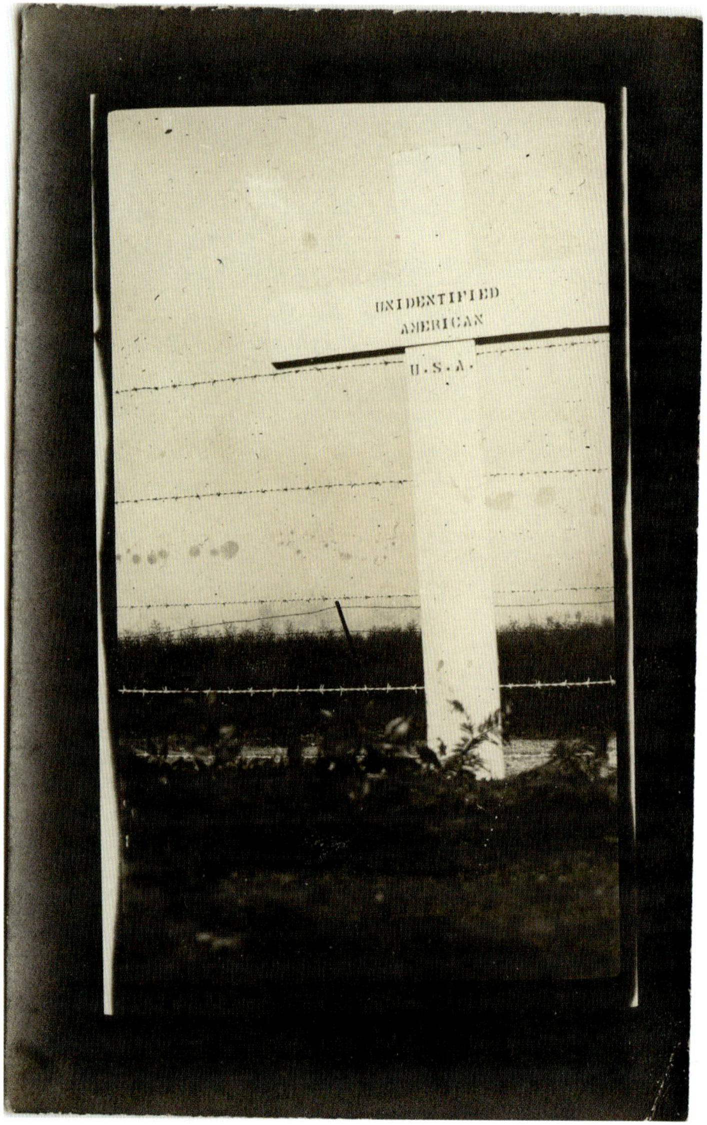

The grave of an unidentified American, location unknown.

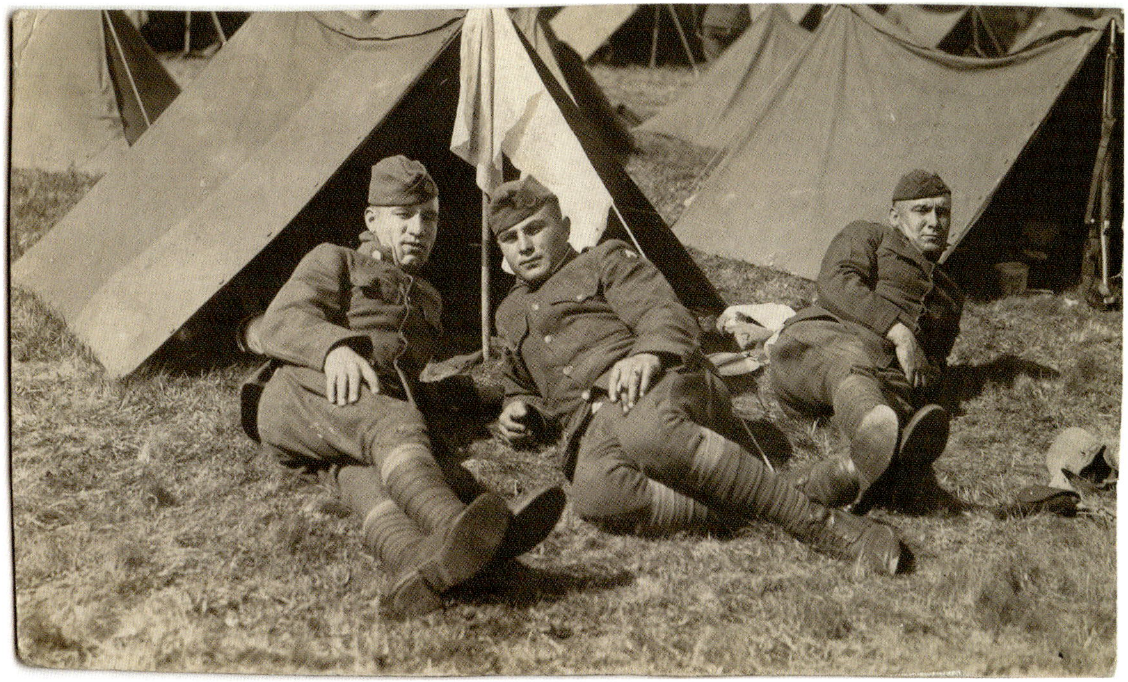

Three Army of Occupation Doughboys in the field. The Doughboys at right and left appear to have had their boots re-soled without hobnails. The center Doughboy is wearing the Metallic Fastened Field Shoe, as the toe cleat is clearly visible. All three have cloth backings behind their cap and collar insignia—likely in their branch color. Given the sunny setting and vigorous turf, this image was likely taken just after their return to the USA in spring of 1919.

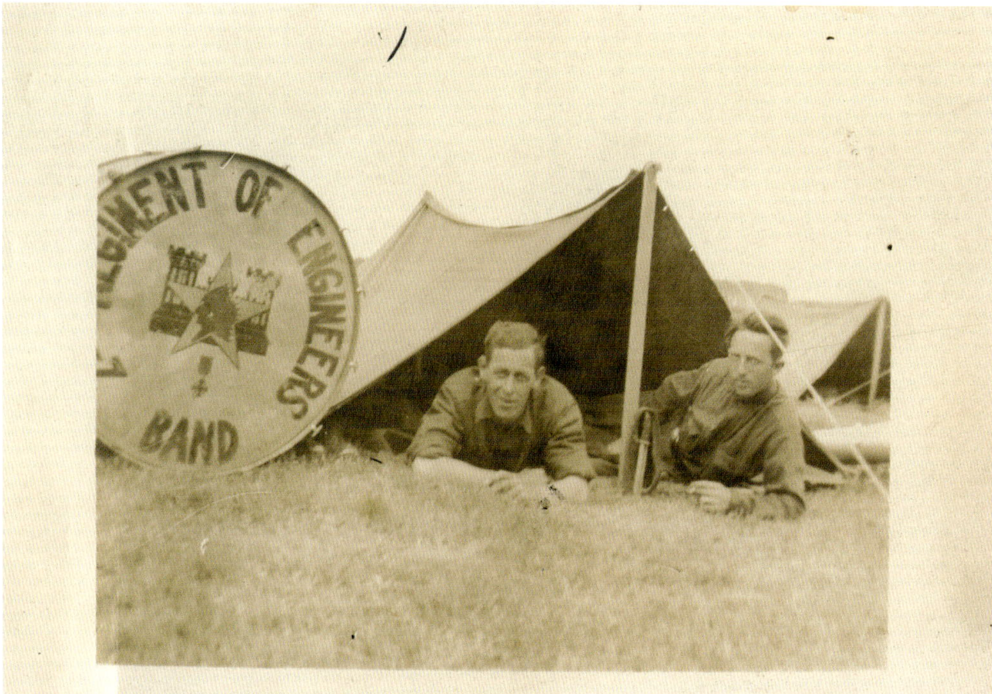

Two members of the 2nd Engineers Band, 2nd Division in the field, after the Armistice. A solid stick of wood has replaced the standard folding pup tent pole. Adjacent to it is a German bayonet thrust into the ground serving as a hat rack for an overseas cap.

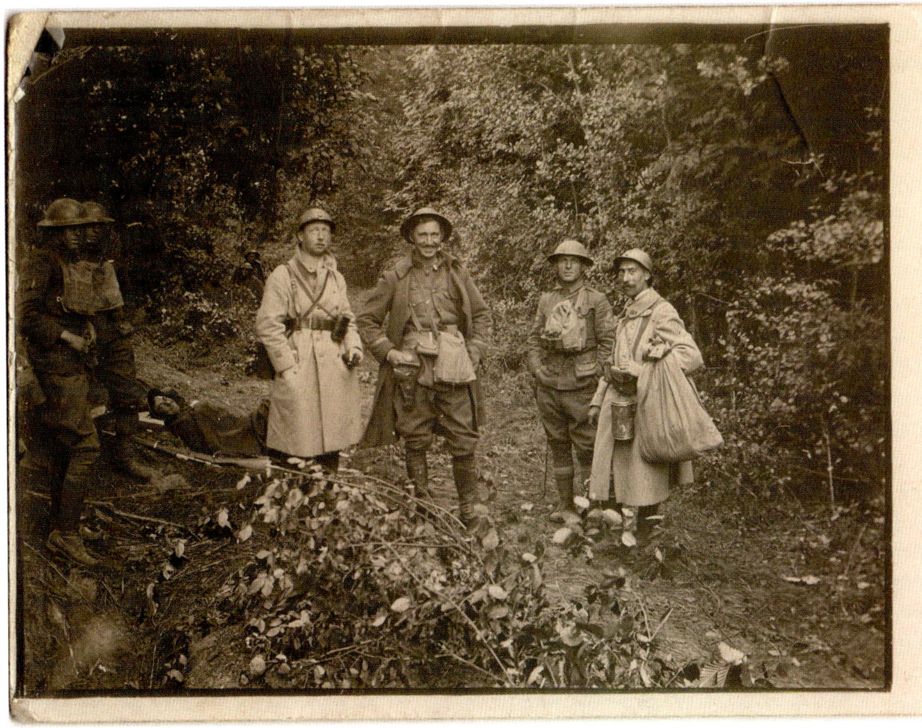

This image appears to be a rare personal snapshot taken during active service. The subjects are a captain of Marines and his first sergeant taken with their opposite numbers from the French Army. Given the luxuriant foliage this was almost certainly taken in summer 1918, possibly at Belleau Wood or Soissons. The Marine captain wears his overcoat with rank indicated by the lace insignia on the sleeve. The sergeant wears the distinctive Marine Corps chevrons for that rank on both sleeves. It is unclear as whether he is wearing the Marine green uniform or Army olive drab. The distinctive 1911 Marine pattern first aid pouch is clearly evident as well as Marine Corps button snap canteen cover. The French soldiers both carry French ARS gas masks in its distinct carrying can.

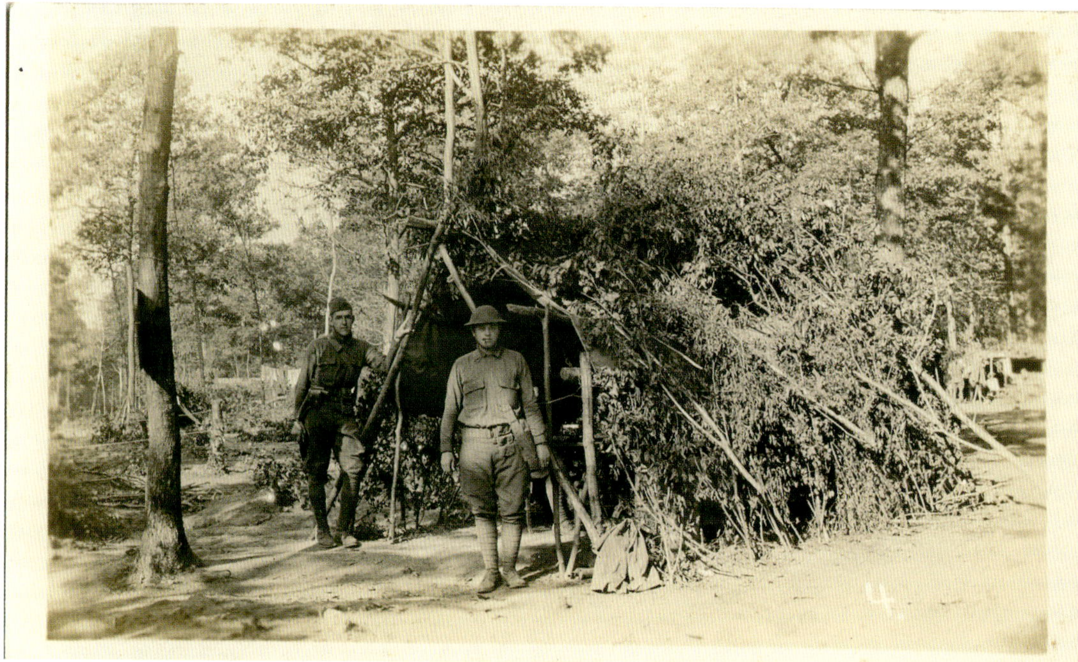

A sheltered and camouflaged orderly room in a forested bivouac area. A Corona portable typewriter is just visible inside the tent. This was the "personal computer" of its day, indispensable in an Army that required ever more paperwork. Other shelters and clotheslines are visible in the background. The two Doughboys clearly visible in the image are armed with Model 1917 revolvers. As their masks are in the carry position they are close to the frontlines.

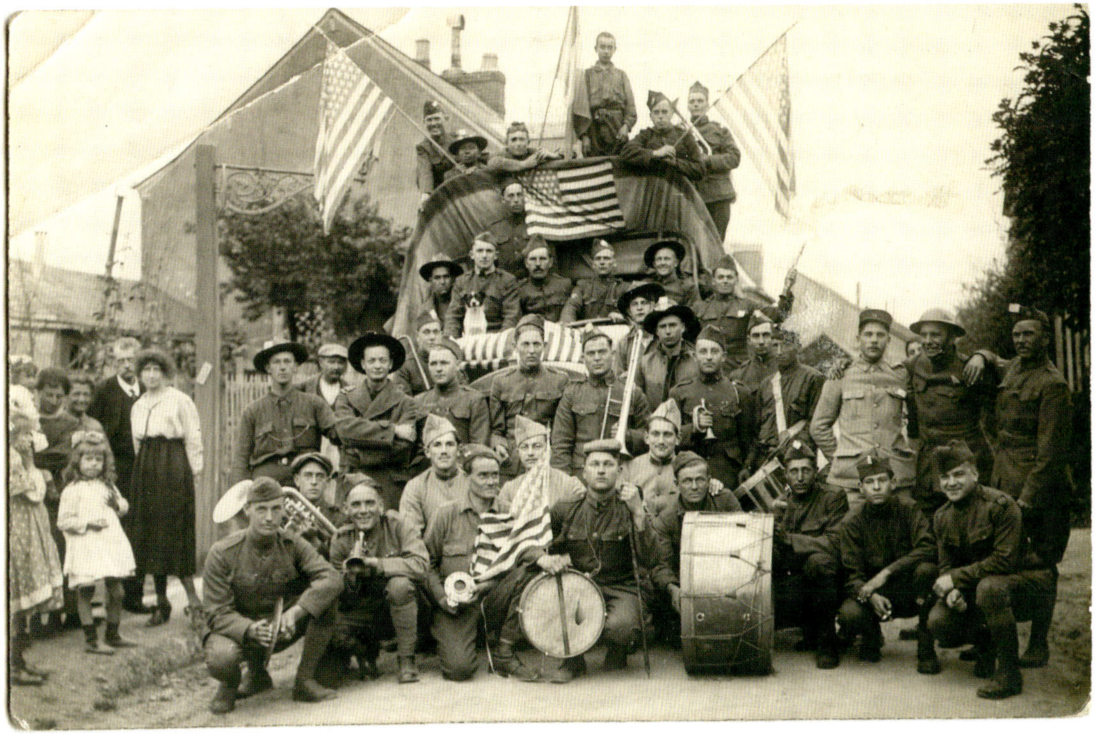

Trucks, drums, bandsmen, French civilians, French soldiers, American flags, small mascot dogs, this celebratory image has it all!

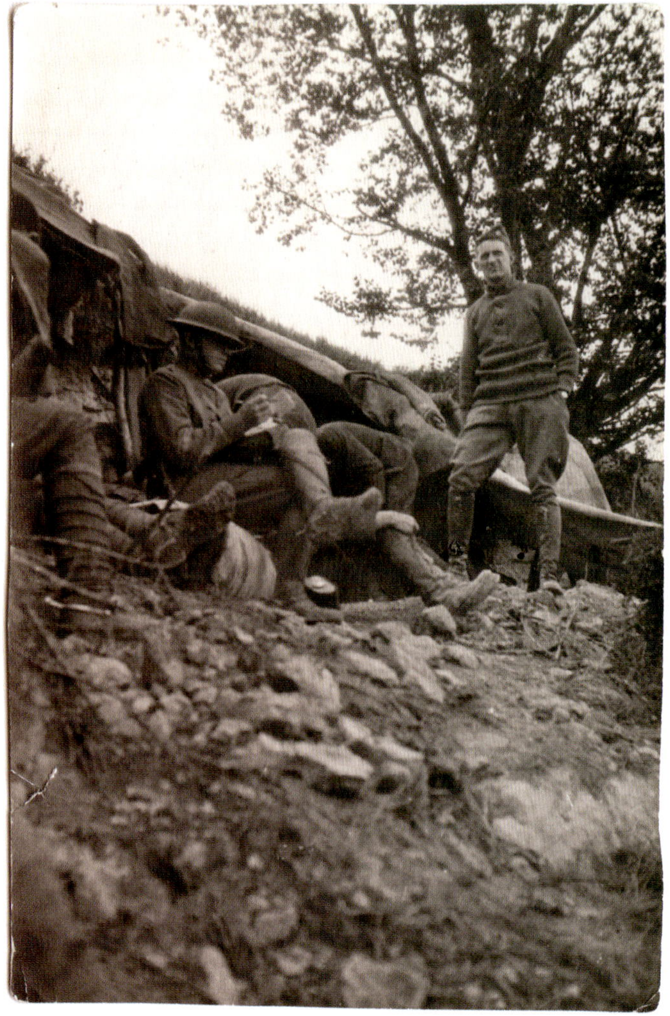

Another snapshot taken close to the shooting. The typewritten caption on the reverse of this image reads, "Major Beckwith at Death Valley." It is unclear as to whether Maj. Beckwith is standing at right, or the seated officer with pencil and notebook at center. In any case the partially dug-in position with emplaced tarpaulin for at least cover from the weather has all the marks of a hasty command post.

Two 3rd Army artillerymen photographed in studio setting against a painted library backdrop. Both are armed with Model 1917 revolvers, and both display brassards low on the left sleeve. These are most likely either the red brassard, denoting runners or possibly the blue brassard for signalmen. Other Army of Occupation images also show brassards worn low on the left sleeve versus the more common war time wear of brassards high on the left sleeve. The Doughboy at right displays a single overseas service chevron. He also appears to be wearing the revolver belt Model 1910, with its unique pockets designed to hold loose .45-caliber ammunition. By contrast his partner on the left wears the later, more common pistol belt but with no ammunition pouches visible.

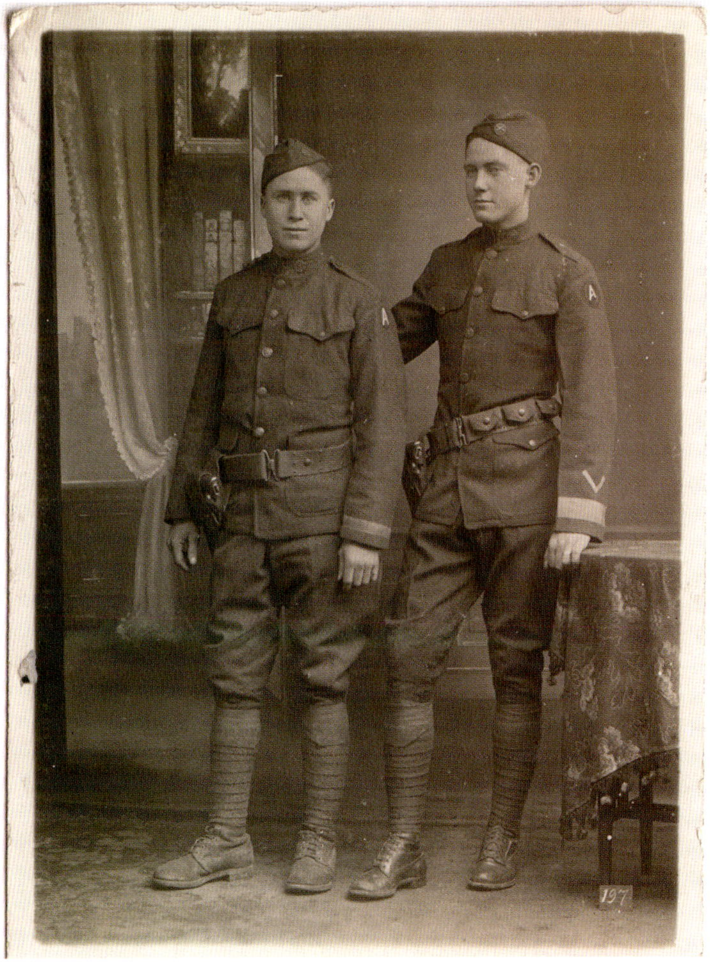

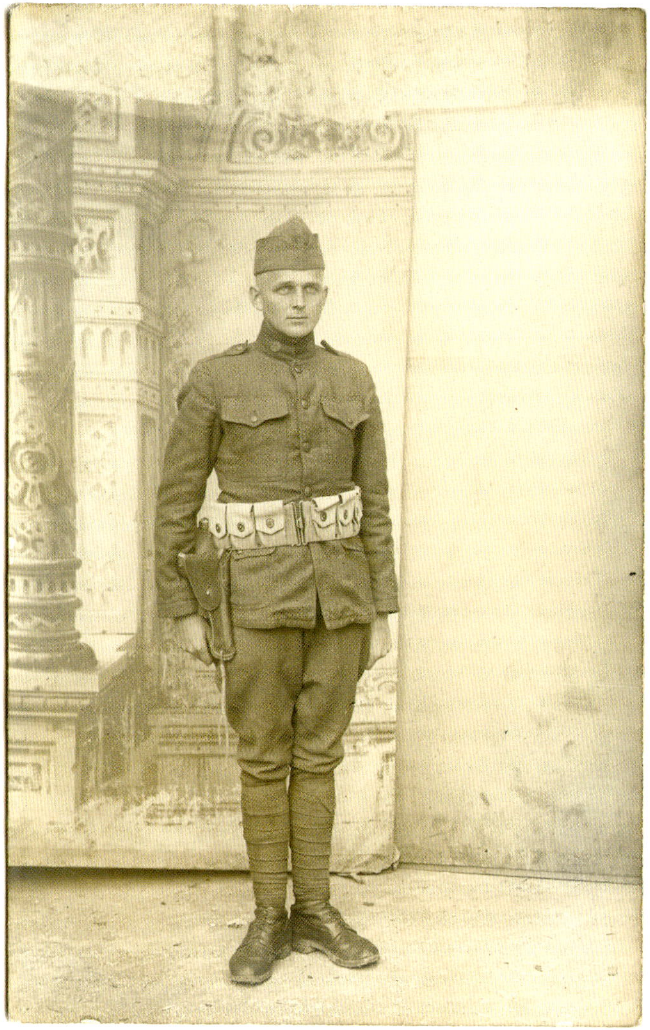

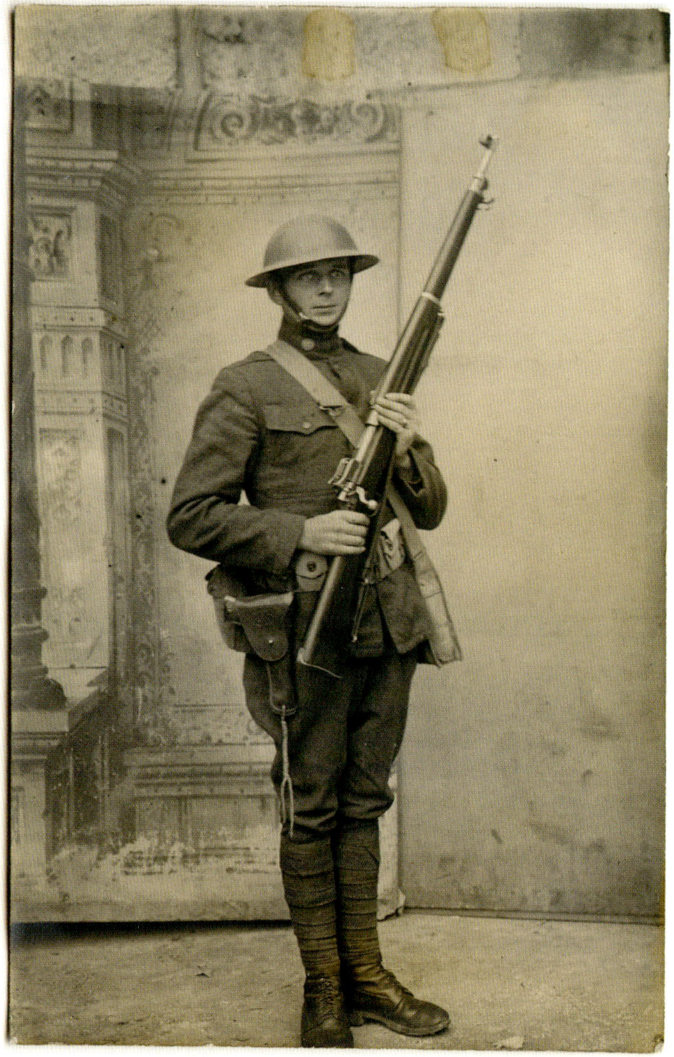

Two images of the same Doughboy; one with helmet, rifle (Model 1917), and gas mask, and the other with cartridge belt and French-style overseas cap. Though armed with a Model 1911 pistol there is no evidence of a magazine pouch for it. This is perhaps explained in part by his cartridge belt, which is the ten-pocket dismounted pattern, having no provision for easy mounting of the magazine pouch. The setting includes a classical painted backdrop.

An interesting study of two artillerists. The Frenchman's Adrian helmet clearly displays the artillery badge on its front. Over his shoulder is the cloth strap, almost certainly that of the French M-2 gas mask fabric carrying bag. Barely visible is a delicate set of pince-nez glasses perched on his nose. Also quite nearly invisible is his belt which, under magnification, is revealed to be a US pistol belt and possibly a US revolver holster. The Doughboy appears quite regulation, wearing the pistol belt, Model 1917 revolver in its holster, and the appropriate three-pocket ammunition pouch. His small box respirator is slung in the carry position, and he also carries what appear to be standard US 6 x 30 power Type EE binoculars in a leather case slung on his right side. He wears a standard Brodie helmet.

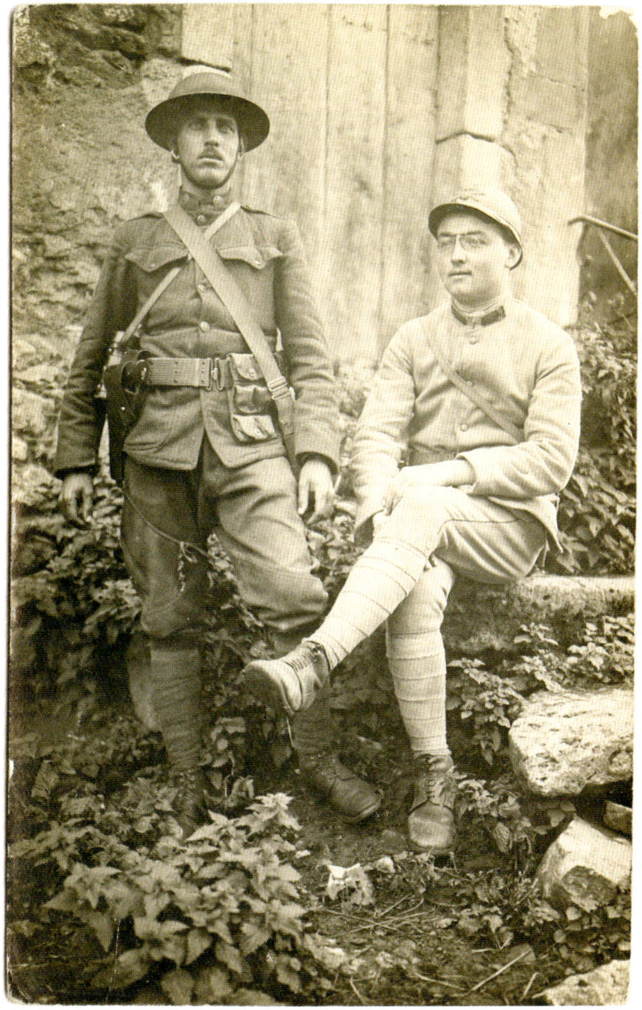

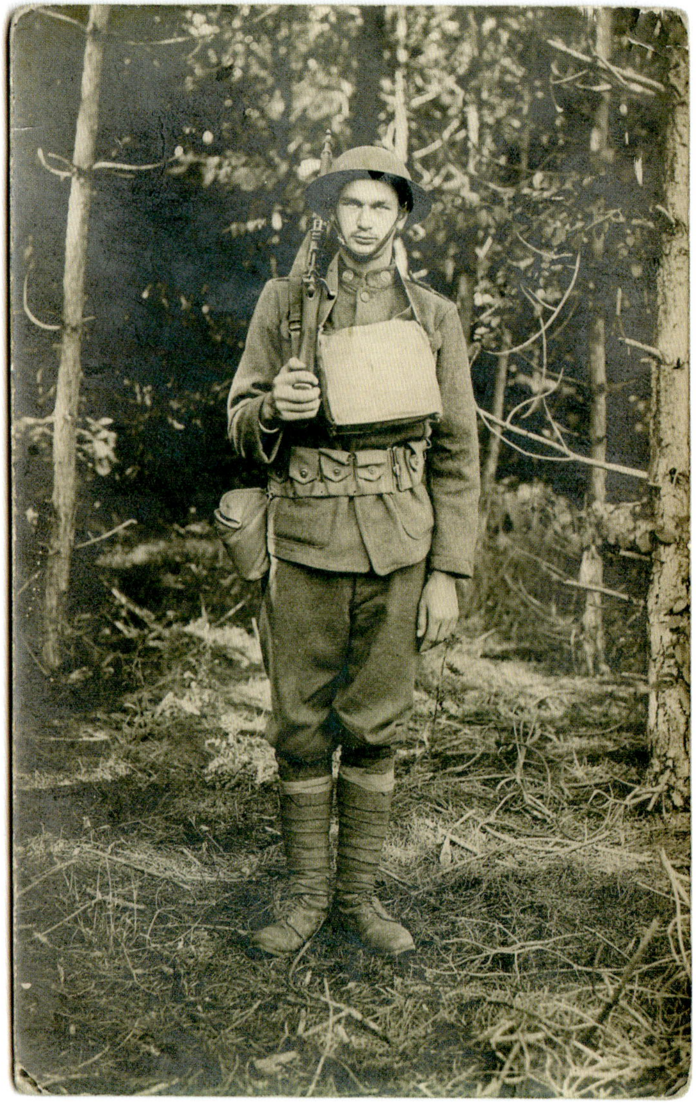

A fully armed Doughboy photographed in the open air. He carries a Model 1903 Springfield rifle. The mask is worn in alert position, but his empty cartridge belt indicates he is actually behind the lines. The empty canteen cover seems to be one of the early eagle snap versions.

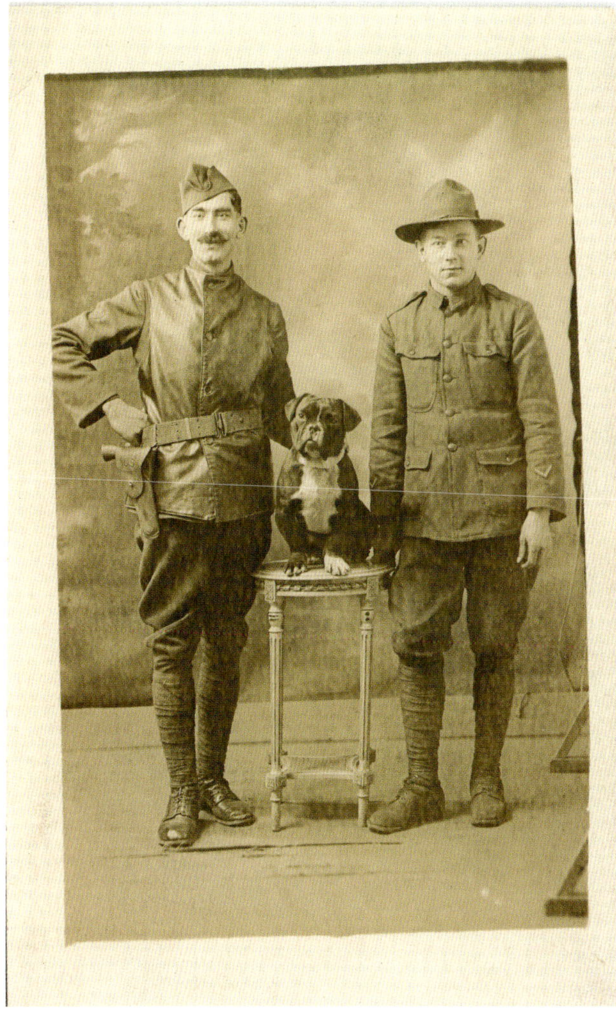

The dog mascot takes center stage in this studio image. In spite of wearing the campaign hat, for the most part worn solely by Doughboys in rear areas, the doughboy on the right wears both a wound stripe and a single overseas service stripe. The Doughboy at left wears a leather jerkin, French-style overseas cap, and carries a Model 1917 revolver in the Model 1916 holster, that was designed for the Model 1911 automatic pistol.

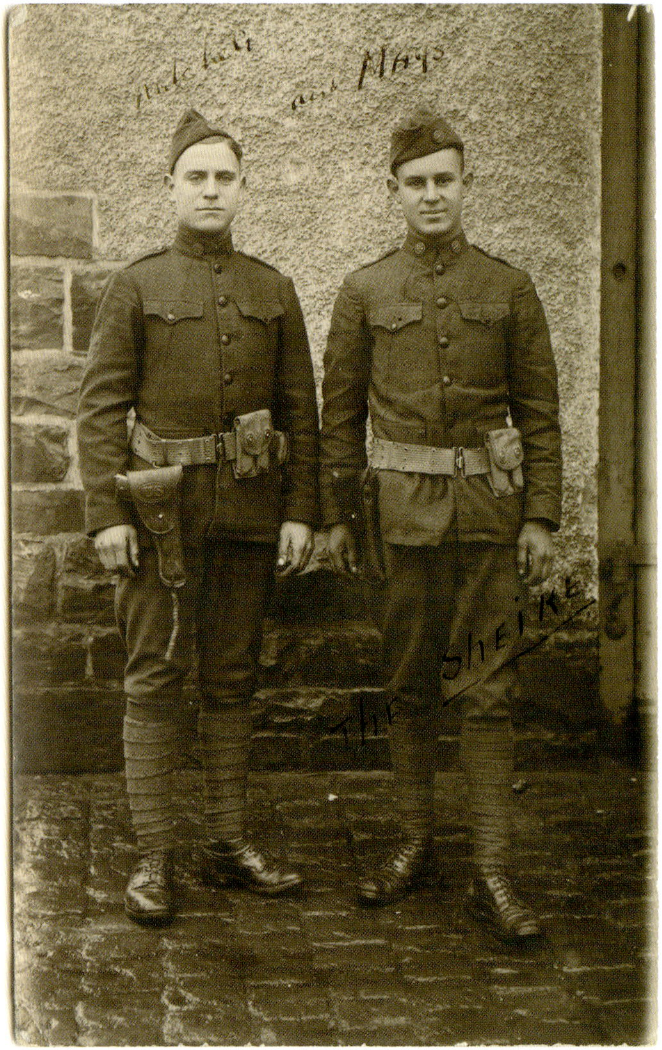

Two Doughboy artillerymen in an Army of Occupation image. Their names appear to be Michaels and Hayes. Hayes has also been styled "the Sheike." Both wear the standard belt rig for the M1911 pistol. Interestingly, both wear the model 1918 "Pershing" pattern service coat. This pattern replaced patch pockets with interior hung pockets to give a more sleek and streamlined appearance. It also appears both are wearing straight-leg trousers vice the earlier breeches. A good study of the uniform the average Doughboy would have worn if the Armistice had not gone into effect in November 1918, and the AEF had conducted a Spring 1919 offensive.

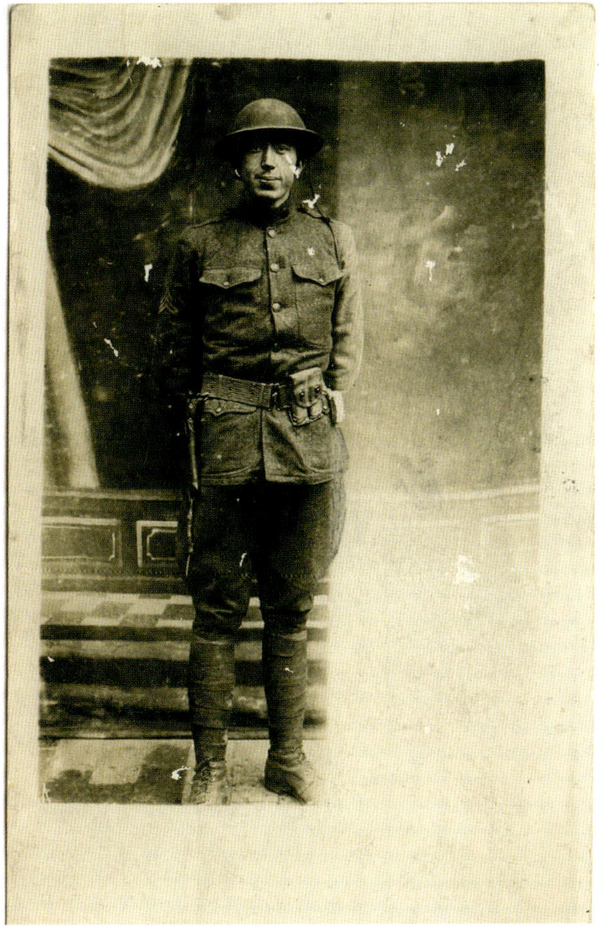

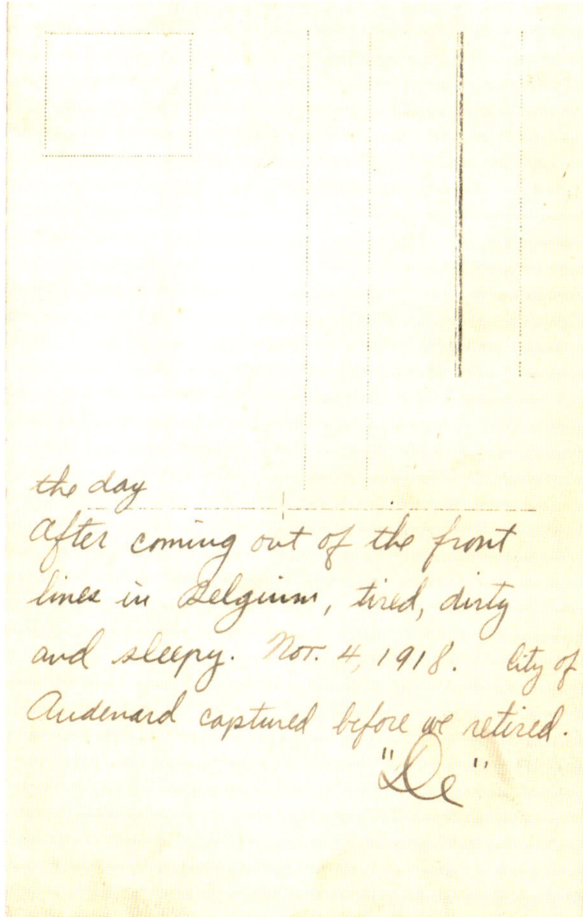

A very interesting study in a studio image of a Doughboy fresh out of the lines in Belgium. Given the date of relief, November 4, this Doughboy was a member of the 37th Division, withdrawn from the line just after the capture of Audenarde, Belgium. This sergeant wears a standard belt rig for the M1911 pistol, and his first aid pouch is just visible on his left hip. Most interestingly, his steel helmet is worn with a lanyard from the helmet to his left shoulder. Such helmet lanyards are rarely seen, but explained in the works of 3rd Division veteran Leonard Nason, as a means to maintain control of the helmet when quickly donning the gas mask. The use of a lanyard like this would also keep the helmet from rolling about in gas drenched ground. Reverse reads: "the day after coming out of the front lines in Belgium, tired, dirty and sleepy. Nov. 4 1918. City of Audenard captured before we retired. 'De.'"

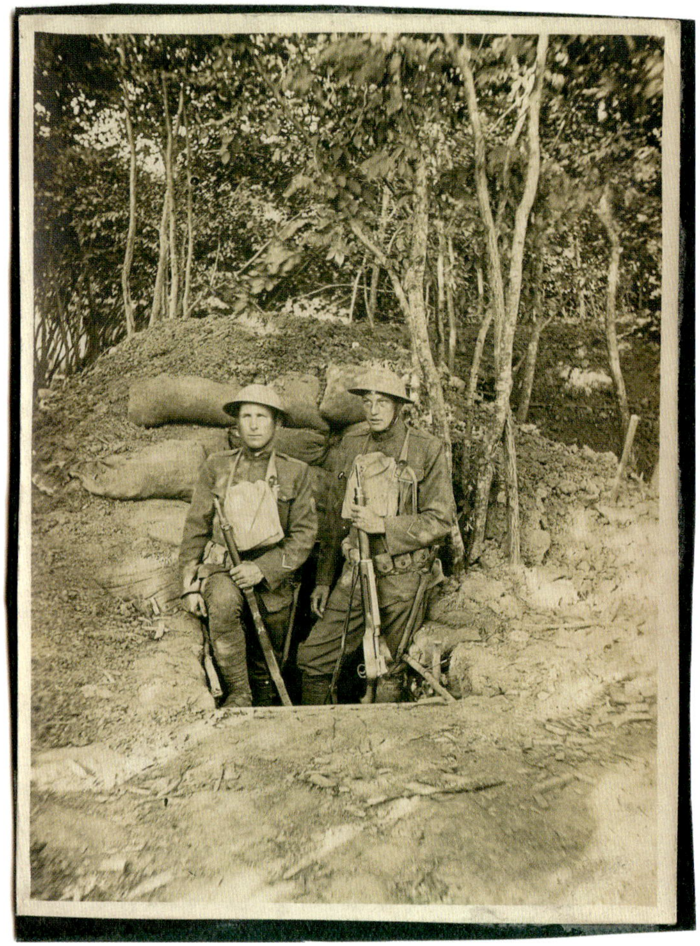

An interesting image of two Doughboys standing in a dugout entrance. Both display chevrons indicating six months overseas service, and both wear British small box respirators, as evidenced by the leather take-up tab used to bring the mask to the alert position. Their cartridge belts look to be filled with ball ammunition. The Doughboy at right, while armed with a Model 1917 rifle, inexplicably carries the Model 1910 scabbard and a Model 1905 Springfield bayonet.

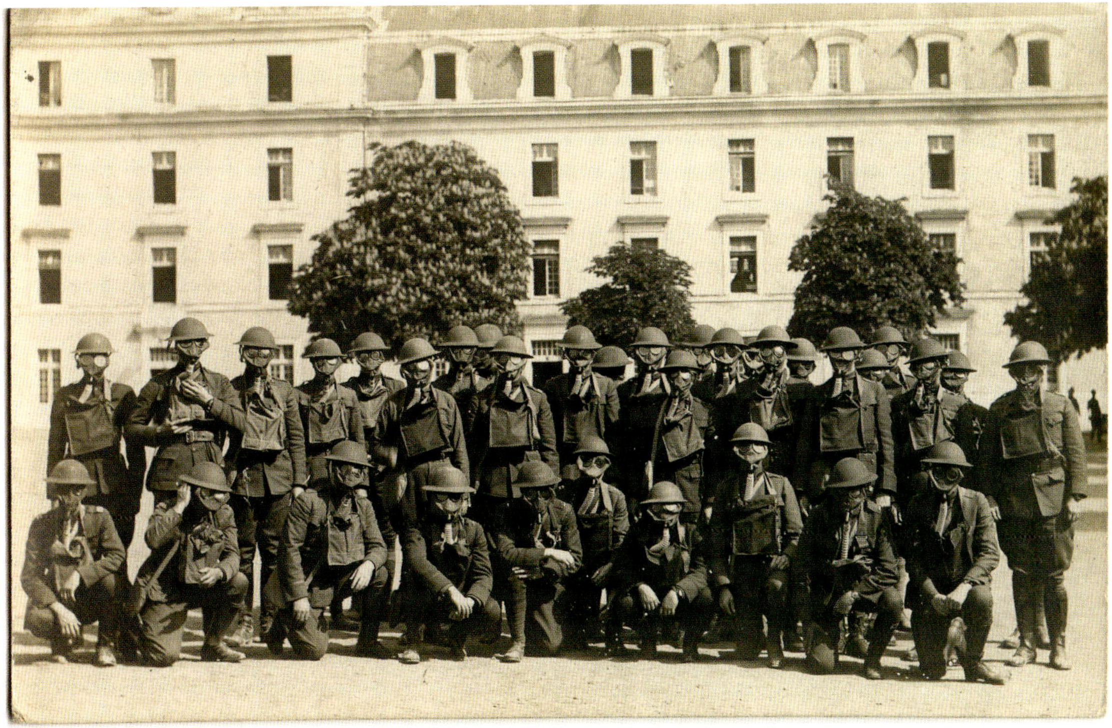

The obligatory class photo! This is clearly a cohort of students at gas officers school taken somewhere in the AEF. This image may be from early in the AEF's service overseas, as there is not a single overseas service chevron to be seen. Close examination reveals nearly every mask being worn is absolutely new. In addition there is a mix of British SBRs and American CEM (Corrected English Model) masks being worn. The officers exhibit a typical mix of leather leggings and spiral woolen puttees. The Sam Browne belt is clearly evident throughout as is the officer cuff braid.

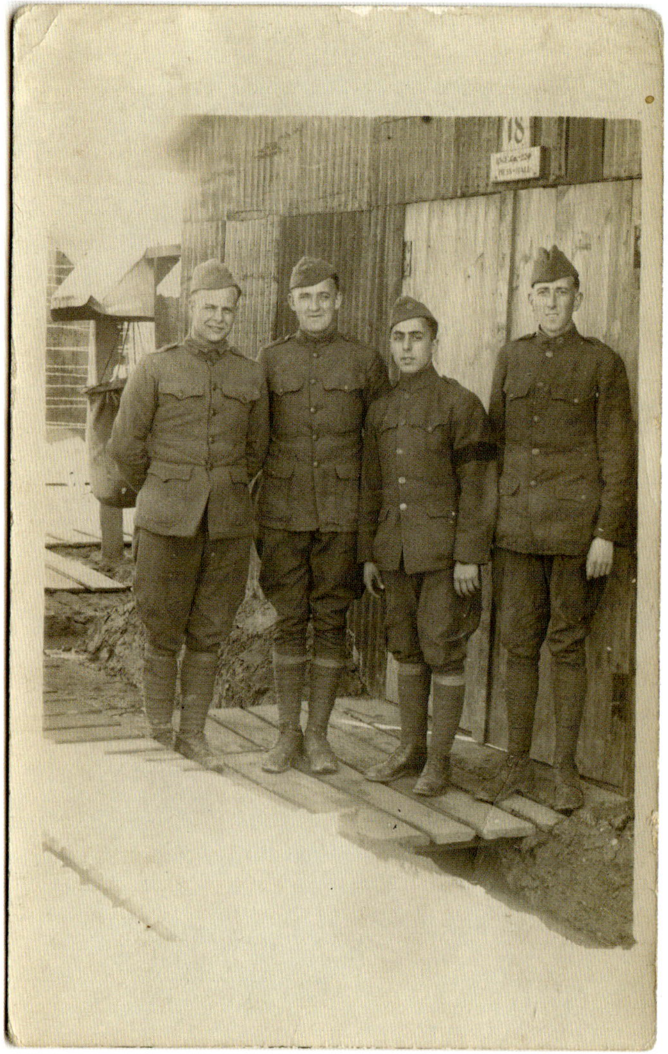

Four Doughboys from Prisoner of War Escort Company, 239 (PWE Company 239), which was organized in the AEF in December 1918, and demobilized in the US in October 1919. The Doughboy third from left, identified as Frankie Valluzzo, of Danbury, Connecticut, wears what is most likely an MP brassard, or possibly a red runners brassard. He lacks any collar ornamentation. While the location is unknown, deep drainage ditches and extensive duckboards indicate quite a muddy camp. A water sterilizing "Lister Bag" hangs under the eaves in the background. Valluzzo's service record indicates he was Italian-born, originally inducted in September 1917, and served in the 304th Infantry, part of the 76th Division, a National Army Division composed largely of New England draftees. Upon its arrival in the AEF, the 76th became the 3rd Depot Division. Harry Rowe, second from left, was English-born and inducted in the same draft as Valluzzo, and also served in the 304th Infantry before his assignment to PWE Company 239. Likely all of them arrived in PWE Company 239 in similar fashion.

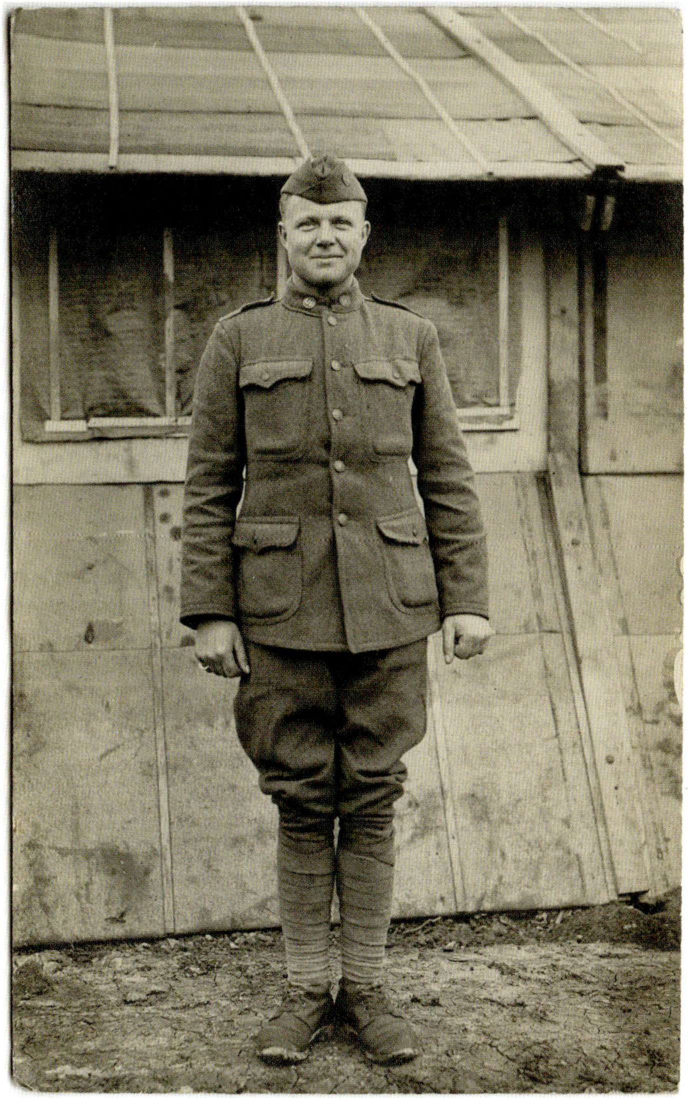

An engineer private photographed against the side of his "Adrian" barracks building somewhere in France. He wears his US and engineer collar ornaments as prescribed and has an engineer disk on his overseas cap. The cap itself shows evidence of pins or stitching to hold the center fold closed. Close examination reveals his service coat is roughcut, and most likely unlined, with pockets and flaps unhemmed, and the collar rather crudely sewn to the coat body. This image reveal much of the details of Adrian barracks type construction. The wall flares out from vertical about three feet above ground level. The construction is no frills; tar paper over rough lumber. The tar paper is held in place by narrow wooden lath, tacked in place. The window appears to be oiled paper again tacked in place with narrow wood lath. This would allow at least some light into the barracks interior. Adrian barracks are often commented on in the period as only marginally better than living in tentage, especially when unfloored.

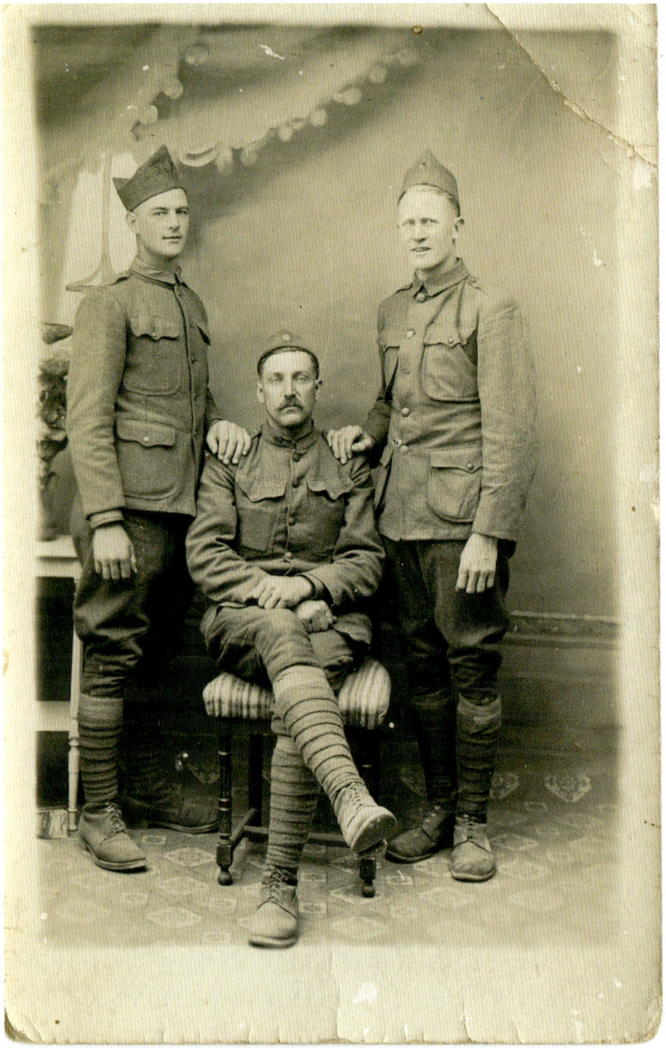

Three Doughboys in a typical studio portrait. The Doughboy seated at center apparently captioned the photo, as he refers to the testament which has nearly worn through his coat pocket, and his moustache. The Doughboys flanking him wear French-style overseas caps. The Doughboy at right wears an early pattern of the olive drab service coat, pattern prescribed in 1904, as evidenced by the construction details of bellows pockets, pointed cuffs, and low standing-falling collar. Service coats of this early vintage are sometimes seen in images of the AEF, but they were apparently not at all common.

Two ordnance men, a corporal and private first class in an interesting exterior image. Both wear gas masks in the carry position indicating some proximity to the front. Curiously, while both wear pistol belts, neither is armed. The PFC at left wears his steel helmet and nearly hip-length rubber boots. These were originally thought to provide protection against "trench foot" but impermeable rubber construction caused sweating and foot injuries of its own. Additionally, these boots were fairly fragile and unsuited for any real front line service. Their issue was restricted fairly early in the AEF to those who had to deal with extended work in mud and standing water.

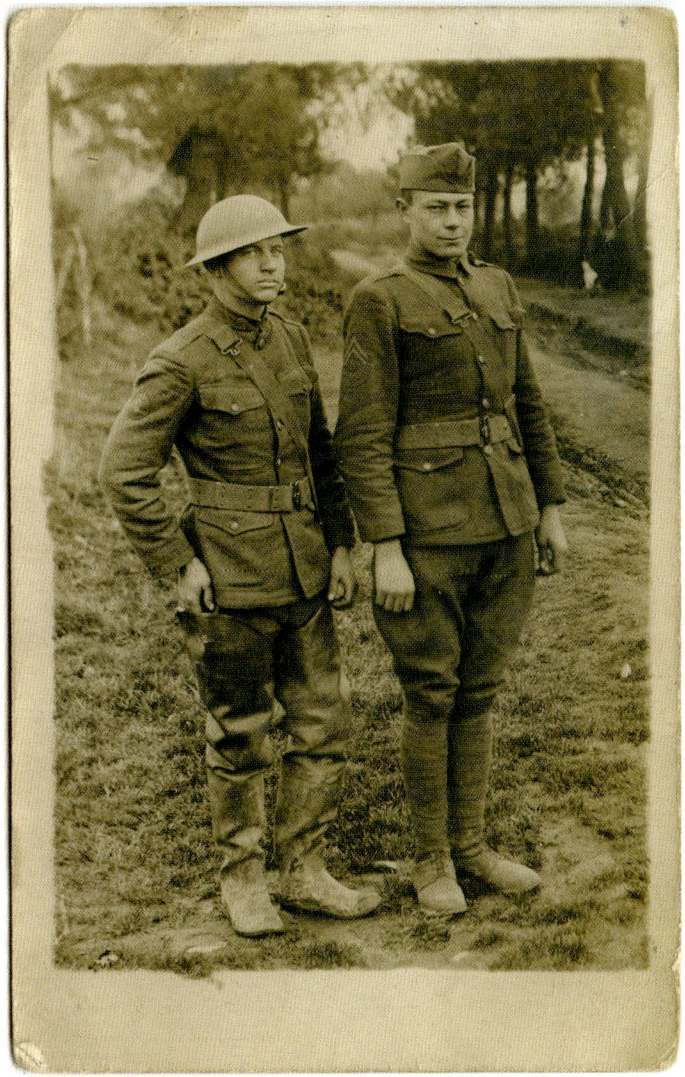

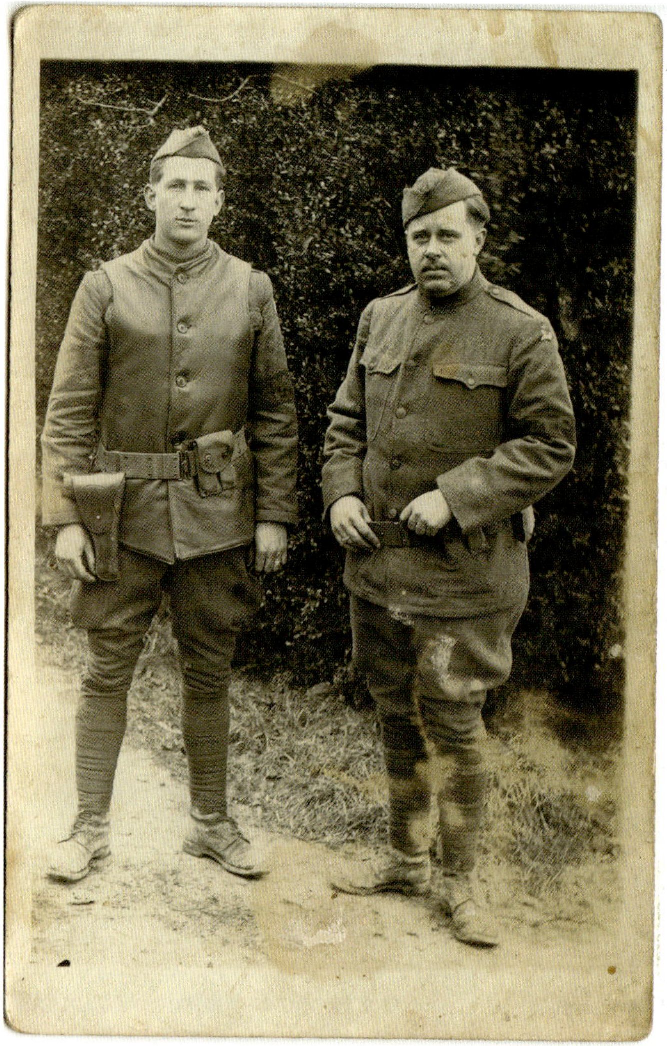

"Who won the war?" A nice exterior shot of two 2nd Army MPs. Both wear the standard MP brassard, most commonly with letters MP in red on a dark or navy-blue band. The MP at right is totally devoid of any collar or cap ornaments. His partner at left wears the leather jerkin. Both are armed with the M1911 pistol and carry the standard belt rig for same. Their lack of gas mask indicates this is a post-Armistice image.

A very nice study of two Doughboys in denim fatigue clothing. Both appear to be wearing the blue denim working jumpers, first adopted in 1908 as the "Coast Artillery Jumper." This basic pattern remained in use until adoption of a full button front "Working Jacket" in 1917. The standing Doughboy wears blue denim trousers while his seated companion wears bib overalls, likely the pattern first adopted in 1917. The seated Doughboy has a crudely bandaged right index finger. Both wear standard olive drab flannel shirts and French-style overseas caps. The standing soldier has his cap embellished with French-made numerals which appear to read 162. This could signify 162nd Infantry, which was part of the 41st Division, broken up as replacements and used to form the cadre of the AEF 1st Depot Division. In infantry organizations, cooks are often seen wearing a variety of denim work clothes.

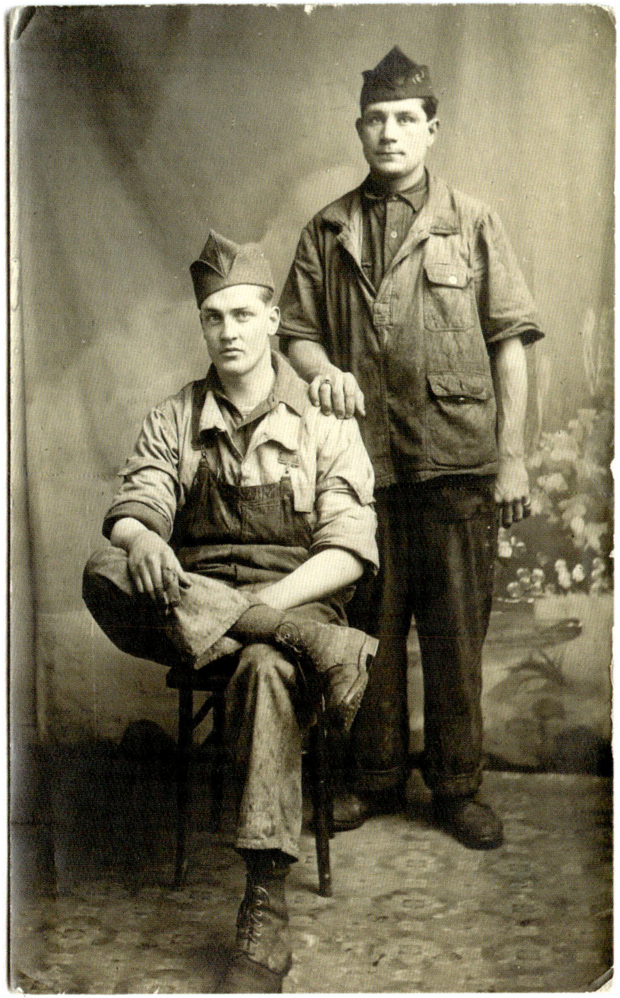

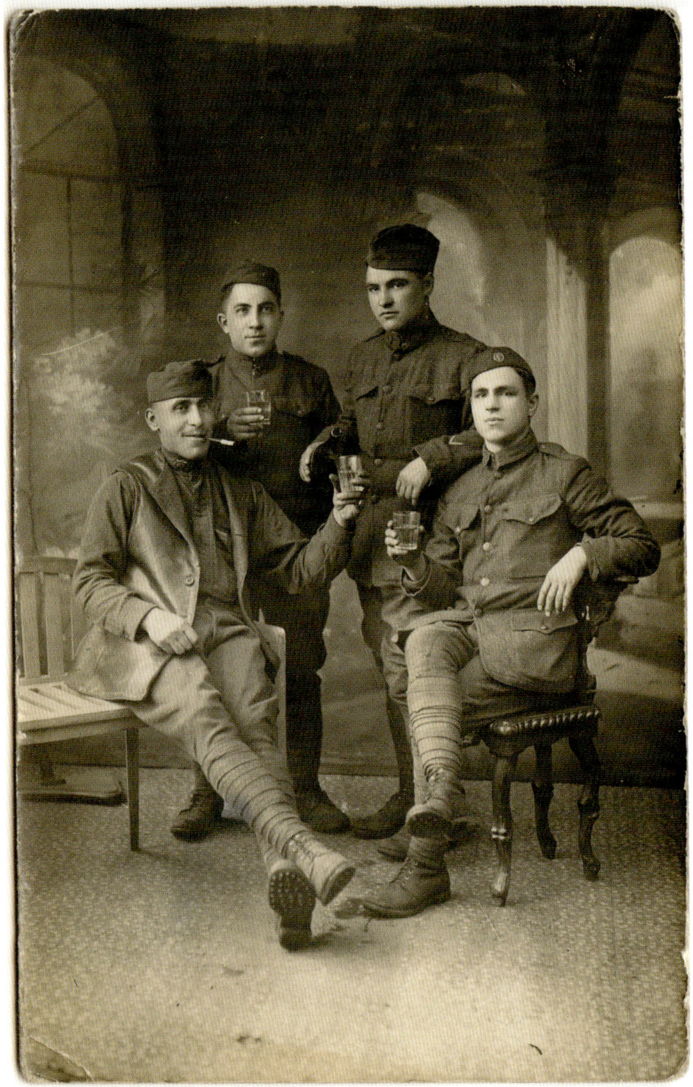

“Pillrollers.” A group of 4th Medical Corps soldiers enjoying some vin blanc. One of them sports a six months overseas service chevron. The dapper fellow seated at left front with cigarette holder appears to have pinned his shirt collar together at the top. He wears the standard US issue jerkin.

Three Doughboys plus one roll of toilet paper must have been an invitation to clowning around. The Doughboy seated at center is completely uniformed in British service dress, including the Pattern 1907 service dress coat and straight-leg trousers. He also wears British issue boots as does his companion standing at left. The left standing Doughboy has wrapped his puttees so as to have the tape at the ankle versus the knee. His shirt appears to be a private purchase item, as the breast pockets are noticeably smaller than a regulation shirt, and it also closes with the regulation three buttons. He wears a British web waist belt of unknown origin. The Doughboy standing at right seems to be uniformed entirely in US issue clothing. He wears smooth-side-out cap toe boots.

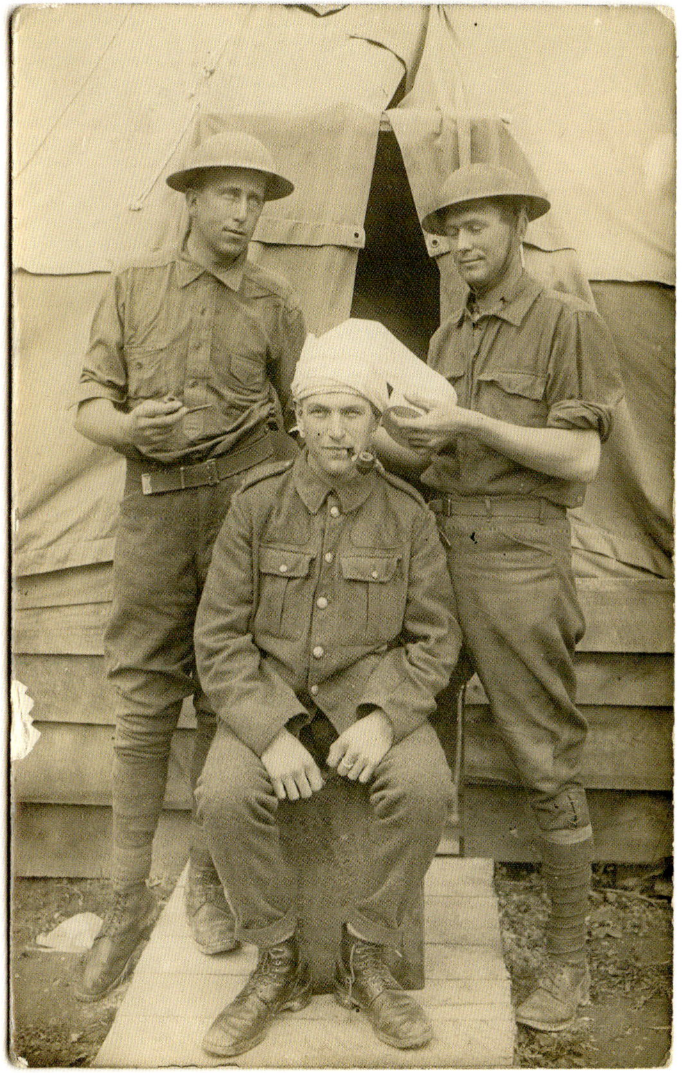

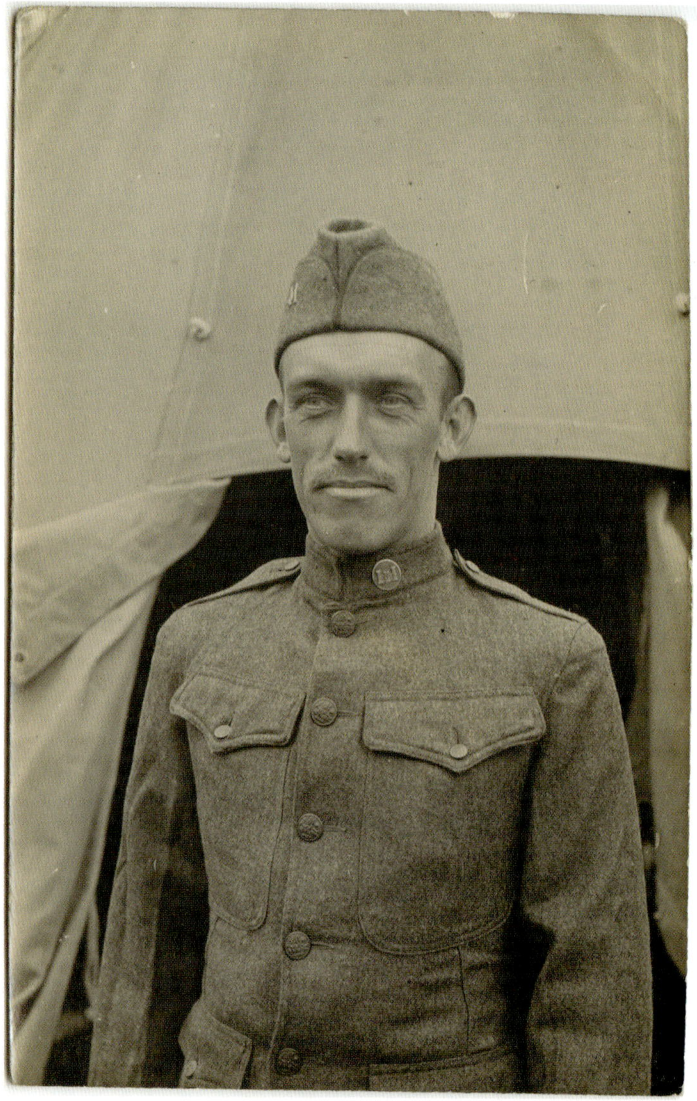

An engineer Doughboy fairly unremarkable but for his cap. The cap is French style but on close examination seems to be piped in, presumably, a branch-signifying color. The cap also carries the number 41, identifying this soldier as a member of 41st Regiment of Engineers. This image was found in a group along with the previous image. Both images are almost certainly of members of the 41st Engineers. The 41st Engineers were originally formed as an "Auxiliary Forestry Battalion" at American University, Washington, DC. The unit arrived in France in February 1918. In October 1918, it was absorbed into the 20th Engineers (Forestry) Regiment. This regiment in its final organization included twenty-nine battalion headquarters, 145 companies, and 46,025 assigned enlisted men—making it the largest regiment in the AEF.

A grouping of Ordnance men with their trusty mascot. The two men seated left are Ordnance sergeants, the others are most likely junior enlisted men. The Ordnance sergeant seated at center wears the model 1907 winter hat. His service coat appears to be an odd variant with pointed cuffs but none of the other identifying features of earlier service coats prescribed from 1904 to 1907 such as the bellows pockets and standing-falling collars. The soldier seated at right front wears a rather large wristwatch on typical wide leather band. Perhaps spiffed up for the photo, none of the subjects has the commonly seen and indeed authorized shirt collar folded over his coat collar.

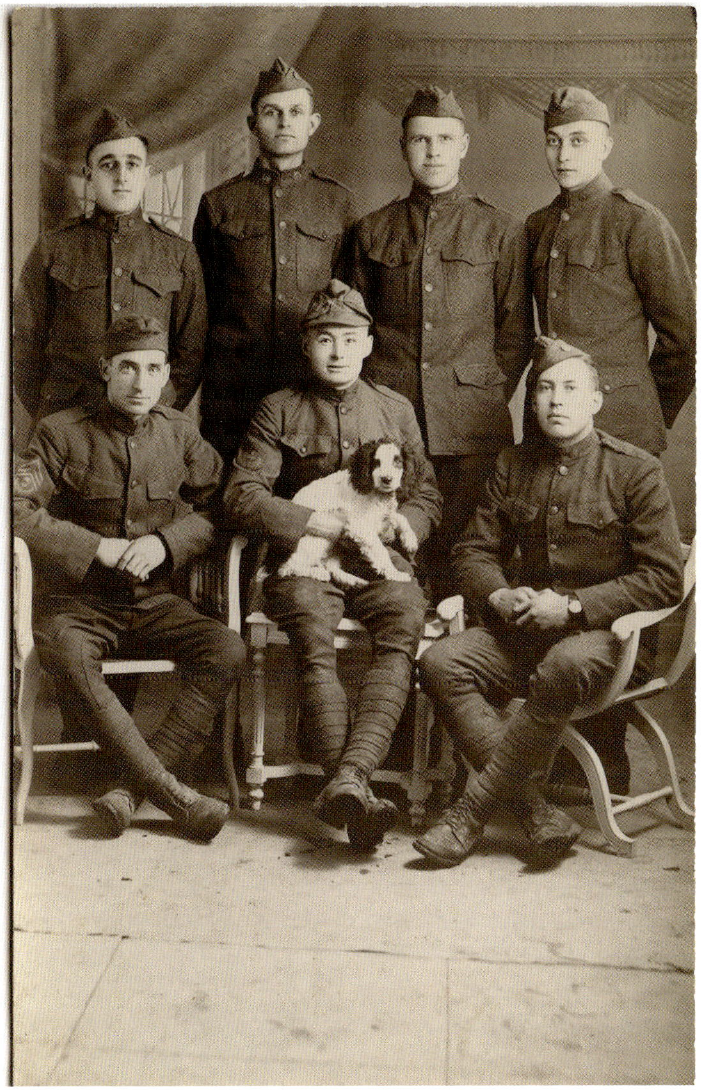

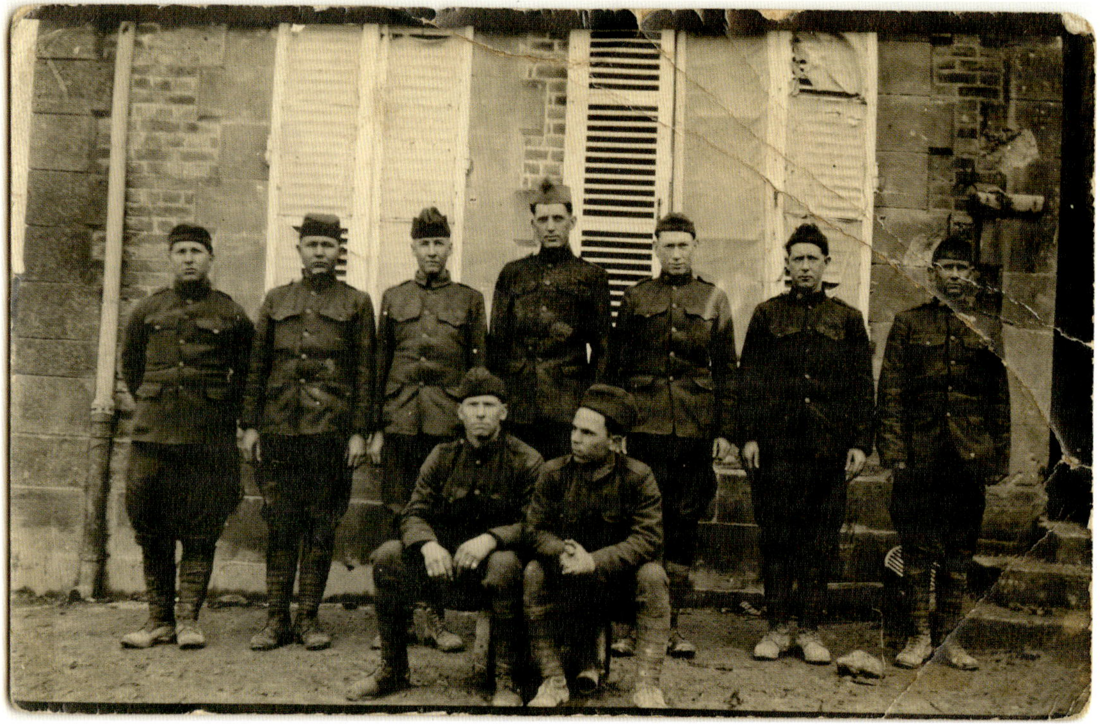

A rather grim-looking group of Doughboys photographed in front of a somewhat battered building in Sechault, France. The image is dated March 1st, 1919. These men are identified as Group 3, Unit 306 GRS (Graves Registration Service), which almost certainly accounts for their grim demeanor. Sechault was the site of desperate fighting from September 26 to October 7, 1918, by the 369th, 371st, and 372nd Infantry Regiments, three of the four African American regiments of the 93rd Division, but fought under French command. Sechault is located roughly between Mont Blanc on the west, and the Argonne Forest to the east. These men may well have been surveying the area for isolated American burials in the region. The building behind them appears to have some battle damage, and the windows and shutters appear to have been papered over, likely due to shattered glass. Barely visible against the building and behind the two Doughboys at right is an upended German steel ammunition box for the MG08 machine gun. A small section of cloth machine gun belt is protruding from beneath the box.

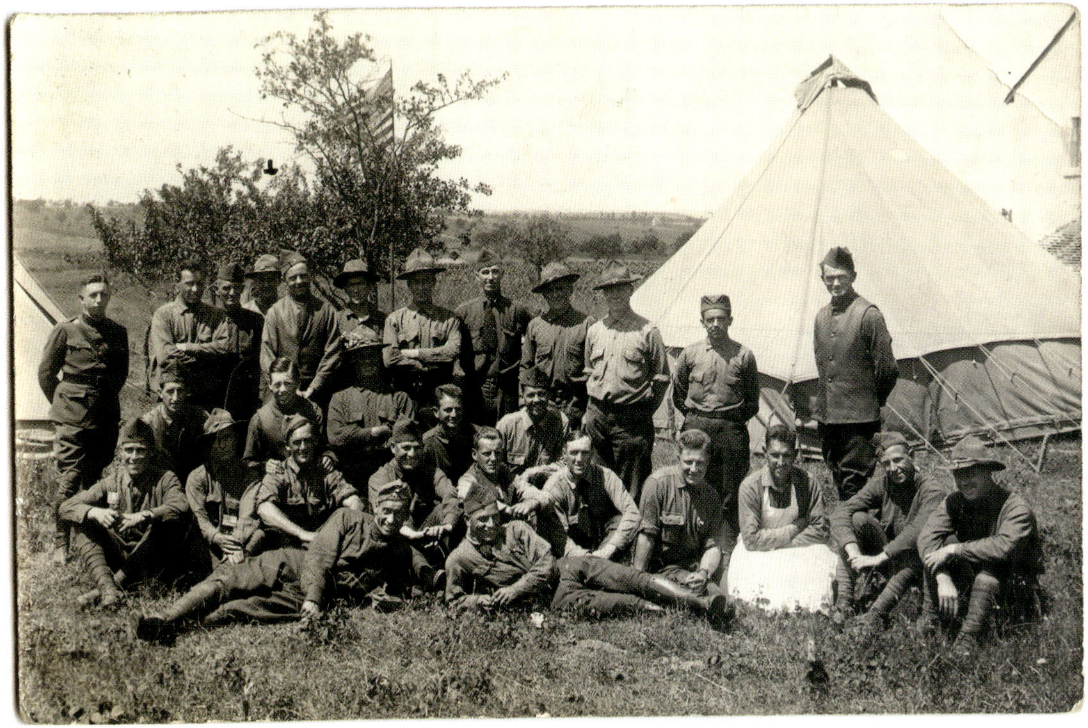

Men of Company E, 401st Telegraph Battalion celebrating a "safe and sane 4th of July 1918." The officer at left is in proper uniform which would meet with Gen. Pershing's approval . . . the men, not so much. The variety of headgear is broad, and all the overseas caps appear to be of French-style manufacture, though some have added two ornamental buttons to the front peak as seen in British-style caps. Cap ornaments include brass numerals 401 and officer-style Signal Corps insignia. Several men wear neckties and several of the men seated foreground have small American flags in hand. Three wear leather jerkins in spite of what appears to be a warm and pleasant day. In the background are two of the standard pyramidal squad tents of the period. One of the two reclining men at center wears officer-style leather puttees. Rounding out the image is a white aproned cook. The 401st Telegraph Battalion arrived in France in March 1918.

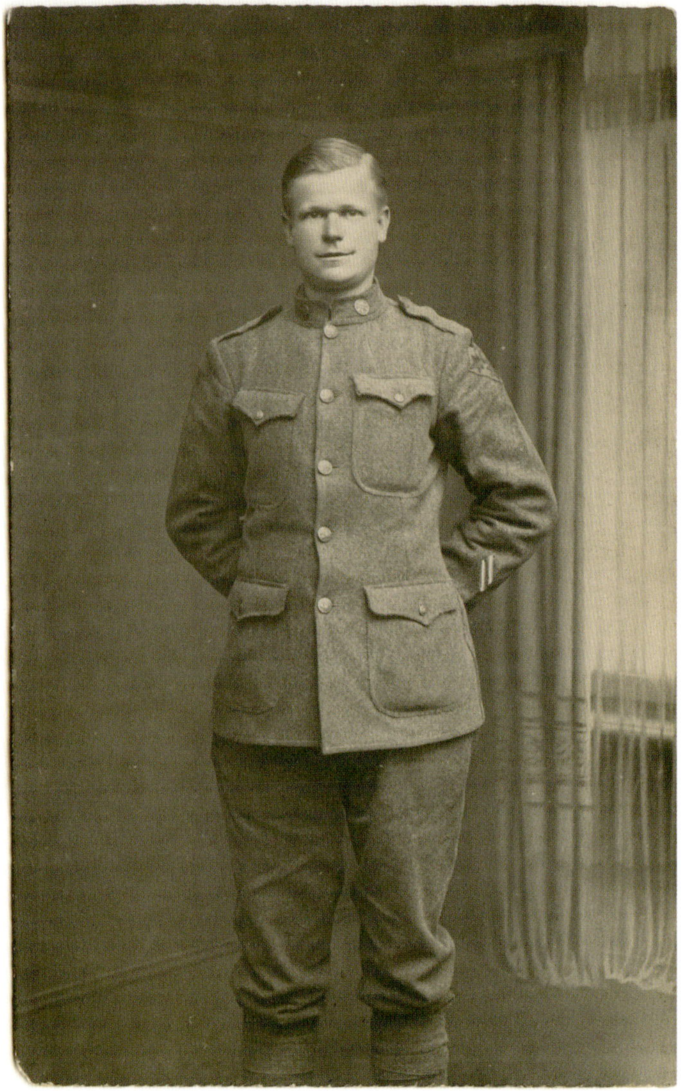

At first glance a straightforward post-Armistice image of a young 4th Division soldier, with one year of overseas service, likely taken in Belgium or Germany. A close look at his coat shows that his right breast pocket is set about two inches lower than the left. The coat looks clean and freshly issued, likely a manufacturing defect missed in the inspection process.

“The long and the short of it.” The soldier at left has been identified as cook Harvey Billings of the Supply Company, 58th Infantry, 4th Division, AEF. At first unremarkable, it can be seen that Billings has added a sixth button to his service coat at about the mid-level of his lower front coat pockets. His unnamed partner has but a single overseas service chevron.

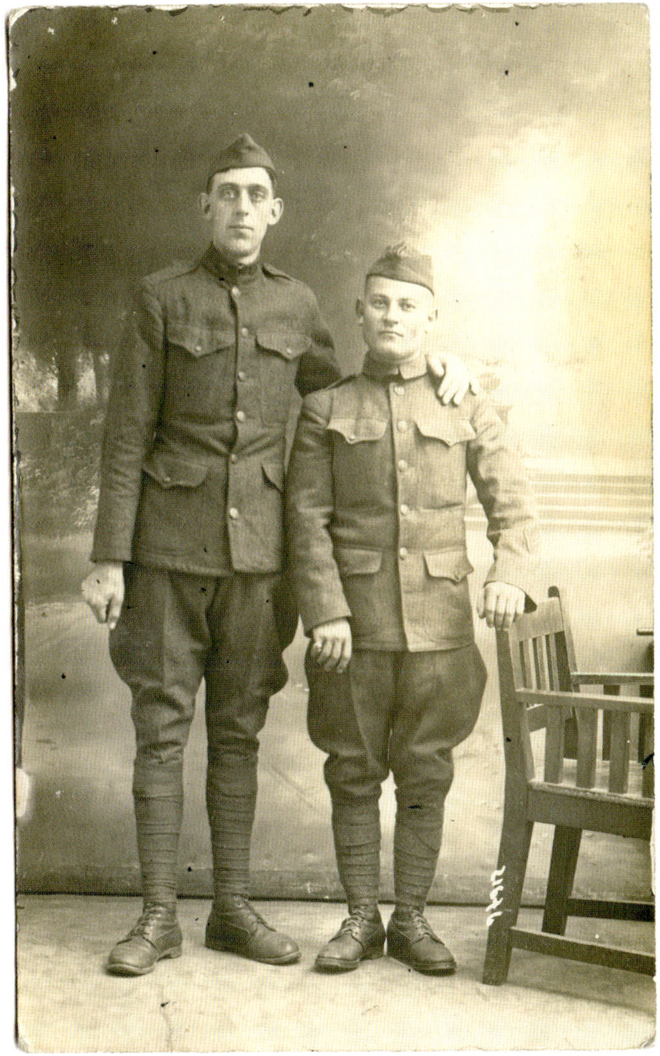

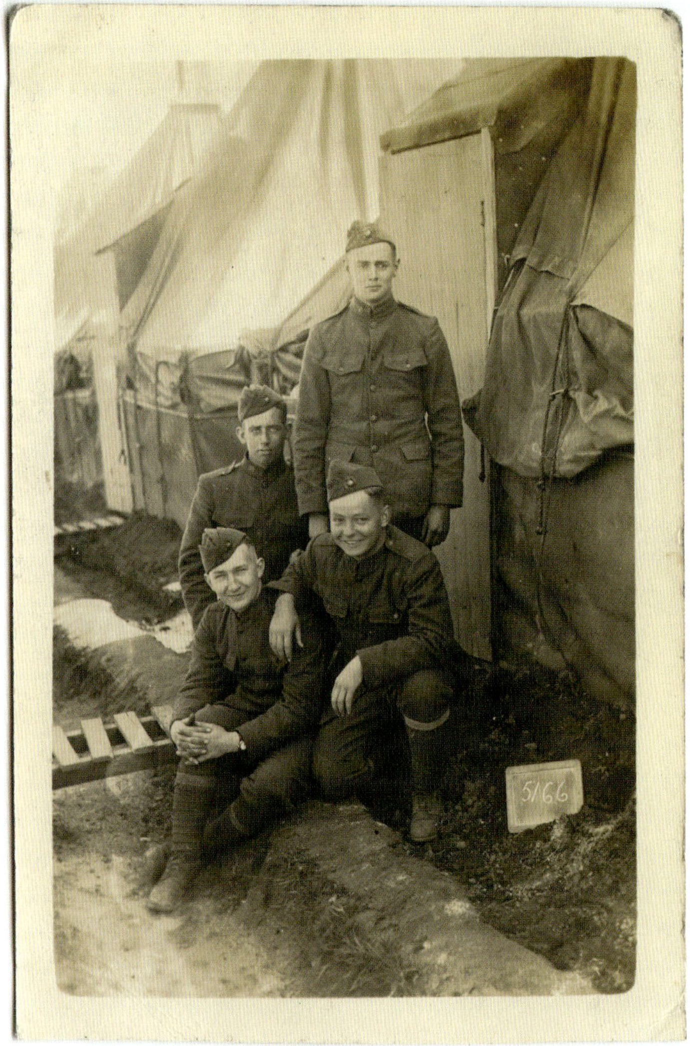

A group of four young Marines in France. These are likely replacements newly arrived in France, or possibly members of the late-arriving 5th Marine Brigade. They wear Army uniforms with the addition of USMC eagle, globe, and anchor (EGA) collar insignia. All four wear standard Army issue overseas caps with the addition of USMC EGA cap badges. The young "devil dog" seated left is wearing a wristwatch. Of note is the small chalk board bearing number 5166—used by the photographer to identify the group. They are billeted in an established tent camp as can be seen from the deep drainage ditch and framed pyramidal squad tents with added entry doors.

A bemused Doughboy in shirtsleeves, with collar turned up.

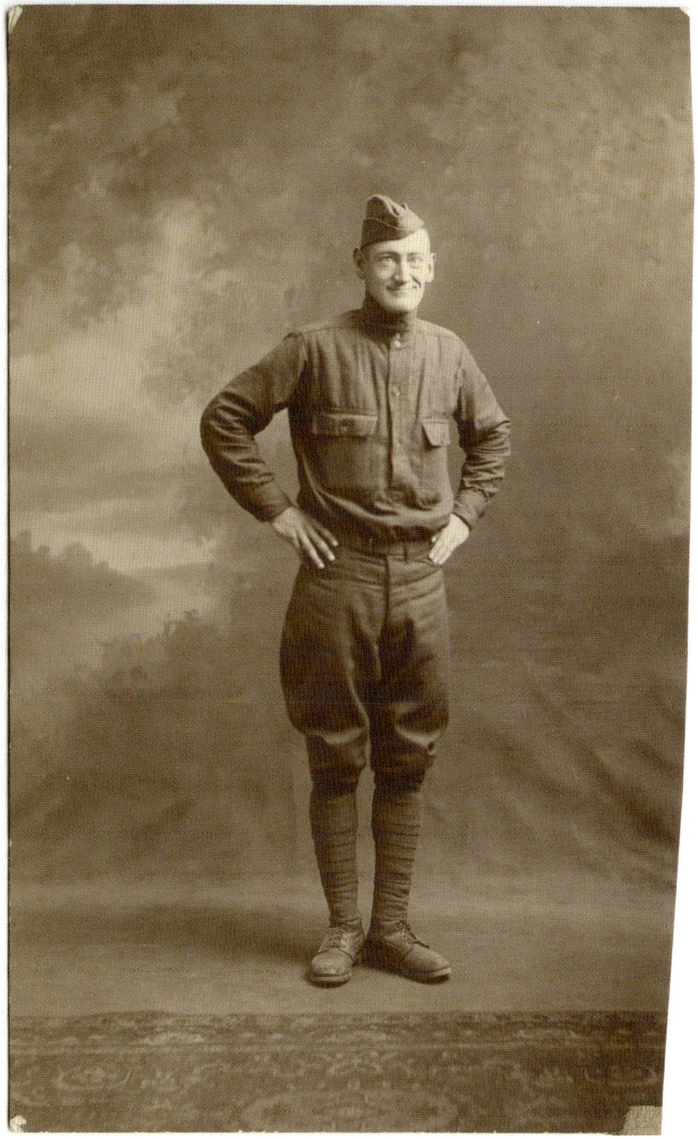

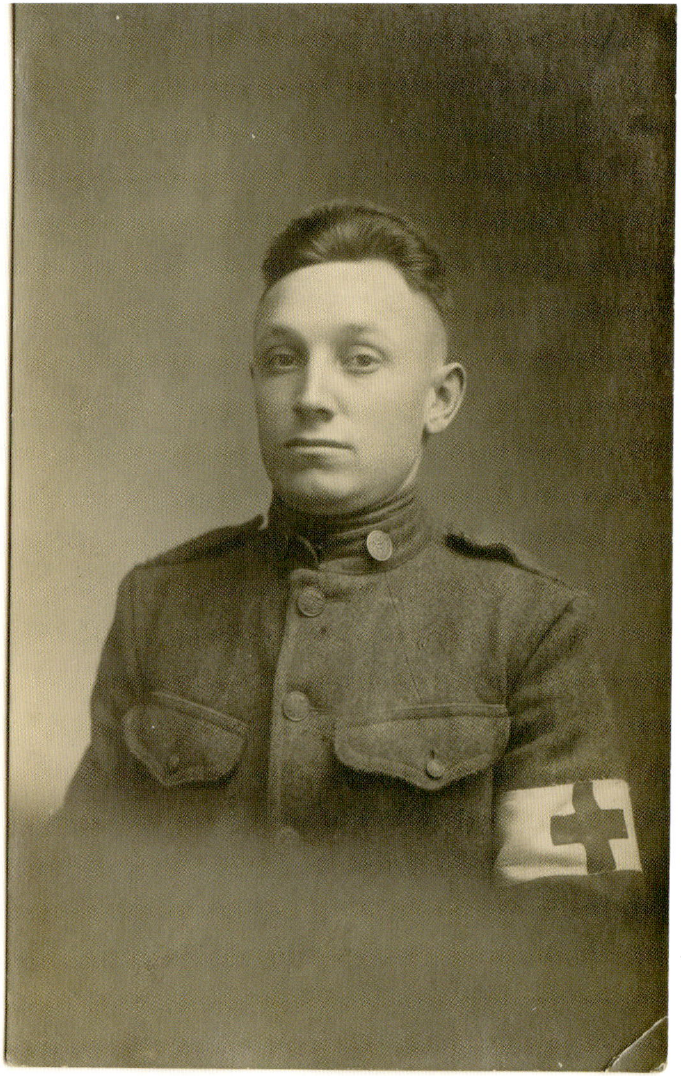

A medic with a distinctive white wall haircut. Close examination reveals the upper edge of his Red Cross brassard is crudely sewn to his service coat. The brassard also lacks a visible serial number stencil, indicating he may be a late arrival in the AEF. Both numbered and unnumbered brassards have been observed in the AEF.

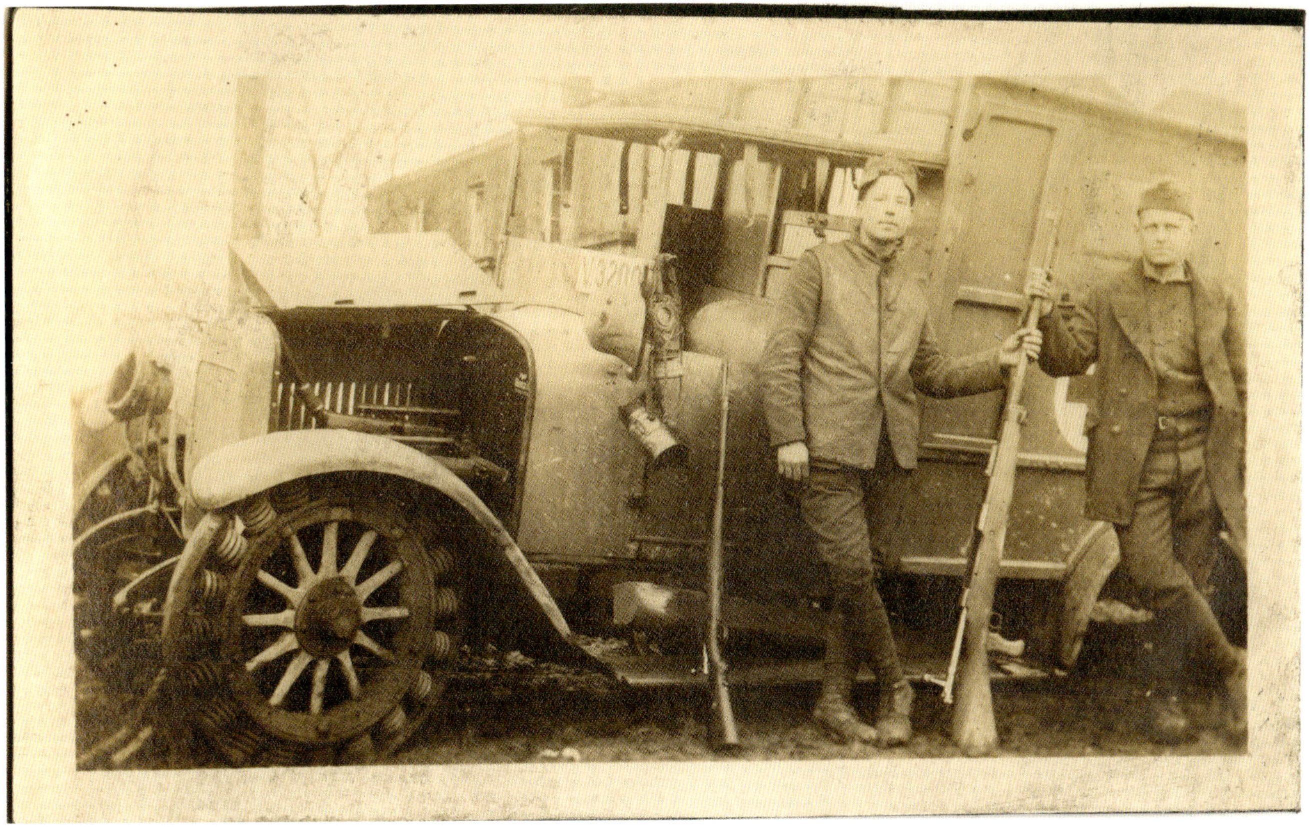

Two Doughboys with perhaps the most often photographed and unusual German souvenir; the 13.7 mm 1918 Mauser T-Gewehr. This was Germany's first attempt at an antitank rifle, more or less a standard Mauser Gew. 98 rifle chambered for a 13.7 mm round. The T-Gewehr looks fairly intact and is missing only its bipod. They stand in front of a somewhat worse for wear German ambulance with further evidence of German ersatz ingenuity—sprung solid tired wheels in lieu of standard pneumatic rubber tires. The ambulance is further festooned with a German stahlhelm and gas mask. The Doughboy at left wears a model 1907 winter hat with the brim folded up and a leather jerkin worn over his service coat. His partner at right wears the mackinaw-style overcoat over shirtsleeves. The lack of gas masks and helmets likely indicates this image was taken sometime well after the Armistice.

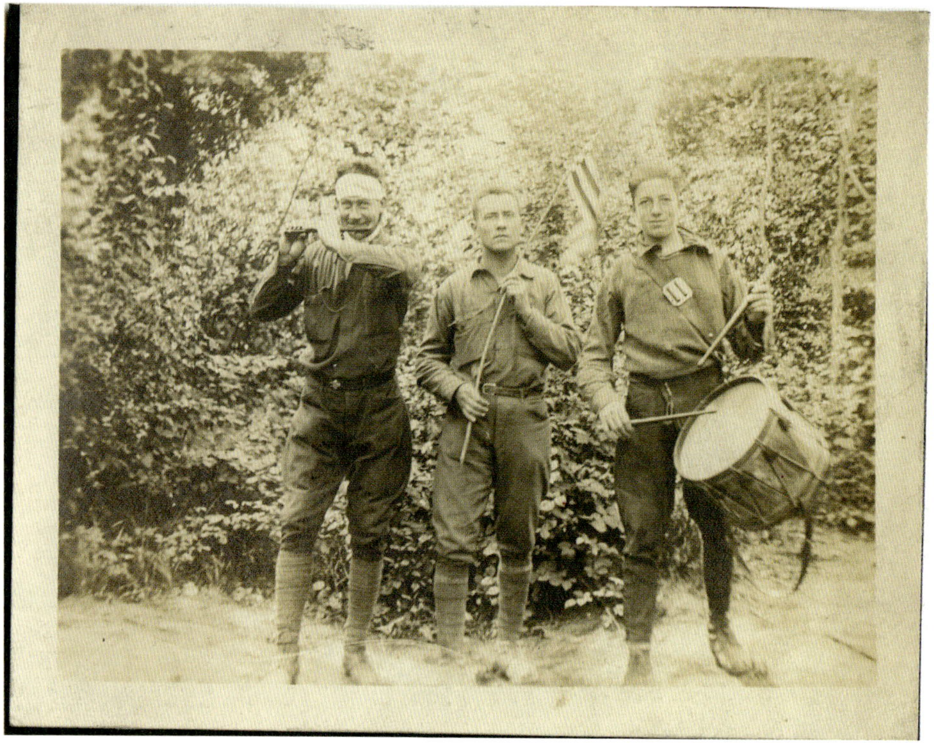

Three Doughboys playfully mimicking the famous and often-reproduced painting "The Spirit of '76," painted by Archibald McNeal Willard, circa 1876, and exhibited at the Centennial Exposition. The original now hangs in Abbot Hall, Marblehead, Massachusetts. The Doughboy at left has salvaged part of a model 1907 rifle sling to use as a belt. His partner in the center wears what appears to be a civilian leather belt. The drummer wears no puttees. His sleeveless sweater appears to be more finely knit than most of the Red Cross and other relief organization examples observed. His rope-tensioned drum appears to of European origin, possibly French.

Another image of cook Harvey Billings, Supply Company, 58th Infantry, 4th Division, AEF, fraternizing with a local German fraulein. Billings sports an identification wrist bracelet on his right hand and a typical wire lug wristwatch on his left. He wears two overseas service chevrons, and an unknown ribbon over his left breast pocket, possibly the Mexican Border Service Ribbon. His overseas cap appears to have no ornamentation at all.

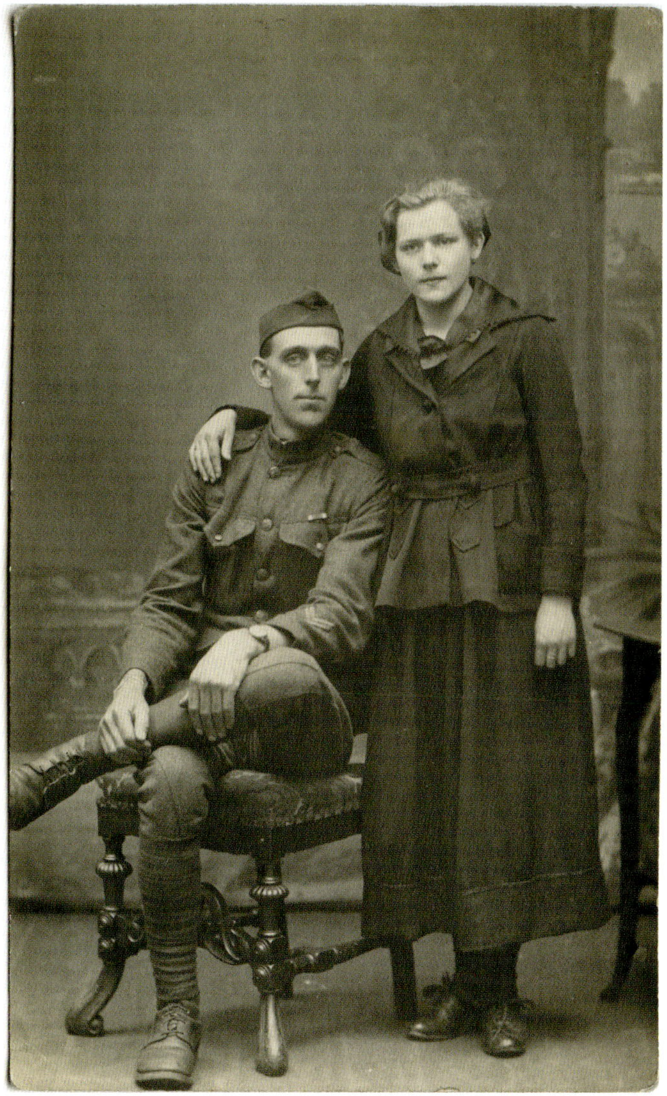

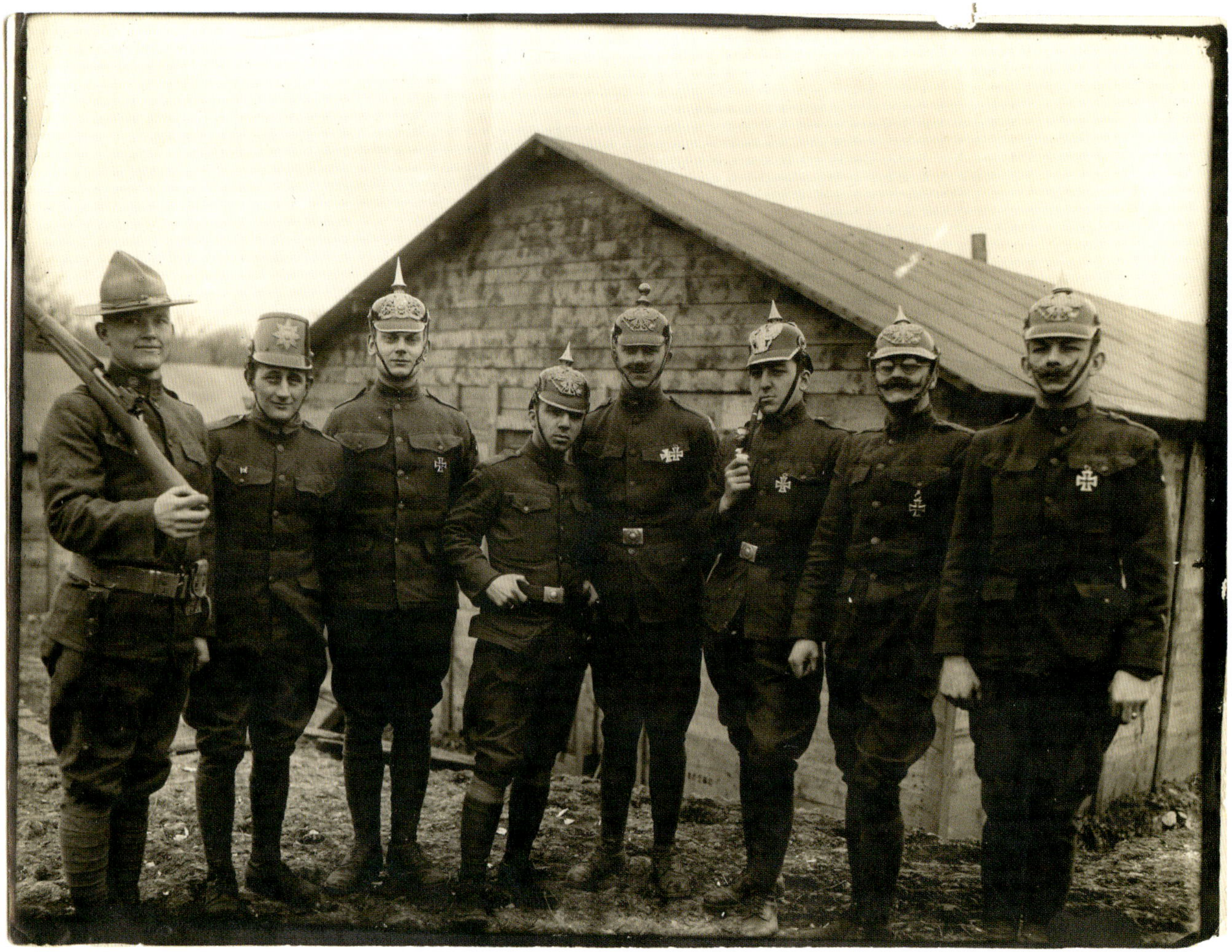

Members of the 5th Photo Section ham it up with their souvenirs. The two clearly visible shoulder sleeve insignia are 1st Army "A" with the air service roundel below, which is confusing since the Order of Battle lists 5th Photo Detachment as corps troops. This photo section had the mission of developing and printing aerial reconnaissance photographs. The Doughboy at center wearing two Iron Crosses and a German artillery *picklelhaube*, as denoted by its balled spike top, appears to be wearing a 5th Corps shoulder sleeve insignia. All the visible branch collar insignia are Signal Corps. In addition to a magnificent collection of spiked helmets, most of which look to be officer quality, there are three German belts, Iron Crosses 1st and 2nd class, a bayonet, and a long-stem porcelain pipe. How an aerial photo detachment amassed this booty is a mystery. The corporal of the guard bears a US Model 1917 rifle, lacking a sling, and wears a pistol belt with empty ammunition pockets, and the scabbard for his rifle. Presumably, the bayonet is fixed so he can properly guard his charges. How they made their false mustaches is another mystery.

A Doughboy photographed quite likely in the course of a post-Armistice battlefield tour. The lack of any arms and a gas mask indicates the "Guerre is fini." Although there is no insignia of grade visible, he does wear a whistle chain from front buttonhole to left breast pocket. His souvenir stahlhelm looks to be a plain example in standard feldgrau finish. He stands in front of what clearly is a wartime barbed wire entanglement as the wire has very closely placed barbs.

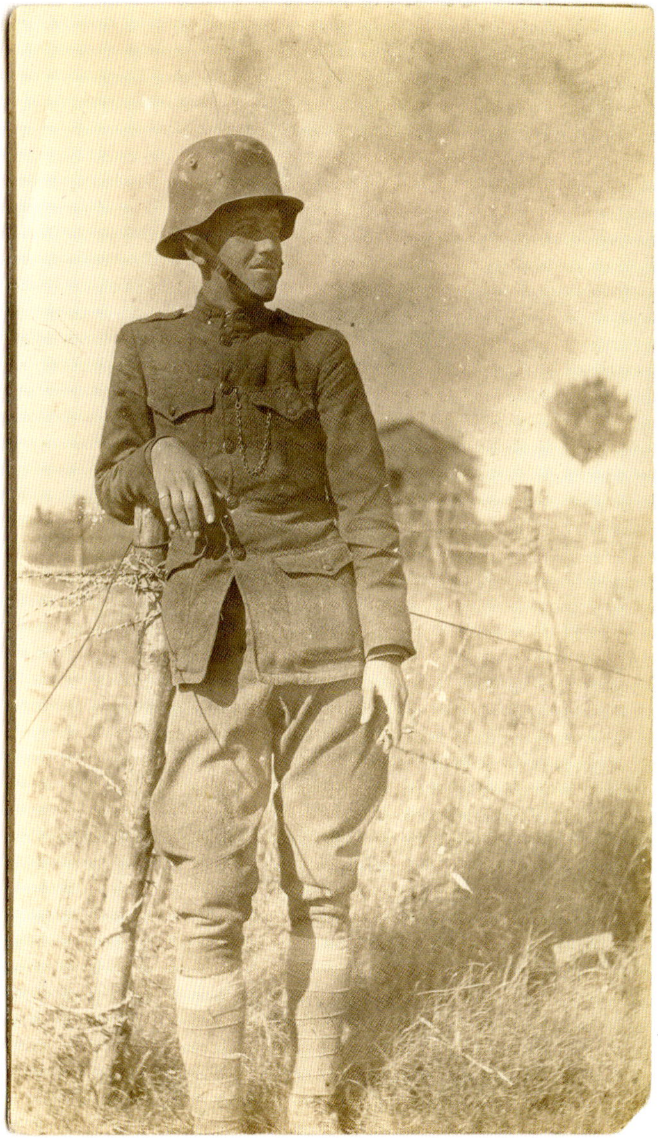

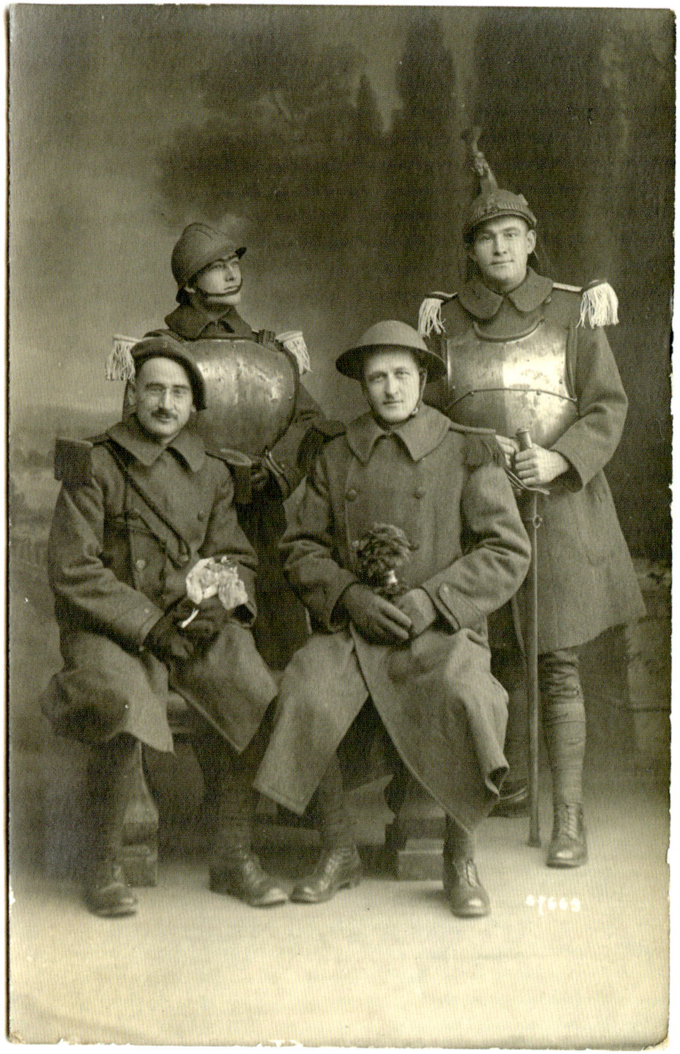

Four Doughboys photographed with the props of a very well-stocked studio. The armor appears to be that of a nineteenth-century French cavalry cuirassier. The soldier standing left is wearing then-back plate as a breastplate. Interestingly he is wearing the 1915 Adrian helmet backwards. All have adorned their overcoats with fringed epaulets. The soldier sitting left a fouragere, possibly in green and red signifying award of the Croix de Guerre, and wears a French Chaussers Alpine "tarte" (beret) adorned with a small brass numeral, either a 3 or 5. The sword is a mid-nineteenth-century French dragoon saber. The meaning of the bouquet and feathered pom-pom in the hands of the two seated Doughboys is unknown. The Doughboy standing right wears the 1918 pattern overcoat without wrist tabs, and has added what appear to be metallic snaps to the collar. The remaining three are wearing the 1917 pattern overcoat. The two seated Doughboys wear standard olive drab wool knit gloves.

Four redlegs of a 155 mm artillery unit during a "Gas Shoot." They wear the French-made semi-impermeable anti-gas suits over their standard uniforms. These were constructed of oiled cotton material, and provided protection from vesicant gases, mustard being the most dangerous. These suits were often worn particularly when handling mustard gas shells to avoid injury from any leaking rounds. The same suits were worn by medical personnel handling gas patients. All four wear the elbow-length mittens which were part of the suit. The Doughboys second and fourth from left have elected to don the hood portion of their suits tightly cinched around their faces. The Doughboy at left wears his souvenir stahlhelm, which appears to be camouflage painted. All four wear their small box respirators in the ready position. The two redlegs at right and left wear canvas leggings while the center two have woolen wrapped puttees. Behind them is a pallet of 155 mm rounds under a camouflage net.

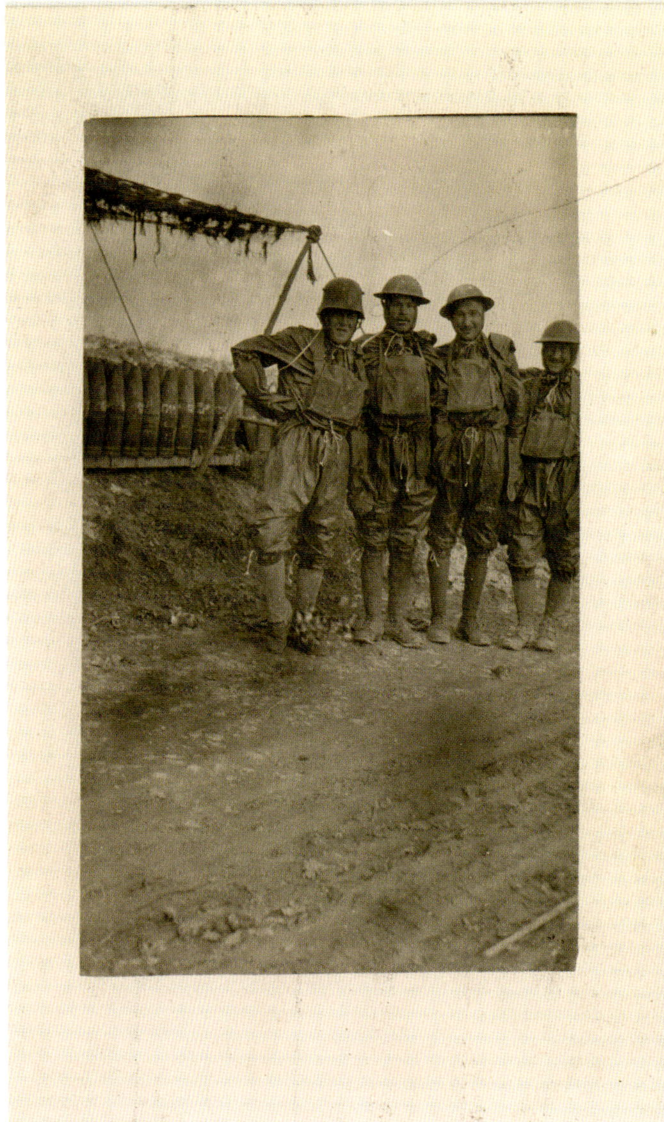

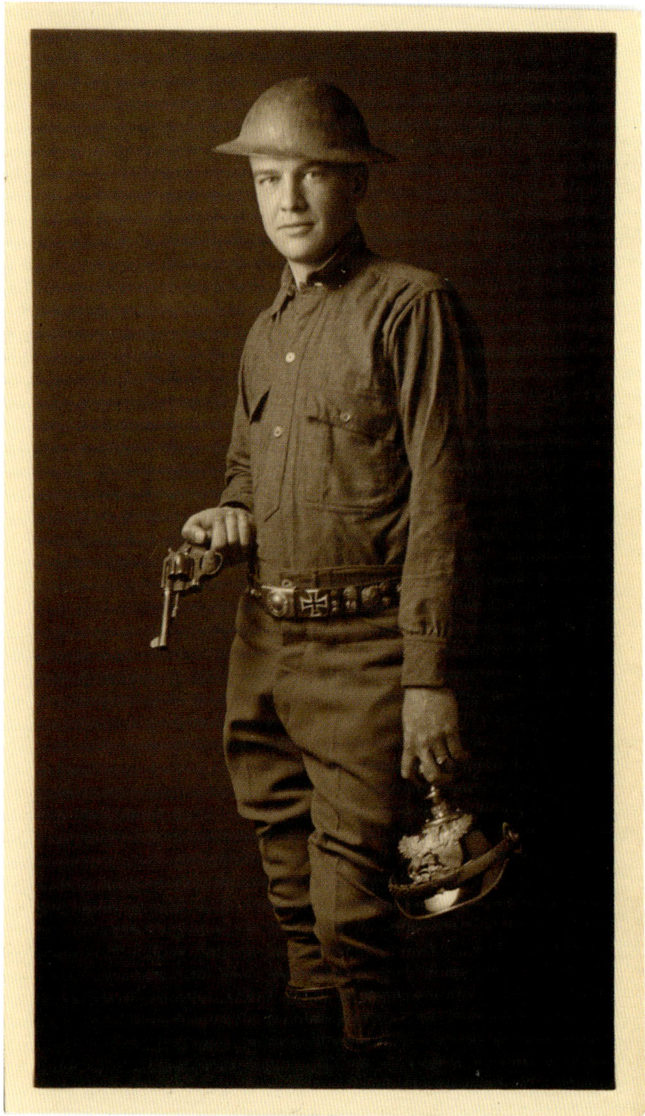

A handsome young Doughboy photographed with some impressive souvenirs, a Model 1917 Smith & Wesson revolver, ornate "hate" belt (prominently displaying a German Iron Cross), and an artillery pikelhaube. The tops of his leather officer-style leggings can just be seen.

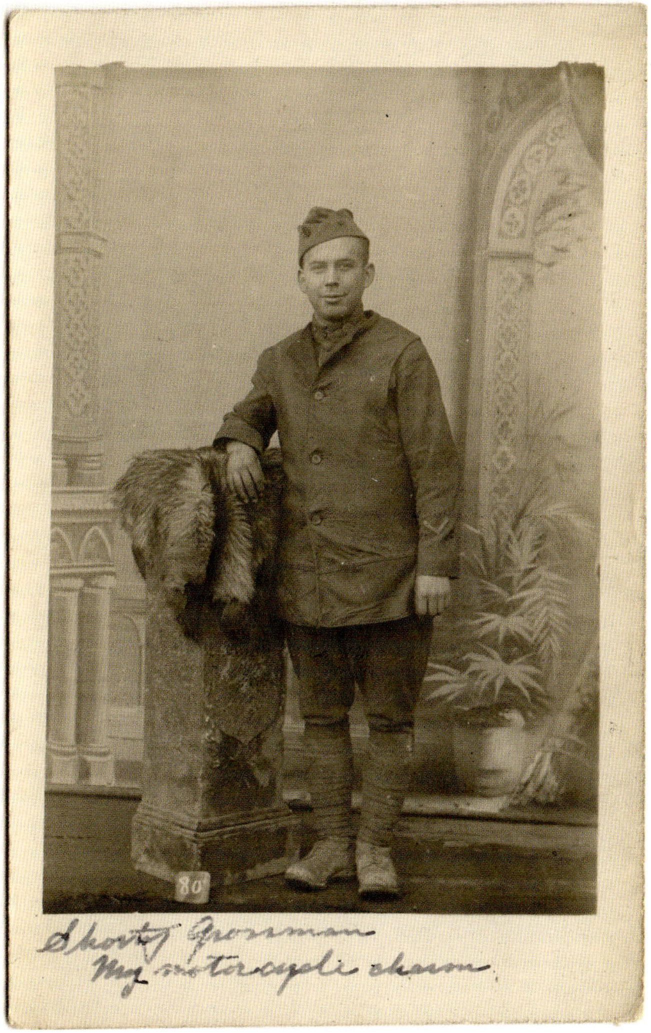

"Shorty Grossman" in a studio setting. His cap seems to have both US and engineer ornaments. A small slate at the base of the column (adorned with some type of animal pelt) is numbered 80, a photographer's aide to identify the subject. Grossman wears the standard leather jerkin over his service coat, and has a single war service chevron.

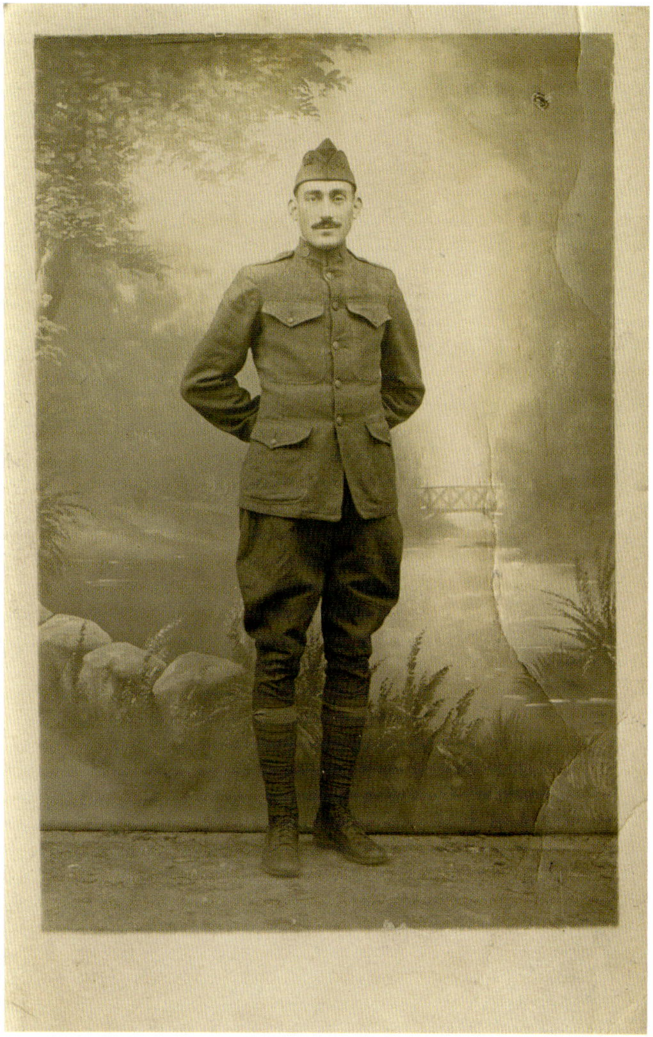

A dapper engineer in standard uniform. His French-style overseas cap bears a large engineer castle and brass numeral 42. This most likely denotes his unit as 42nd Engineers, an auxiliary Forestry Battalion, which arrived in France in May 1918. In October 1918, this battalion was absorbed into the 20th Engineer Regiment (Forestry). This was the largest engineer regiment in the AEF, with twenty-nine battalion headquarters, 145 companies, and an aggregate enlisted strength of 46,025 men.

Two medical corps soldiers photographed in the open air. The Doughboy at left is wearing a privately purchased service coat and breeches. The collar is significantly taller than that of his comrade in standard issue uniform. In addition, button closure of the breeches legs can be seen. Finally, the coat in particular looks to be made of finer material than the standard service coat, and the shape of the pocket flaps is more scalloped. He is wearing smooth side out service shoes. His partner at right is wearing all standard issue uniform items and wears a single overseas service stripe. His boots are hobnailed Trench boots.

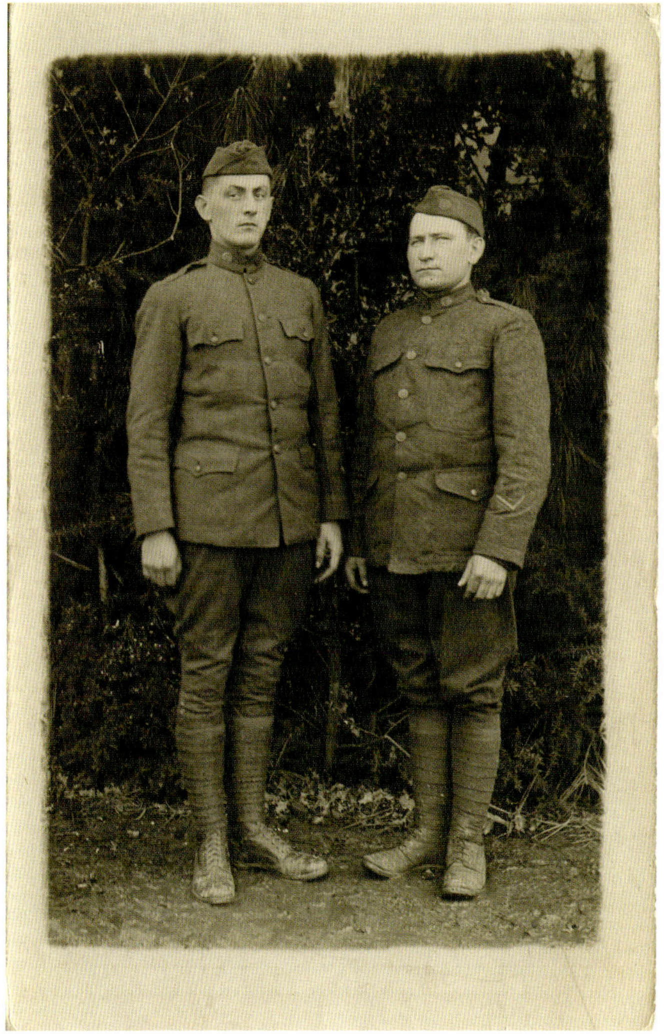

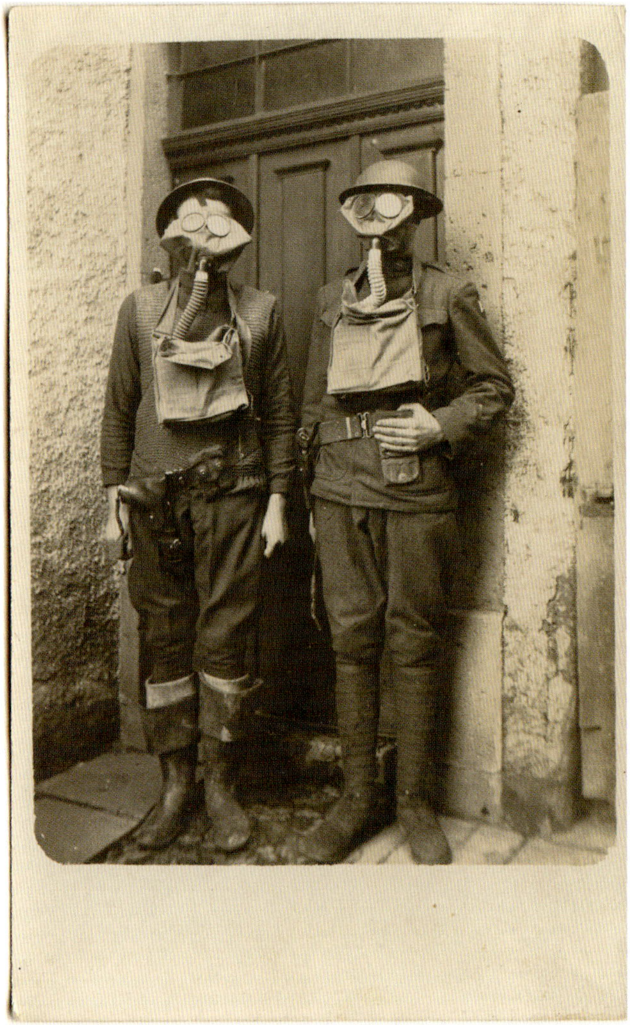

The obligatory photo taken with steel helmets and gas masks on. This image was clearly taken in the Army of Occupation as the soldier on the right wears the 3rd Army shoulder sleeve insignia, as well as a single overseas service chevron. His single visible collar ornament is that of the field artillery. He is armed with a Model 1917 revolver of either Colt or Smith & Wesson manufacture, and has the unique three-pocket ammunition pouch for carrying rounds in the three-round half-moon clips for revolvers. His partner on the left wears the standard flannel shirt and a hand-knit sweater vest of the type donated to and issued by relief organizations to the members of the AEF. He is armed with a model 1911 .45-caliber automatic pistol. Interestingly, it is being carried in a model 1912 swivel style holster which has been doubled over the pistol belt, so it no longer has the drop it would have if worn normally. The substantial leg tie down strap can be seen wrapped around the body of the holster. A spiral wrapped thong seems to be routed through the pistol's lanyard loop. His thigh-length rubber trench waders are folded down, as was often seen when not actually in deep muddy trenches.

A jaunty fellow with rather unusual facial hair for a member of the AEF. While moustaches were common (and quite a fad in the Army of Occupation), the addition of an "imperial" is unusual. He wears two US collar ornaments. His brassard is the very uncommon maroon and white-trimmed narrow version worn by engineer field clerks. Since engineer field clerks had no distinguishing collar insignia this may explain the choice of wearing two US collar ornaments. He wears a tall peaked French-style overseas cap without ornamentation.

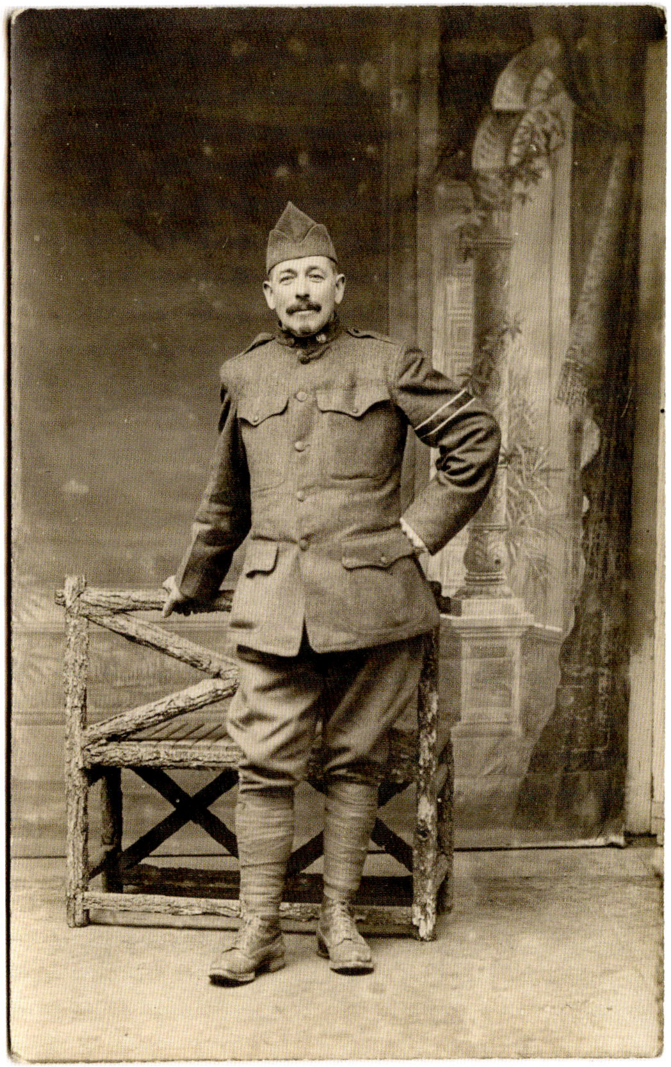

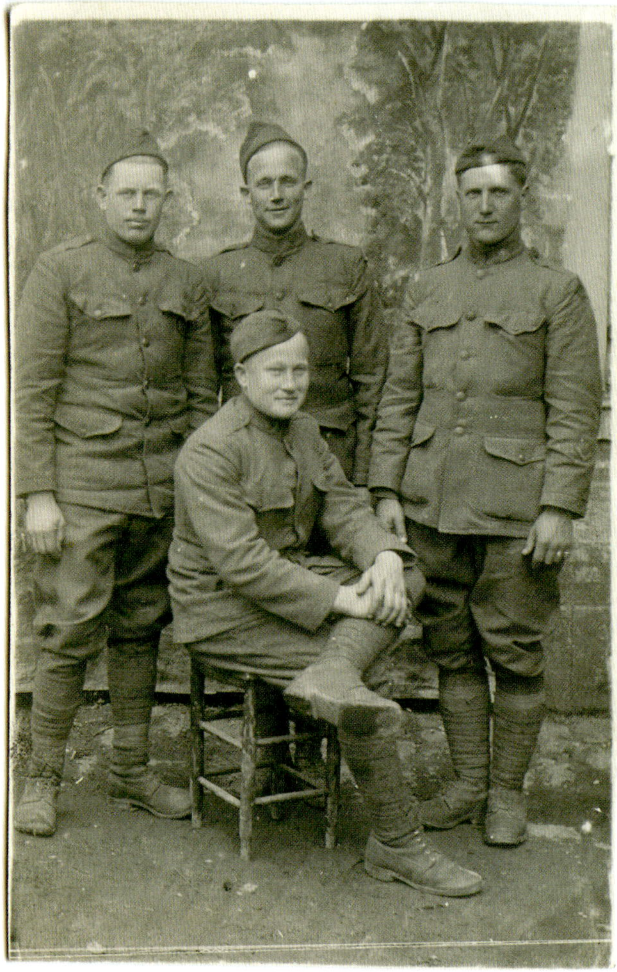

A grouping of Doughboys taken in open air with a painted backdrop. The Doughboy standing at right wears a single overseas service chevron and a "T," for trains, collar insignia. His boots appear to be British pattern "ammunition" boots which have a toe plate. The seated Doughboy wears boots, which may have been reclaimed by QMC repair activities. They look to have been half-soled and had hobnails added around the periphery of the heels in lieu of iron horseshoes. All seem to be wearing standard US issue overseas caps. The standing Doughboy at left has chosen to wrap his puttees with the tie tapes terminating around the ankles. His service coat looks to have had two sets of hooks and eyes added below the bottom button to prevent the coat gapping.

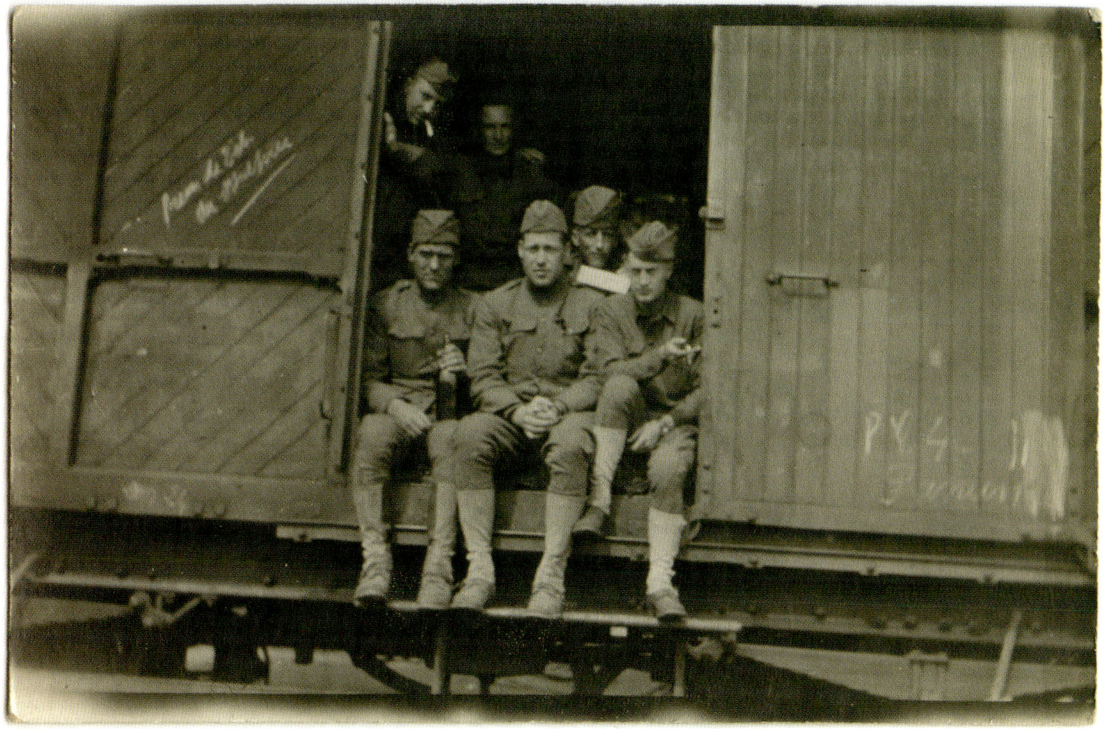

A group of Doughboys sitting in the door of a "40 and 8" or "side door Pullman" as French boxcars were known. The three Doughboys seated in the door wear canvas leggings, the leftmost of which are the leather-reinforced mounted pattern. All are wearing standard US overseas caps.

Conclusion

One hopes that most of the Doughboy images in this book speak for themselves. It is certainly an unscientific survey of images and not in any way intended to be a definitive work on uniforms and equipment of the AEF. Still, some general observations are in order.

Since all the AEF images in this book were taken in France and Germany, 1917–19, they do represent a snapshot in time. On close examination it is striking how "un-uniform" the uniforms worn in the AEF were; even in the notoriously spit and polish APG (apres la Guerre) Army of Occupation.

The most obvious example is the newly authorized overseas cap. Manufactured by the United States, France, and Britain, the overseas cap is seen in bewildering variety of cuts, patterns, and shapes. Olive drab service coats also appear in a variety of patterns and cuts. By the time of arrival, and some months service in France, most of the earlier patterns such as the 1904–07 coats with pointed cuffs, standing-falling collar, and bellows pockets had been worn out and replaced by the 1911 and 1917 pattern coats with standing choker collars and patch pockets.

Similarly, a wide variety of footwear is evident with multiple patterns of boots in use from the 1911 smooth side out cap toe marching shoes, to the triple-soled, rough out, Metallic Fastened Field Shoe, or "Pershing Boot."

The British were the largest source of uniform items (primarily service coats and trousers, boots, and spiral puttees) purchased by the AEF due to delays in US production. The Chief Quartermaster AEF reported in April 1918, the purchase of 100,000 pairs of British Field Shoes, and the same number of "suits of uniform clothing," presumably British Service Dress coats and trousers. These do occasionally appear in period photos. By the post-Armistice period, American-made straight-leg trousers begin to show up, replacing the tightly fitted breeches. The issuance of "British Service Dress Coats and Trousers" excited little comment except in the 165th US Infantry—the old "Fighting 69th." Their chaplain, Father Duffy, is reported to have quelled near mutiny after issued British Service Dress coats with English buttons to the Irish regiment of the "Rainbow Division."

The issues of British boots were problematic. The British sizing system was different than American, and by most accounts the upper leather was much stiffer than any American-issue boots. Some accounts point to a low instep in the British boot pattern as the cause of difficulties, while others maintain the cut of the pattern was too narrow. These complaints reached a crescendo with the march of units into Germany to form the Army of Occupation. In the immediate post-Armistice weeks before beginning the march into Germany, 3rd Army units received significant issues of new uniforms and shoes. The 1st, 2nd, 42nd, and 89th Divisions all reported extensive foot injuries on the march, and most attributed the injuries to the hated British boots. Had there been some time to break these boots in before several weeks of hard marching, results might have been different. Nonetheless, medical and line officers in each of these divisions unanimously reviled the British boots. Even after arrival in the Army of Occupation in Germany in December 1918, British boots remained an issue. First Division Administrative Bulletin No. 7, dated December 16, 1918, decried the practice of turning in serviceable boots in order to draw larger sizes enabling the wear to two pair of heavy socks, and stated, "Should this practice continue the stock of American shoes will become exhausted and will result in resumption of issues of British and French shoes."

In the AEF during hostilities and into the post-Armistice period, the out-and-out shortage of collar insignia is surprising. Again, even in the Army of Occupation a very large number of men did not have the correct combination of ornaments for their service coats and caps.

Unauthorized mixing of uniforms and other insignia were also fairly common. This is especially the case with unauthorized numerals worn on overseas caps, officer insignia worn on enlisted mens' overseas caps, enlisted men wearing tall officer's style lace up boots and/or officers's leather puttees, and in the post-Armistice period wear of a myriad of unauthorized and unofficial campaign ribbons. GHQ AEF G.O. No. 31, dated February 14, 1919, was the first of several orders forbidding wear of unauthorized "fourrageres and other decorations" and describing penalties for such wear up to a $300 fine, and imprisonment for up to six months.

Among students of the AEF, and especially those with interest in uniforms and equipment, the usual conclusion is "never say never." The most unlikely combinations of uniform, equipment, and insignia invariably appear . . . with or without rational explanation. Researchers encounter unending variations of unauthorized and nonsensical combinations of uniform and insignia in the American Army from 1917 to 1920.

Bibliography

American Battle Monuments Commission. *American Armies and Battlefields in Europe.* Washington, DC: US GPO, 1938.

Britten, Thomas A. *American Indians in World War I: At Home and at War.* Albuquerque: University of New Mexico Press, 1997.

Derby, Richard. *Wade in Sanitary: The Story of a Division Surgeon in France.* New York: G. P. Putnam's Sons, 1919.

Hatler, Margaret. *The M. Waldo Hatler Story.* Joplin, MO: Smith Printing Company, 1968.

Lee, Charles H., ed. *History of the Twenty-Sixth Engineers (Water Supply Regiment) in the World War, September 1917 – March 1919.* N.p.:1920

The Medical Department of the United States Army in the World War, sixteen volumes. Washington, DC: US GPO, 1923.

United States Army in the World War, seventeen volumes. Washington, DC: Center of Military History, 1988.

About the Author

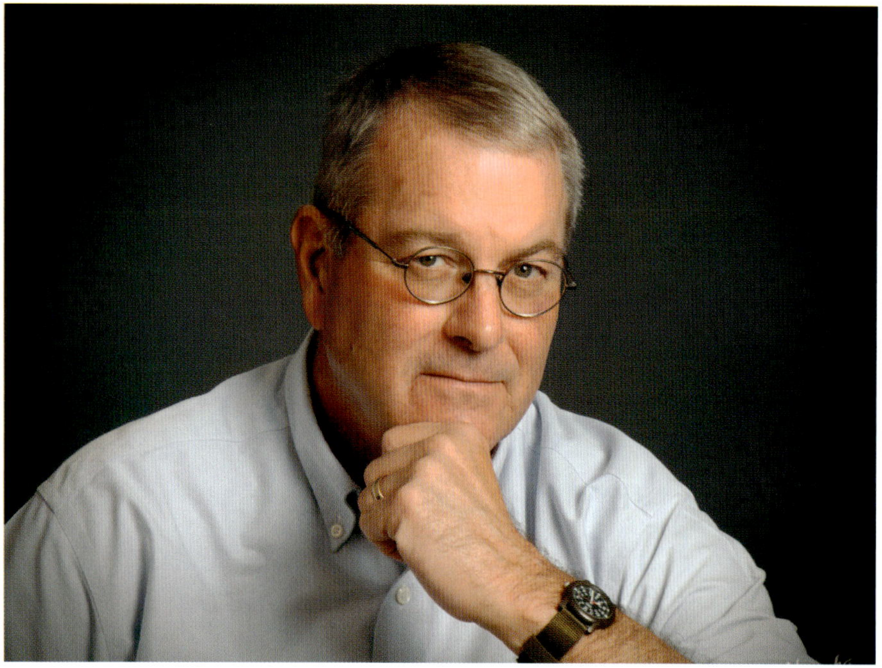

Stephen C. McGeorge has served as deputy chief historian, US Army Training and Doctrine Command (TRADOC) since April 2007. While a serving Army officer he completed an MA in history under Dr. Ted Wilson and served on the Leavenworth faculty with Combat Studies Institute as a military history instructor. Following retirement he was director of the Oregon Military Museum, TRADOC historian for the Stryker Brigade Combat Teams at Ft. Lewis, Washington, and chief collections curator for the National Museum of the United States Army.